Microsoft® Gui

OPTIMIZING
WINDOWS™

Microsoft
P R E S S

DAN GOOKIN

PUBLISHED BY
Microsoft Press
A Division of Microsoft Corporation
One Microsoft Way
Redmond, Washington 98052-6399

Library of Congress Cataloging-in-Publication Data
Gookin, Dan.
    Microsoft guide to optimizing Windows : proven advice for
  configuring, expanding, and maximizing your Windows 3.1 system / Dan
  Gookin.
        p.   cm.
    Includes index.
    ISBN 1-55615-506-9 : $17.95 ($24.95 Can.)
    1. Windows (Computer programs)   2. Microsoft Windows (Computer
  file)   I. Title.
  QA76.76.W56G66   1992
  005.4'3--dc20   92-31891
                                                            CIP
Printed and bound in the United States of America.

1 2 3 4 5 6 7 8 9   AGAG   8 7 6 5 4 3

Distributed to the book trade in Canada by Macmillan of Canada, a division of Canada Publishing Corporation.

Distributed to the book trade outside the United States and Canada by Penguin Books Ltd.

Penguin Books Ltd., Harmondsworth, Middlesex, England
Penguin Books Australia Ltd., Ringwood, Victoria, Australia
Penguin Books N.Z. Ltd., 182–190 Wairau Road, Auckland 10, New Zealand

British Cataloging-in-Publication Data available.

Acquisitions Editor: Mike Halvorson
Project Editor: Tara Powers-Hausmann
Technical Editor: Mary DeJong
Editing and Production: Online Press, Inc.

Contents

Acknowledgments

Hi. I'm Dan Gookin and I really did write this book. Every word. It took six intense weeks to do it, and it wasn't without the help of many fine people at Microsoft Press. Above all I'd like to thank Mike Halvorson, who is one cool dude and came through with Windows and related software including the *Knowledge Base* on CD-ROM. Dean Holmes and Lucinda Rowley also helped immensely, especially when Mr. Halvorson played hooky to do his income tax (on April 15, no less). Lucinda, Dean and I really didn't mean to break your monitor.

Thanks go to Tara Powers-Hausmann, Russell Borland, Mary Dejong, Dail Magee, and David Rygmyr of Microsoft Press, who were all friendly and helpful—even when they couldn't talk because they were "in a meeting." Thanks also go to Joyce Cox, Polly Fox Urban, Christina Smith, and Bill Teel of Online Press.

Special thanks goes to Jon Kechejian in the MS-DOS group, and to Bob Ferguson (whom I didn't quote at all!). Also, thanks to Kenny Jacobsen, formerly of Novell now of Dell, who helped with the networking stuff and sent Jordan a SuperSoaker 150.

On the home front, Sandy deserves a big hug of thanks for my incredible caffeine-induced mood swings during the final weeks. Jordan was cool, as always, especially when he stopped by the office to show me all the trash he was throwing away, one piece at a time.

Introduction

What do you make of Windows? Let's be honest: It's a cute graphical shell with nifty advantages for beginners. That's common knowledge. Intermediate and advanced computer users can accept that; after all, a uniform environment makes learning new software easier for everyone. Soon, however, even seasoned users realize that there's more to Windows than just graphics, menus, and the mouse.

Beneath Windows' surface is a complex, powerful engine. Like any engine, Windows can be coddled and coaxed into higher levels of performance. In Windows, this all starts with a few simple tricks: using a disk cache, creating a "permanent swap file," learning how to quickly switch between running programs, and so on. Eventually, the attraction to optimizing Windows becomes magnetic. Improving performance becomes an obsession. Soon, even beginning users will want to know how to make things work faster, more efficiently, and better. It's all possible. But like pampering an engine, pampering Windows requires patience, subtle skill, a drop of oil here, and a dab of grease there. There are no secrets, just techniques. That's what this book shows you.

Optimizing Windows involves no undocumented switches or hidden tricks, and this book won't show you how to do something that will become obsolete when the next version of Windows appears. Instead, this book shows you how to:

- Create ideal CONFIG.SYS and AUTOEXEC.BAT files for Windows

- Optimize memory under Windows by working with SMARTDrive, RAMDrive, and expanded memory managers

- Work with the mysterious WIN.INI and SYSTEM.INI files, honing them to perfection

- Optimize your existing hardware, or make upgrades you might not have thought of before

- Share information among programs with DDE and OLE

- Completely control MS-DOS programs running under Windows, tuning them for top performance

- Use your printer to its fullest extent

- Explore the "fun" aspects of Windows' fonts, graphics, networks, and multimedia

This is all amazing stuff, and it's all within Windows' capabilities. This book is heavy with optimization information, loaded with tips and suggestions, and ready to help you make Windows explode with power on your PC.

Is This Book for You?

I'll be honest: You probably consider yourself an adept Windows user. Maybe the label "advanced user"—or worse, "power user"—is a bit too egotistical for you. Say you understand Windows and know what you want from it. And you're tired of reading books that explain what a dialog box is, how to click the mouse, or what File Manager is all about. If, instead, you crave solid information, then this is your book.

Here, you won't find any information about learning Windows or any redundant information about using the *applets* (I'm told that's what Windows' bundled applications are called). What I've done is write a Windows book for people who enjoy working in the environment and want to see it run better. Consider this your problem solving text. Maybe you're reluctant to call technical support to ask why your printer's Pumpernickel font doesn't look right on the screen. Don't bother! I've already done the calling, and I tell you why in Chapter 7.

Windows contains lots of treasures, some of which aren't readily obvious. This book explores each of them, showing you ways to make Windows work better with your hardware and how to make you work better with Windows. And because I consider myself a regular guy, you won't find any condescension or patronizing in this book. So if you're into lofty prose, self-importance, or technobabble, consider buying another book instead. I'm a real person—one of you.

Modes and Moods

Depending on your PC's processor and amount of RAM, Windows 3.0 operated in one of three modes: real mode, standard mode, and 386 enhanced mode. Windows 3.1 operates only in the latter two modes, and it can run only on a PC with an 80286 or higher processor.

In this book, I refer to *standard mode* as such and to 386 enhanced mode as *enhanced mode*. All 80286 or IBM PC/AT compatibles are referred to as *80286 PCs*, and all 80386, i486, and 586 computers are lumped together as *'386-based PCs*.

The bulk of the commands and techniques in this book apply to Windows 3.1 running in enhanced mode. Information for standard mode is included when it's notably different from enhanced mode. I also assume that you're running MS-DOS version 5.0 or later. If you aren't, then my first tip is to upgrade to the latest version of your PC's operating system.

This book assumes that drive C is your primary hard drive, that MS-DOS is installed in the C:\DOS directory, and that Windows is installed in the C:\WINDOWS directory. Windows' system files are all stored in a SYSTEM directory under the main WINDOWS directory, which I call WINDOWS\SYSTEM.

Windows for Workgroups and This Book

Windows for Workgroups is Microsoft's networking version of Windows 3.1. In addition to the regular features of Windows, it includes peer-to-peer networking capabilities, an enhanced File Manager and Print Manager, and some new applets. Because Windows for Workgroups is an extension of Windows 3.1, you optimize its performance the same way you do Windows. Nearly everything I suggest in this book pertains to Windows for Workgroups. If it doesn't, I'll let you know.

How to Use This Book

This book was written with information in mind. It's short on personal experience and exposé. It has enough humor to make you smile once in a while, but not enough to detract from the subject matter. I took a stack of information I thought would be beneficial to Windows users wanting to get the most out of their system, organized that stack into chapters, and the end result is in your hands—a lean, tight book, packed with useful information, not filler or meaty by-products.

You can read the chapters in this book in any order. I start the book the way Windows starts on your PC: Chapter 1 is about booting your PC and setting up AUTOEXEC.BAT and CONFIG.SYS for Windows, and Chapter 2 covers running Windows and what makes it start. The remaining chapters can be read in any order, though I recommend reading about the INI files in Chapter 2 before you perform the INI file surgery mentioned in the chapters that follow. Chapter 9 is about multimedia, and I put it last because I think of that subject as dessert. Here's a quick chapter overview:

- Chapter 1 is about starting your PC, configuring CONFIG.SYS and AUTOEXEC.BAT to run Windows, and setting up MS-DOS's memory management.

- Chapter 2 discusses how Windows itself starts—the files involved and what you can do to customize the process.

- Chapter 3 deals with Windows and your hardware, specifically how to optimize or upgrade your hardware for Windows. It includes information on using your printer and running Windows on a laptop computer.

- Chapter 4 is all about optimizing Windows' performance, preserving resources and memory, and optimizing hard drive performance. It provides tips for making Windows run faster, and (as if that weren't enough) tells you where to find some "secret" files you may not know about.

- Chapter 5 covers running MS-DOS applications under Windows and making them work best in a multitasking graphical environment.

- Chapter 6 discusses the way Windows can run more than one program at a time and ways in which you can share information among programs.

- Chapter 7 deals with the graphic side of Windows, covering fonts, icons, and Windows' desktop.

- Chapter 8 covers the broad topic of networking under Windows and Windows for Workgroups, and provides information about telecommunicating and sending and receiving faxes under Windows.

- Chapter 9—dessert—is about using Windows for multimedia. This chapter covers using a sound card and CD-ROM drive with Windows and answers the question "What is multimedia all about?"

I hope you'll find Windows as interesting, surprising, and fun to use as I have. It truly does get better and better. And my hope is that, after reading this book, you'll not only enjoy Windows as much as I do, but you'll also have a greater understanding of and appreciation for what it can do. And you'll be able to impress the heck out of your friends. Alt-Spacebar, X!

Chapter 1

Configuring MS-DOS for Windows

Microsoft Windows makes it possible for you to avoid MS-DOS completely, which is great because we all know how painful that can be. Still, MS-DOS is what starts and configures your computer and is the place from which Windows is launched. Windows then takes over the controls. MS-DOS is like an ugly rest area between your house and Wally World— a cold, cinderblock way station that nevertheless performs a necessary function.

For you to get the most from your PC's hardware, Windows and MS-DOS must work together. This chapter discusses how to configure MS-DOS to run Windows best. It offers suggestions for setting up CONFIG.SYS and AUTOEXEC.BAT, as well as housekeeping information, memory management suggestions, and a whole host of useful tips. The idea is to set up MS-DOS as a solid foundation for Windows and then leave that bleak environment behind.

THE BIG PICTURE

There's a group of nutritionally correct people out there who wouldn't dream of starting the day without a good breakfast. Then there's the majority of us who skip breakfast for one reason or another. For Microsoft Windows, MS-DOS is breakfast. However, it's not a delightful meal—the electronic equivalent of gruel.

It is very important to feed Windows just the right amount of gruel— er, MS-DOS. Windows is more than just a "shell"—a program that makes MS-DOS pretty and easier to use. Starting with version 3.1, Windows is a complete "operating system" (it says so right on the box), bypassing

MS-DOS to access your computer's devices. Your screen, mouse, keyboard, printer, and so on are all controlled directly by Windows, not MS-DOS. Windows can even control your disk drives directly, which makes disk access under Windows much faster than under plain ol' MS-DOS. However, Windows still cannot start the computer by itself.

When your PC starts, or boots, a complex series of events takes place. First, the computer performs an internal diagnostic self-test, asking itself several reflective questions: Am I alive? Do I have all my parts? Does everything work? Then if the computer likes the answers to these questions, it tries to load MS-DOS from disk.

MS-DOS is loaded in several complicated steps. I won't bore you with the details here, except to say that MS-DOS uses five files to boot and set up your computer. For convenience, I've listed the files in Table 1-1. Of the five, the two you should concern yourself with are CONFIG.SYS and AUTOEXEC.BAT. These files are basically text files that contain special commands for configuring your system. Setting them up properly can make or break Windows.

Filename	What It Does
IO.SYS	The input/output device setup file. Loads all of MS-DOS's files and sets up system device drivers that allow MS-DOS to talk with your screen, keyboard, printer, and so on.
MSDOS.SYS	The MS-DOS kernel. The core of the operating system. Controls disk access, manages files, keeps the date and time, manages memory (well, somewhat), and does other similar stuff.
CONFIG.SYS	The system configuration file. Sets up MS-DOS and its file system, plus loads installable device drivers.
COMMAND.COM	The command interpreter or shell program. Produces the infamous command prompt and allows you to use basic file manipulation and other MS-DOS commands (the "internal" commands).
AUTOEXEC.BAT	The MS-DOS configuration batch file. Allows you to run startup programs and configure COMMAND.COM.

Table 1-1. *MS-DOS's five startup files.*

CREATING THE IDEAL CONFIG.SYS FILE

CONFIG.SYS is one of the MS-DOS boot files over which you have direct control. You create it as a text file by typing a series of configuration commands that set up your PC. You then store the file in the root directory of your boot disk, which I'll assume is drive C. What you include in this file is important because a well-written CONFIG.SYS file is vital to getting the most out of MS-DOS and Microsoft Windows.

MS-DOS reads the configuration commands in CONFIG.SYS each time your computer boots. Based on those commands, MS-DOS configures its file system and loads special programs called *device drivers* into memory. Device drivers allow MS-DOS and other programs to access the hardware attached to your system. For example, the MOUSE.SYS device driver allows you to use your mouse. Device drivers also provide extended control over basic hardware. For example, the ANSI.SYS device driver gives you extra control over your screen and keyboard.

When running Windows, you don't want an elaborate CONFIG.SYS file. Most of the commands in a CONFIG.SYS file that are designed for use with MS-DOS programs aren't needed for Windows. Having such a CONFIG.SYS file isn't bad; Windows still runs. But you might waste precious memory on device drivers that Windows doesn't need or configure your system for MS-DOS in a way that's counterproductive for Windows.

For running MS-DOS programs, CONFIG.SYS is, in fact, optional. If you don't have a CONFIG.SYS file, you can still run your computer. However, MS-DOS will undoubtedly make some foolish assumptions about your PC, and you won't end up with an optimized system. (Windows is a different story. Windows won't run at all unless you have a CONFIG.SYS file that loads the HIMEM.SYS device driver.)

Configuration Commands

You can use 15 configuration commands in CONFIG.SYS. All but one command (the Rem command) is followed by an equal sign and one or more values. The type of values used depends on what's being configured. Each command sits on a line by itself and must be no longer than one line, so turn off the word-wrap feature in your word processor or text editor when you're editing CONFIG.SYS. Blank lines are okay.

The 15 configuration commands are listed below, along with suggestions for proper settings on a computer running Windows.

Break

This command controls how often MS-DOS checks to see whether a cancel key (Ctrl-C or Ctrl-Break) has been pressed. A cancel key is not needed in Windows, so don't bother putting a Break command in your CONFIG.SYS. (You might want to have MS-DOS check for the cancel key as often as possible when you run MS-DOS from Windows. If so, use the MS-DOS command *break on* in the MS-DOS window. See the sample RUNDOS.BAT file in Chapter 5 for an example.)

Buffers

This command sets aside memory for MS-DOS to use when accessing your disks. The more buffers you have, the better, but you pay for them with memory. For Windows, the optimal number of buffers is 20, so you need the following command in your CONFIG.SYS:

```
buffers=20
```

However, I strongly suggest using the SMARTDrive disk cache to boost MS-DOS's disk performance beyond the capabilities provided by the Buffers command. If you're using SMARTDrive, you can set the number of buffers to 10 with this command:

```
buffers=10
```

Note: In systems with 256 KB to 511 KB of RAM, buffers=10 *is the default setting, so if your computer has that amount of memory, you don't really need a Buffers command in CONFIG.SYS at all! Just remember to run the SMARTDrive disk cache, and you'll be fine.*

Country

This command configures MS-DOS to use a specific country's conventions for date and time format, currency symbols, decimal separators, and more. Note that this command doesn't change the language MS-DOS uses.

If you're using MS-DOS in a country other than the United States, you are probably using a version localized for your country, so you don't have to worry about using this command.

Device and Devicehigh

These commands load device drivers into memory. You can use Device-high only if you have loaded the MS-DOS memory management device drivers, HIMEM.SYS and EMM386.EXE, and included the Dos command. Otherwise, you use Device. You follow either command with an equal sign and the name of a device driver file. The Device command loads drivers into conventional memory (the first 640 KB of memory). Devicehigh saves conventional memory for your programs by loading drivers into upper memory blocks (UMBs), which are located in upper memory, between the 640-KB and 1-MB marks. The section titled "Configuring Device Drivers," later in this chapter, describes in detail how to set up device drivers for Windows.

Dos

This command loads MS-DOS's files into a special area of memory called the high memory area (HMA). Loading into the HMA is possible only on a '386-based PC that has been properly configured with memory management software. This command helps to configure your system so that you can use the Devicehigh command in CONFIG.SYS, as well as the Loadhigh command in AUTOEXEC.BAT. More information about commands that manage memory is provided in "Memory Management Issues," later in this chapter.

Drivparm

Use this command only if it's required by your system's disk drive hardware. This command specifies characteristics of your disk drive that are different from the MS-DOS defaults.

Fcbs

Unless you are connected to a network, or using the Share command in your AUTOEXEC.BAT file, you won't need to use the Fcbs command. This command specifies the maximum number of file control blocks, which manage how networks access files on your disk. On a network workstation, a good setting for Fcbs is:

```
fcbs=20,8
```

This command sets the maximum number of file control blocks to 20 and specifies that 8 files are protected from automatic closure. (The second parameter isn't used in MS-DOS 5.0.) However, your network software probably adds the Fcbs command to CONFIG.SYS, and if it uses different values, leave them as they are.

Files

This command specifies the number of files you can have open under MS-DOS at one time. Setting Files to 30 with the command

```
files=30
```

is best for Windows. Setting a higher value only uses up more memory. However, if you ever see this error message in Windows,

```
Insufficient file handles, Increase Files in CONFIG.SYS
```

you should set this value higher. A setting of *files=50* usually solves the problem.

Install

This command loads terminate-and-stay-resident (TSR) programs from within CONFIG.SYS. You shouldn't mess with Install when setting up MS-DOS for Windows. However, I've often seen the Install command used to load the SHARE.EXE program for networks.

Note: Do not use Install to load the FASTOPEN.EXE program. Fastopen is deadly and causes conflicts between many MS-DOS utilities and programs. Do not even load it from within AUTOEXEC.BAT! Use the SMARTDrive disk cache program instead.

Lastdrive

This command sets the highest drive letter MS-DOS can use. The letter can range from the number of hard drives you have—plus any RAM drives you install—all the way up to Z. For example, if you have two hard drives and three RAM drives, they are automatically assigned drive letters

C through G by MS-DOS. If you want to use additional drive letters for network drives, you can set the Lastdrive command like this:

```
lastdrive=z
```

This Lastdrive setting is fine for nearly all computers using Windows. Setting the value lower—or not setting it at all—saves you a few bytes of memory, but not enough to make an appreciable difference in performance. It's like tossing out three ties to make more room in your closet.

Rem

This command allows you to insert comments in your CONFIG.SYS file. Follow Rem with a space and then the text of the comment. MS-DOS ignores lines that start with Rem when it reads CONFIG.SYS.

Shell

This command tells MS-DOS where to find COMMAND.COM, the command interpreter. You can also use the Shell command to specify an alternative command interpreter, such as J.P. Software's 4DOS or Norton's NDOS. For Windows, you should use the Shell command to load COMMAND.COM and create a large environment space. (The environment contains strings that programs can access to get information about the system.) If COMMAND.COM is in the root directory of drive C, here is the command you should use:

```
shell=c:\command.com c:\ /e:2048 /p
```

The first part of the setting, *c:\command.com*, is the full pathname (the location and name) of the command interpreter. This pathname is followed by COMMAND.COM's directory, C:\. You must be sure to specify the correct location for COMMAND.COM. For example, if the file is in your C:\DOS directory, you use this Shell command in CONFIG.SYS:

```
shell=c:\dos\command.com c:\dos /e:2048 /p
```

The */e* switch sets the size of the environment. In the above example, the size is set to 2048 bytes or 2 KB. Such a large environment might seem a bit excessive, but Windows runs better on some systems when the environment is set to 2 KB.

The /p switch makes COMMAND.COM the permanent command interpreter and directs COMMAND.COM to load and execute the AUTO-
EXEC.BAT batch file that is stored in the root directory of your boot disk.
(I cover AUTOEXEC.BAT in "Creating the Ideal AUTOEXEC.BAT File,"
later in this chapter.)

Stacks

This command sets aside space for MS-DOS's internal "stacks," which are
the storage places MS-DOS uses when it does things that are too complex
to discuss here (switching stacks for hardware interrupts if you really want
to know). The Windows Setup program adds the following command to
CONFIG.SYS, which sets up 9 stacks, each with 256 bytes:

```
stacks=9,256
```

After running Windows Setup, you can reset Stacks using the following
command:

```
stacks=0,0
```

This setting saves about 3 KB of memory. If you subsequently see a *Stack
overflow* message or if your machine crashes unpredictably, reset the command to *stacks=9,256*.

Switches

This command does two things, only one of which is important to Windows—and it's important only when you're running Windows version 3.0
on an MS-DOS 5.0 computer and you want to store the WINA20.386 file in
a directory other than your root directory. If that's you, see the tip box on
page 134.

Configuring Device Drivers

MS-DOS comes with several device drivers you can load from within
CONFIG.SYS by using either the Device or Devicehigh configuration
commands. Several of these drivers are vital to Windows' performance;
others aren't. Depending on your system's hardware and whether that
hardware is necessary to run Windows, you might also need to load third
party drivers.

Note: Always use the most recent version of HIMEM.SYS, EMM386.EXE, RAMDRIVE.SYS, and SMARTDRV.EXE. Check the file dates. If two files exist on your system, one in the MS-DOS directory and another in the Windows directory, use the one with the latest date.

The most important device drivers to load from within CONFIG.SYS are those that set up your disk drives. You need these drivers only if you're using special types of drives or external drives that must be configured before you can use them. (Most PCs don't require any disk configuration device drivers.) If you have special drives, these device drivers are probably already set up in your CONFIG.SYS file; don't mess with them.

Note: Disk doubling programs, such as Stacker, set up their device drivers in CONFIG.SYS. Unlike the device drivers for hardware disks, the device drivers for disk doubling programs must appear at the end of your CONFIG.SYS file so that they are loaded after all other device drivers.

After the device drivers that configure special disk drives come the memory management device drivers. For MS-DOS, the important device drivers are HIMEM.SYS and EMM386.EXE. Windows requires HIMEM.SYS in order to run. EMM386.EXE is necessary if you use MS-DOS's memory management commands on a '386-based PC. These commands are covered in detail in "Memory Management Issues," later in this chapter.

If you're running a multimedia PC, you'll need to load your sound and CD-ROM drivers from within CONFIG.SYS. These device drivers should come after the disk configuration and memory management drivers. And if you've set up memory management properly, you can use the Device-high command to load the drivers, saving that much conventional memory.

Some caching controllers as well as some SCSI and ESDI controllers use physical memory addresses. This is a problem if you're running Windows in 386 enhanced mode, which uses virtual memory. To solve the problem, load the double-buffer driver contained in the SMARTDrive program by adding the following command to CONFIG.SYS:

```
device=smartdrv.exe /double_buffer
```

This command creates a buffer in memory whose virtual and physical addresses are the same. Note that you can't use the Devicehigh command with this driver because it needs the physical addresses of conventional memory.

The Windows Setup program automatically adds this Device command to your CONFIG.SYS file if you need the double-buffer driver, so worry about adding the command only if you install a device after you set up Windows. To check whether you need the command, type *smartdrv* at the MS-DOS prompt. You should add the command to CONFIG.SYS only if *yes* appears in the column labeled *buffering*.

The only other device drivers you should load from within CONFIG.SYS are those that are vital to your system—for example, network drivers, virus scanning software, MS-DOS's SETVER.EXE "version fooling" device driver, and drivers for your scanner or any other hardware you use in Windows.

If you have an EGA video adapter, you might want to load the EGA.SYS driver. Stick the following command in CONFIG.SYS:

```
device=c:\dos\ega.sys
```

EGA.SYS should be stored in your DOS directory; be sure to specify the proper path. This device driver provides extra help for Windows when it switches from an MS-DOS application back to the Windows graphics screen. It's not needed for VGA-equipped PCs.

Two common drivers to avoid are MS-DOS's ANSI.SYS screen and keyboard device driver and the MOUSE.SYS device driver. ANSI.SYS controls the MS-DOS command line environment. Load this driver only if you will be running MS-DOS from Windows and you need ANSI.SYS. Otherwise, skip it and save yourself 4.5 KB of RAM. Likewise, because Windows has its own mouse device drivers, you can skip MOUSE.SYS, as well as its AUTOEXEC.BAT counterpart, MOUSE.COM. (However, you will need to load MOUSE.SYS if you want to run an MS-DOS program that uses a mouse under Windows. This subject is elaborated on in Chapter 5.)

The most important "bonus" device driver to load for use with Windows is RAMDRIVE.SYS, which creates a superfast RAM drive that Windows can use to store temporary data. (In case you forgot, a RAM drive is a section of memory that simulates a disk drive.) Loading RAMDRIVE.SYS is covered in the following section.

Note: With versions of Windows earlier than 3.1, the disk cache portion of the SMARTDrive program was loaded as a device driver from within CONFIG.SYS. Starting with version 3.1, the disk cache portion of SMARTDrive is a TSR and is loaded from within AUTOEXEC.BAT. See "Loading the SMARTDrive Disk Cache," later in this chapter.

Creating a Windows RAM Drive

Windows receives a small performance boost when you set up a RAM drive for storing temporary files. Before charging ahead, however, you should weigh the cost: Do you have enough spare memory for a RAM

Efficient RAM Drives

Creating a RAM drive any larger than 1 KB is a waste of memory under Windows unless you're swimming in RAM. If you're using disk doubling software, check whether you can create a small RAM drive and then double its size. For example, you might use Stacker to create a 512-byte RAM drive and then use the SCREATE.SYS device driver to "stack" the RAM drive, doubling its size to 1 KB. You would place this command right after the command that creates the RAM drive in CONFIG.SYS, like this:

```
devicehigh=c:\dos\ramdrive.sys 512 /e
device=c:\stacker\screate.sys d:

devicehigh=c:\stacker.com d:
```

Here, SCREATE.SYS doubles the size of the RAM drive—assumed to be drive D—which is created by the preceding line. Note that SCREATE.SYS isn't a resident device driver, so there's no need to load it high with Devicehigh.

drive? If you have a PC with 6 MB or more of extended memory, you have plenty of room for a 512-byte or 1-KB RAM drive. Or if you're configuring a diskless workstation, a RAM drive is an ideal way to speed up Windows. If your situation is any different from these, the memory you'd give up for a RAM drive would be better used by Windows itself.

To create a 512-byte RAM drive, insert this command in CONFIG.SYS:

```
device=c:\windows\ramdrive.sys 512 /e
```

If you've set up MS-DOS's memory managers, you can load the RAM-DRIVE.SYS device driver high by using the Devicehigh command:

```
devicehigh=c:\windows\ramdrive.sys 512 /e
```

The 512 in both of these commands sets the size of the RAM drive to 512 bytes. If you want a larger RAM drive—say 1 KB—specify 1024.

The /e switch puts the RAM drive in extended memory. This switch is required for Windows; without /e, the RAM drive would be created in conventional memory and you wouldn't have enough memory left to load Windows. (RAMDRIVE.SYS also has an /a switch that puts the RAM drive in expanded memory. But you haven't loaded an expanded memory manager because Windows doesn't use expanded memory, so specifying the /a switch would result in an *Expanded Memory Manager not present* error message.)

Note: RAMDRIVE.SYS comes with both Windows and MS-DOS. Be sure to use the most recent version.

To make the RAM drive most useful, you need to direct Windows to store its temporary files there by setting the TEMP environment variable from within AUTOEXEC.BAT, as discussed in "Creating Environment Variables," later in this chapter. Additional information about RAMDrive's options is provided in Appendix A.

Building a CONFIG.SYS File for Windows

Figure 1-1 shows an outline of the CONFIG.SYS file required to run Windows. You simply replace the entries in angle brackets with the necessary information for your system, ignoring them if they don't apply.

```
REM CONFIG.SYS file for Windows
REM <the date of modification>

<Hardware disk device drivers>

device=c:\dos\himem.sys
dos=high<,umb>
<Other memory management drivers, including EMM386.EXE>

files=30
<buffers=10>
stacks=0,0 <or stacks=9,256>
<fcbs=20,8 for networked PCs>
<lastdrive=z>
<shell=c:\command.com c:\ /e:2048 /p>

<device (or devicehigh)=c:\dos\setver.exe>
<device (or devicehigh)=c:\dos\ega.sys (EGA systems only)>
<device (or devicehigh)=c:\windows\ramdrive.sys 512 /e>
<device (or devicehigh)=c:\mouse\mouse.sys (for MS-DOS apps)>
<Multimedia sound driver>
<CD-ROM driver>
<device=smartdrv.exe /double_buffer>

<Other important device drivers>
<Device drivers for disk doubling programs, such as Stacker>
```

Figure 1-1. *The CONFIG.SYS file for Windows.*

Nothing in Figure 1-1 is etched in silicon. For example, you'll want to substitute the names of your own directories in your CONFIG.SYS. Also, you might want a 1024-byte RAM drive instead of the 512-byte example. Whatever the case, customize your CONFIG.SYS file accordingly, and remove anything not required by Windows.

CREATING THE IDEAL AUTOEXEC.BAT FILE

AUTOEXEC.BAT is the last of the five files MS-DOS uses when it boots your computer, and it's the second of the two files over which you have direct control. AUTOEXEC.BAT lets you set environment variables and allows you to run MS-DOS programs automatically every time you start your computer. For Windows, that means logging onto your network and loading the TSRs that you use with both Windows and the MS-DOS programs you run under it. You can also use AUTOEXEC.BAT to configure

COMMAND.COM, though that's a moot issue when you're running Windows.

Like all batch files, AUTOEXEC.BAT consists of commands you'd normally type at the command prompt. MS-DOS executes them one after the other when it runs AUTOEXEC.BAT. A good AUTOEXEC.BAT file contains all the commands you'd regularly type every time you start your computer. You can take advantage of special batch file commands, but they aren't often used in AUTOEXEC.BAT.

Like CONFIG.SYS, AUTOEXEC.BAT is a text file. You edit it using a text editor, such as Windows' Notepad program or the SysEdit program discussed in Chapter 2. Each command sits on a line by itself, and you can't use word wrap. AUTOEXEC.BAT must be saved as a text file when you finish editing, and you must reboot your computer for the changes to take effect.

Setting Up AUTOEXEC.BAT for Windows

What you put in AUTOEXEC.BAT depends on how you use your system. Many detailed MS-DOS scriptures offer guidance about the best startup file. In the following sections, I will cover several items that you should

Disabling Configuration Commands

An easy way to disable a command in CONFIG.SYS or AUTO-EXEC.BAT is to precede it with a Rem command (plus a space):

```
REM device=c:\mouse\mouse.sys
```

The command is still visible in the file, but because the line starts with *REM*, MS-DOS ignores the command. If you want to reactivate the command at a later date, edit out the Rem command.

Because MS-DOS reads CONFIG.SYS and AUTOEXEC.BAT every time you boot your PC, the changes you make to the file won't have any effect until you reboot. So the normal procedure is to edit CON-FIG.SYS, save it to disk, quit your editor, exit Windows (if you're running Windows), and then reboot to test everything.

consider putting in your AUTOEXEC.BAT, as well as rules for including additional items that I don't cover here. I'll present the ideal Windows AUTOEXEC.BAT file in "Building an AUTOEXEC.BAT File for Windows," later in the chapter.

Setting the Ideal Windows Path

Windows needs its own directory to be in your *search path*—the collection of directories specified by the Path command. MS-DOS and Windows use the search path to help hunt down programs to run. For an MS-DOS–only computer, the search path is vital for your efficiency. For example, it's a good idea to include your MS-DOS directory and a utility or batch file directory on the path so that you don't have to "cd" (change directories) all over your drive to run programs. To run Windows and its programs under MS-DOS, you should also put the WINDOWS directory on the search path, like this:

```
path c:\windows;c:\dos
```

This command puts the C:\WINDOWS directory in the path, followed by C:\DOS, your MS-DOS directory. Typically, the Windows Setup program adds the Windows directory to the Path command. As you install other

Resetting Your Search Path

If you need to access programs in other directories, such as a UTIL or BATCH directory, you can reset the path *after* Windows runs. You simply create a new Path command that puts necessary subdirectories in the path after you run WIN.COM. For example, you might put these two commands at the end of your AUTOEXEC.BAT:

```
win
path c:\dos;c:\util;c:\batch
```

If you need to access the directories in an MS-DOS window in Windows, you can use a special RUNDOS.BAT batch file that sets the path when you open an MS-DOS window. This batch file is covered in Chapter 5.

Windows-based applications, they will want to put themselves in the path, too. For example, both Microsoft Excel and Microsoft Word for Windows like their directories to be in the path. During the application's setup process, select the option that modifies your search path. You can also add the application's directory manually by editing your search path to look something like this example:

```
path c:\windows;c:\dos;c:\excel;c:\winword
```

Remember to specify the full pathname—including the drive letter—for all the directories you add to the path.

Setting a Prompt

Setting an MS-DOS prompt is totally unnecessary for Windows. The object of Windows is to avoid the MS-DOS prompt. However, you should include a Prompt command in AUTOEXEC.BAT to create a prompt for use when you run MS-DOS from Windows or after you exit Windows.

If you plan to run MS-DOS only from Windows, here's a command that creates an ideal prompt:

```
prompt In Windows; type EXIT to return$_$p$g
```

Putting Pathnames in WIN.INI

If Windows is unable to locate a program file, you'll be prompted to enter a path. To avoid the prompt, you can put that program's directory in the path in AUTOEXEC.BAT, or you can modify your WIN.INI file to specify the program's pathname directly. Put the pathname in WIN.INI under the [programs] section using this format:

program=pathname

Here, *program* is the name of the program you want Windows to run, and *pathname* is the full pathname (drive letter, directory path, and filename) of the file, showing its location on disk.

Further information about modifying WIN.INI is given in Chapter 2.

Assuming that you are working in the WINDOWS directory, this command creates the following MS-DOS prompt:

```
In Windows; type EXIT to return
C:\WINDOWS
```

The prompt reminds you that you're running Windows, not MS-DOS. Use the Exit command to close the MS-DOS window and return to Windows' friendly graphical environment.

Note: If you decide to use a special "in-Windows" prompt, remember to change it after you exit Windows. Put a new Prompt command after the win *command at the end of your AUTOEXEC.BAT file.*

Creating Environment Variables

You should create environment variables for use by certain programs. These variables and their contents are stored as character strings in the MS-DOS environment. Programs can examine the variable's contents in the environment and then make decisions based on what they find. An example of an environment variable that is used by both MS-DOS and Windows is TEMP, which sets a location for the storage of temporary files. You create the TEMP variable with the Set command. For example, the command

```
set temp=d:
```

sets TEMP equal to drive D. Temporary files are then stored on drive D, which is probably a RAM drive. (For more information, see "Creating a Windows RAM Drive," earlier in this chapter.)

Note: Do not end the TEMP variable's contents with a backslash. For example, specify D: for the root directory of drive D. If you specify D:\ for the root directory of drive D, some programs might not run. Similarly, specify a directory as C:\DIRECTORY, not C:\DIRECTORY\. That trailing backslash has been known to cause trouble.

If the programs you use require other environment variables, you should edit AUTOEXEC.BAT and create the variables using the Set command. On my system, I create special variables that describe how the system is running. For example, the WIN variable is set to *yes* or *no* to tell certain batch files whether Windows is running. The command looks like this:

```
set win=yes
```

Here, the WIN variable is set to *yes*, which means Windows is running. Batch files that I run in Windows can examine this variable and respond accordingly. I also set the NETWORK variable to *yes* or *no* depending on whether I'm logged onto the network. Of course, you must remember to reset the variables you create if the situation they describe changes. In any case, WIN is reset to *no* when I exit Windows, and NETWORK is reset to *no* when I log off the network.

Loading the SMARTDrive Disk Cache

Windows comes with a special program called SMARTDrive that can be used to perform *disk caching*. A *disk cache* (pronounced *cash*) is a place in memory where information read from disk is stored. The disk cache portion of SMARTDrive monitors all disk activity and diverts a copy of information read from disk to its cache. When a program requests information from disk that is already stored in the cache, SMARTDrive fetches the information from memory instead of reading the disk again. The SMART-Drive cache is also used when you write data to a disk. SMARTDrive saves the data in its cache and actually writes the data to disk only when the cache is full or when your computer isn't doing anything else. Because memory access is much faster than disk access, your system's performance is greatly improved.

Using the SMARTDrive program, you can set up a disk cache for use by Windows. Here is an abbreviated format for the SMARTDrive command:

smartdrv [*drive±*] [*InitCacheSize*] [*WinCacheSize*]

Here, the optional *drive±* indicates a drive letter to cache (+) or not cache (–). If you omit a value for *drive±*, SMARTDrive caches all your hard drives. If you indicate a drive letter but give no plus or minus sign, SMARTDrive won't cache the information you write it to disk, but it will cache the information you read. *InitCacheSize* indicates the initial size of the cache in KB, and *WinCacheSize* indicates the minimum size for the cache in KB. Windows can reduce the cache size from *InitCacheSize* to

WinCacheSize when it runs short of memory. (The full format for SMART-Drive and all its options is provided in Appendix A.)

The ideal size for the cache varies. SMARTDrive is quite intelligent about allocating only as much memory as it needs, depending on how much memory you have in your PC. Table 1-2 shows the memory sizes SMARTDrive automatically uses.

Total Memory (megabytes)	InitCacheSize (bytes)	WinCacheSize (bytes)
1 or less	256	0
2	1024	256
4	1024	512
6	2048	1024
8 or more	2048	2048

Table 1-2. *Cache sizes used by SMARTDrive.*

The values in Table 1-2 are selected by SMARTDrive when it's installed. They are also the values I suggest, which means you really don't need to specify any options when you use the SMARTDrive driver. Simply stick the following command in your AUTOEXEC.BAT file:

```
c:\windows\smartdrv.exe
```

This command directs SMARTDrive to automatically cache all the drives in your system. If you don't want to cache some of your drives, such as RAM drives (which are fast enough already and waste memory when cached) or Stacker drives (which shouldn't be cached at all), you can exclude them from caching by specifying the drive letter followed by a minus sign when you load the SMARTDrive driver. If you don't want to cache the information you write to a disk, specify the drive letter without a minus sign. The following command disables write caching for drive C and disables caching altogether for drives D and E:

```
c:\windows\smartdrv.exe c d- e-
```

Here are additional rules of thumb for using SMARTDrive:

■ SMARTDrive is automatically loaded high; there's no need to use the Loadhigh or Lh command, which loads TSRs into upper memory. To prevent it from being loaded high, follow the SMARTDRV command with the /l switch.

■ Because you're running SMARTDrive, you don't need to run Fastopen. Be sure that FASTOPEN.EXE doesn't appear in either your CONFIG.SYS or AUTOEXEC.BAT.

■ To force SMARTDrive to write to disk any data it has in its cache, enter *smartdrv /c* at the MS-DOS prompt before you turn off your computer.

Dealing with TSRs

Generally speaking, you should load TSRs only when they're absolutely necessary for running Windows. Two big winners here are network and CD-ROM drivers. You usually load these programs from within AUTO-EXEC.BAT before Windows runs so that you can take advantage of them.

Note: Often, a who's-on-first issue arises between network and CD-ROM drivers. Typically, you should load your network drivers first and then your CD-ROM drivers. Otherwise, some networks assume that the CD-ROM driver is another network program in memory and refuse to load when they see it.

You should run memory resident "pop-up" utilities in an MS-DOS window within Windows. To run a utility, you must create a PIF for it and specify that the TSR run in stand-alone mode. See Chapter 5 for more information.

A special TSR you might want to load is DOSKEY, which gives you command line editing capability, command line history, and macro commands at the MS-DOS prompt. DOSKEY is as far from Windows as you can get, so it's a good idea not to load it from within AUTOEXEC.BAT. True, if you do load DOSKEY, you will have access to its power when you run MS-DOS from Windows. However, you can save some memory by using the RUNDOS.BAT batch file (discussed in Chapter 5) to run MS-DOS from Windows with DOSKEY intact.

The MS-DOS TSR most worthy of a place in AUTOEXEC.BAT is Mirror. Mirror offers hard disk protection as well as deletion tracking "disaster recovery" features. The hard disk protection part of Mirror guards against accidental reformatting of your hard drive and is used with the Unformat command. The deletion tracking part allows easy recovery of accidentally deleted files. Both of these features can be set up in AUTOEXEC.BAT with the following command:

```
c:\dos\mirror c: /tc
```

I'm assuming that Mirror is in your DOS directory; be sure to specify the correct path for Mirror in your AUTOEXEC.BAT file.

The first parameter, *c:*, tells Mirror to provide hard disk protection for drive C. The second, */tc*, activates deletion tracking for drive C. Note that the drive letter by itself activates only the hard disk protection. The */t*drive parameter is what switches on deletion tracking.

Additional drives can be protected as follows:

```
mirror c: d: e: /tc /td /te
```

Here, hard disk protection and deletion tracking are provided by Mirror for drives C, D, and E.

Note: Only when Mirror's /tdrive option is specified does Mirror become memory resident. However, the program automatically loads high, so there's no need to use the Loadhigh or Lh commands to put the program in upper memory.

Commands to Avoid

I'm assuming that by now you know to leave the Fastopen command alone. While you're at it, avoid using these MS-DOS commands as well:

- Append
- Assign
- Join
- Mode
- Subst
- Undelete

Most of these commands are unnecessary under Windows. For example, you don't need to use the Mode command to set up a serial printer in

MS-DOS because that's done from within Windows. (Refer to "Using Your Printer" in Chapter 3 for more information.)

Starting Windows

The final thing you do in your AUTOEXEC.BAT file is run Windows by putting the *win* command on a separate line, like this:

```
win
```

If you've created a Windows-only path and prompt in AUTOEXEC.BAT, you can reset them so that they will be more suitable for MS-DOS when you quit Windows, like this:

```
win
REM reset path and prompt here
path=c:\dos;c:\util
prompt $p$g
```

You can also unload any Windows-specific TSRs, flush SMARTDrive's buffers, and optionally log off your network—provided, of course, that you will be turning off your computer immediately after you quit Windows. (For examples of these commands, refer to the sample AUTOEXEC.BAT in "Building an AUTOEXEC.BAT File for Windows," later in this chapter.)

Creating a Windows Batch File

A quick and easy solution to running Windows from within AUTO-EXEC.BAT is to create and use a special batch file that can be *chained* or *called* from AUTOEXEC.BAT. Creating a batch file to run Windows has three advantages:

■ It eliminates a lot of clutter that might otherwise appear in AUTO-EXEC.BAT.

■ It allows you to neatly start Windows-only TSRs and then shut them down after you quit Windows.

■ It allows you to rerun Windows with everything set up properly, without having to reboot your PC.

I recommend this course of action for setting up Windows, though it has one major drawback, which I'll disclose toward the end of this section.

Let's assume that you named the Windows batch file WINDOWS.BAT. You can run the batch file from within AUTOEXEC.BAT in two ways. The first way chains AUTOEXEC.BAT to the WINDOWS.BAT file by making WINDOWS.BAT the last line in AUTOEXEC.BAT, like this:

```
windows
```

The second way is to use the Call batch file command to run WINDOWS.BAT. This method allows you to run the batch file and then return to AUTOEXEC.BAT so that you can run additional startup commands after you quit Windows and finish running WINDOWS.BAT. The last part of AUTOEXEC.BAT then looks like this:

```
call windows
REM finish AUTOEXEC.BAT
```

Inside the Windows batch file, you can set your Windows path, run startup programs to modify Windows, and then undo everything after you quit Windows. Figure 1-2 shows a sample WINDOWS.BAT file.

First, the path is set to WINDOWS, DOS, and related file directories. This command might repeat a Path command in your AUTOEXEC.BAT, but it's required if you reset an "MS-DOS path" after you quit Windows (which is the case in the sample WINDOWS.BAT). That way, when you rerun the Windows batch file, the path will again be set to the one Windows needs.

```
@echo off
REM Windows batch file

path c:\windows;c:\dos;c:\excel;c:\ndw
prompt In Windows; type EXIT to return$_$p$g

smartcan /on /skiphigh
set win=yes
win /b
smartcan /off

path c:\dos;c:\util
prompt $p$g
set win=no
```

Figure 1-2. *A sample WINDOWS.BAT batch file used to run Windows.*

The prompt is set to an "in-Windows" prompt, as discussed in "Setting a Prompt," earlier in this chapter. Note that the prompt is reset to a "normal" MS-DOS prompt at the end of the batch file. The WIN environment variable is similarly set to *yes* and then reset to *no*.

The Smartcan program that is run in the sample batch file is a TSR from the Norton Desktop for Windows. It keeps track of deleted files and is used to delete files from the Desktop. What's important in this example is that after you quit Windows, Smartcan is removed from memory. Your WINDOWS.BAT should similarly load any TSR program before Windows and optionally unload it afterwards, as is done in Figure 1-2.

Note: Setting a Windows path in a WINDOWS.BAT file has a major drawback: Programs that want to modify Windows' path usually make their modifications in AUTOEXEC.BAT—not in the WINDOWS.BAT file where the Windows path is really kept. When that happens, you need to use SysEdit and the Notepad to cut and paste the proper part of the path from AUTOEXEC.BAT into your WINDOWS.BAT file.

Preliminary Housekeeping

As part of good hard disk management, you should perform regular "housekeeping" on your PC. This chore can be done from within AUTO-EXEC.BAT before or after a Windows session. You don't do housekeeping from within Windows because many of the housekeeping utilities, including MS-DOS's Chkdsk command, should not be run in a multitasking environment like Windows.

The subject of hard disk management and Windows housekeeping is covered in detail in Chapter 4. For now, stick a handy placeholder or Rem command in AUTOEXEC.BAT for future housekeeping commands.

Building an AUTOEXEC.BAT File for Windows

Figure 1-3 shows the minimum AUTOEXEC.BAT file required to run Windows. As with the CONFIG.SYS example earlier in this chapter (see the section titled "Building a CONFIG.SYS File for Windows"), the stuff in the angle brackets should be replaced with the information needed for your system according to the guidelines presented in the previous sections.

```
@echo off
REM AUTOEXEC.BAT file for Windows
REM <the date of modification>

path c:\windows;c:\dos;<other directories for Windows>
<prompt=$p$g (or a special "in-Windows" prompt)>
set temp=<temporary drive or directory pathname>
<Set other environment variables here>

REM <housekeeping duties>
smartdrv <drive letters and options>
<The Mirror command>

<Start your network software>
<CD-ROM drivers and extensions>

<Load Windows-only TSRs>
win <or call the Windows batch file>

<Commands to unload TSRs, reset the path, prompt, etc>

<DOSKEY>
<c:\windows\smartdrv /c (to flush the cache)>
```

Figure 1-3. *The AUTOEXEC.BAT file for Windows.*

Nothing in the sample AUTOEXEC.BAT file is sacred. In fact, Figure 1-3 tackles just about every task you'd ever want to handle from within an AUTOEXEC.BAT file. Some of this stuff is complex, so you may just

AUTOEXEC.BAT Finale

Here are the commands I put after *win* at the end of an AUTO-EXEC.BAT file for a dedicated Windows machine:

```
win
smartdrv /c
cls
prompt $a
echo It is now safe to turn off this computer.
```

First, SMARTDrive's cache is written to disk. Next, the *prompt $a* command makes the MS-DOS prompt "invisible." After quitting Windows, all I see is the message *It is now safe to turn off this computer,* which is what I usually do.

want to stick with the basics. For example, consider running the house-keeping commands outside AUTOEXEC.BAT, either by typing them each time or by putting them in their own batch file.

You must reboot your computer to test any changes you make to the AUTOEXEC.BAT file.

MEMORY MANAGEMENT ISSUES

You must take care of memory management before you start Microsoft Windows. Windows is finicky, and your computer must be set up just so for this prima donna to do its thing. The correct setup includes the following:

■ You *must* install an XMS device driver, such as HIMEM.SYS. This device driver creates the HMA and thereby provides Windows (and MS-DOS) with a "bonus" 64-KB bank of memory. (XMS stands for *Extended Memory Specification*, and an XMS device driver controls the extended memory Windows craves.)

■ You should install an expanded memory driver *only* if you plan on running Windows only in standard mode and you have MS-DOS programs that need expanded memory.

■ You should configure your system to load device drivers and memory resident programs high (into upper memory blocks).

■ If you use third party memory managers, you must configure them to run Windows. The big names, Quarterdeck's QEMM-386 and Qualitas's 386MAX, can be configured quite painlessly.

Desperate for Expanded Memory?

Do you really need to use expanded memory? If so, you can edit the SYSTEM.INI file to tell Windows to simulate expanded memory. This is tricky stuff. My advice is to read "SYSTEM.INI Overview" in Chapter 2 and then turn to Chapter 5 and read "Giving MS-DOS Programs Expanded Memory."

To put it bluntly: Windows needs extended memory to run. Gobs of it. Because 8088/8086 computers don't have this kind of memory, Windows cannot run on those platforms. It's limited to running on the old AT class (with 80286 processors) and the newer '386-based PCs (all 386, 486, and 586 varieties and flavors of processor).

Note: For the bottom line on MS-DOS memory management, refer to The Microsoft Guide to Managing Memory with DOS 5, *another book from Microsoft Press.*

Starting with Windows 3.1, it's possible to run Windows in 386 enhanced mode with expanded memory available. This memory is of use only to MS-DOS programs running under Windows that really need it. Windows doesn't use it, and any expanded memory you have directly subtracts from the total extended memory available for Windows.

Memory Management for 80286-based PCs

To get the best memory management for 80286-based PCs running Windows, add the following two commands to your CONFIG.SYS file:

```
device=c:\windows\himem.sys
dos=high
```

The first command loads the HIMEM.SYS extended memory device driver. This device driver does bounteous things for Windows. Primarily, HIMEM.SYS sets up extended memory and the HMA.

Note: Sometimes Windows installs HIMEM.SYS (and other device drivers) in drive C's root directory. In that case, specify c:\himem.sys. *Or, if you like to keep your hard disk organized, move HIMEM.SYS into your WINDOWS directory, and change the Device command in CONFIG.SYS accordingly.*

The Dos command puts part of MS-DOS into the HMA and gives Windows a bit more elbow room. Together with the HIMEM.SYS device driver, this command initiates memory management for both MS-DOS and Windows.

At this point, 80286 memory management stops. If you have a third party 80286 memory manager, such as Quarterdeck's QRAM, or a memory manager that supports the 80286, such as Qualitas's 386MAX, you can also load device drivers and TSRs high. But for MS-DOS, this is all you can do.

Additional information on HIMEM.SYS and the various options that might be required for certain systems is covered in Appendix A.

Memory Management for '386-based PCs

On '386-based PCs, you start with HIMEM.SYS and the Dos command, as shown in the previous section. You can stop there if you like. Windows is happy with that setup. But you can go further and make more memory available by creating upper memory blocks (UMBs) and loading device drivers and TSRs into them.

Creating UMBs with EMM386.EXE

To create UMBs, you must do two things. First, you must modify the Dos command in your CONFIG.SYS file to include its *umb* option, like this:

```
dos=high,umb
```

The Dos command then both loads MS-DOS high and prepares MS-DOS for the creation of UMBs. The second thing you need to do is actually create the UMBs by loading the EMM386.EXE device driver with the following command:

```
device=c:\windows\emm386.exe noems
```

Be careful not to use the SYS extension; EMM386.EXE is the correct name for this device driver. (You also enter the extension when you run the driver from the command line.) The sole option used here, *noems*, directs EMM386.EXE to create UMBs. (Another format of EMM386.EXE converts your PC's extended memory to expanded memory. Some MS-DOS programs like the expanded memory, but Windows can't use it.)

You should now have the following three commands in CONFIG.SYS to set up memory management:

```
device=c:\windows\himem.sys
dos=high,umb
device=c:\windows\emm386.exe noems
```

Loading High

After you create UMBs, you can use the Devicehigh command in CON-
FIG.SYS to load your device drivers high into UMBs and the Loadhigh,
or Lh command in AUTOEXEC.BAT to load TSRs high. For example,
MS-DOS's SETVER and RAMDRIVE device drivers can be loaded high
with the following commands in CONFIG.SYS:

```
devicehigh=c:\dos\setver.exe
devicehigh=c:\windows\ramdrive.sys 512 /e
```

In AUTOEXEC.BAT, you load TSRs high by sticking the Loadhigh, or Lh,
command in front of them. For example, the following three commands
start up a LANtastic workstation from within AUTOEXEC.BAT:

```
lh c:\lantasti\aex irq=15 iobase=300 verbose
lh c:\lantasti\ailanbio
lh c:\lantasti\redir behemoth logins=2
```

These Lh commands load LANtastic's ethernet, LAN BIOS, and redirec-
tion drivers into UMB memory. You can load other TSRs needed by
Windows in the same manner; simply prefix their full pathnames with
Lh. Note that both SMARTDrive and the Mirror command automatically
load themselves high if there's room, so you don't need Lh commands
for them.

If you don't have room to load a device driver or a TSR high, you can
fiddle with the loading order in CONFIG.SYS. For example, loading larger
device drivers first often allows you to stuff them into a UMB where they
wouldn't fit before. You can use the *mem /c ¦ more* command at the MS-DOS
prompt to see what fits where in the upper memory area as well as the
size of your device drivers in KB. Then edit CONFIG.SYS if necessary,
rearranging the device drivers from largest to smallest to load them high.

If a device driver or TSR cannot be loaded high, it will be loaded into conventional memory, as usual.

Including and Excluding Memory

It's possible to increase the number of UMBs that are available by using
EMM386.EXE's *i* (for *include*) option. You can also use the *x* option to
exclude areas of memory, protecting such things as network hardware and

other regions of memory from being trampled on by a device driver or TSR loaded high.

To increase the number of UMBs for MS-DOS—and for Windows—use the *i* option, followed by an equal sign and the region of upper memory you want to include. The unpalatable part of this trick is that you must specify the region in hexadecimal. Fortunately, Windows comes with a utility, MSD.EXE (the Microsoft Diagnostics program), that makes the job somewhat easier.

To run MSD, switch to your WINDOWS directory, and then type *msd* at the MS-DOS prompt. (You can also run MSD from within Windows, but the results are tainted by the PIF associated with MSD. So it's best to run the utility at the MS-DOS prompt before or after you run Windows.)

When MSD starts, select the *M* Memory option from the main menu by pressing M. You then see a graphic map of upper memory, similar to the one shown in Figure 1-4. Note where the ROM areas are located. For example, a ROM area is located in the section labeled *C800* on the left side

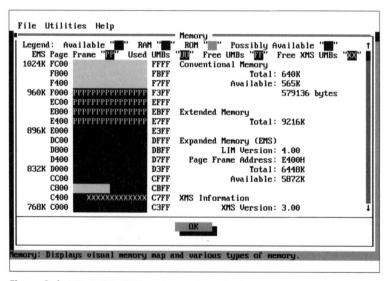

Figure 1-4. *The MSD.EXE memory map, which can be used to locate include or exclude areas in upper memory.*

of the memory map in Figure 1-4. That's the memory my system's network adapter card uses. It resides in upper memory, beginning at address C800 hexadecimal and ending at location CBFF, which can be seen on the right side of the memory map in the figure. (It doesn't fill the whole map, side to side, but there's no need to be picky here.) To exclude that portion of memory, I could add the following option to EMM386.EXE:

```
x=c800-cbff
```

Similarly, if you see any ROM areas in the memory map of your system, note their beginning and ending location numbers. (The locations start with the hexadecimal number on the left side of the memory display and end with the number on the right.) For example, if an adapter's ROM starts at location D800 and ends at DFF, you can exclude it with the following option:

```
x=d800-dfff
```

Note: In addition to excluding any areas of upper memory by running EMM386.EXE from within CONFIG.SYS, you also need to use the EMMExclude command in SYSTEM.INI. This command is covered in the section titled "The EMMExclude Setting," in Chapter 2.

Excluding areas of memory protects them from wanton destruction by wayward device drivers and TSRs. But that's the negative side of the story. On the positive side, you can include areas of memory to increase total UMB storage. As long as you're not using a Compaq or IBM PS/2 computer, you can include all of the bank E area of memory (from E000 to EFFF) for a total of 64 KB of extra UMBs. (Both Compaq and IBM PS/2 computers use parts of bank E for their ROM.) Here is the *i* option that performs this trick:

```
i=e000-efff
```

In hexadecimal speak, this option includes all of bank E for a total of 64 KB. Other areas might be available for inclusion on your system, but this option gives you the most UMBs. On some VGA systems, you can include the monochrome display memory area, like this:

```
i=b000-b7ff
```

This option makes the 32-KB area used by a monochrome display adapter, which goes unused on a VGA system, available as a UMB. (This option might not work with some SuperVGA systems.)

Some third party memory managers automatically include as UMBs the monochrome display memory that is not used on an EGA or a VGA system, by using the MONOUMB2.38_ file included on the Windows distribution disks. (MONOUMB2.38_ is compressed, and you must expand it using the Expand command before you can use the file.) The drawback with that trick is that MONOUMB2.38_ is incompatible with the EMM386.EXE driver that comes with MS-DOS. Oh well...

All include and exclude options must appear on the EMM386.EXE line in CONFIG.SYS, after the program's pathname. It's best to list the excludes first, then the includes, and then follow everything with the *noems* option. Here is an example:

```
device=c:\windows\emm386.exe x=d800-dfff i=e000-efff noems
```

Here, memory between D800 and DFFF is excluded and then memory between E000 and EFFF (all of bank E) is included. Remember to save your changes to CONFIG.SYS and then reboot so that they will take effect.

The full format for the EMM386.EXE device driver is given in Appendix A. Additional information on memory management under Windows can be found in Chapter 4.

Third Party Memory Managers for Windows

The benefit of using third party memory managers is that they can load device drivers and TSRs high much more efficiently than MS-DOS can, often without the setup headache. Two programs worth considering are QEMM and 386MAX. Both are fully compatible with Windows.

Before moving on, note that a major drawback with going the third party route is that their device drivers are usually incompatible with the next version of Windows. This means that you might have to order an upgrade for your memory manager to stay compatible with Windows. However, the memory savings and hassle-free approach to memory management they provide usually makes up for the expense and the wait.

Chapter 2

Windows Startup

With the required tweaking of both CONFIG.SYS and AUTOEXEC.BAT out of the way, all that remains is to quickly duck into Windows and leave the ugly command prompt behind forever. You do this by typing *win* at the MS-DOS prompt or, better yet, by somehow including the command in AUTOEXEC.BAT. (See Chapter 1 for the grimy details.) From that point on, using Windows is painless and requires little thought or effort on your part—that is, until you're told to edit your SYSTEM.INI file. What exactly is an INI file—the opposite of an OUTTIE file? And how does that file, as well as its boon companion, WIN.INI, fit into *The Big Picture*?

The purpose of this chapter is to acquaint you with the way Windows starts, the programs that are used, and how everything works together. After reading this chapter, you'll understand why hundreds of files are stored in the various Windows directories. I also introduce the perplexing INI files—SYSTEM.INI and WIN.INI—and tell you how they fit in and what you should and shouldn't do to them.

WINDOWS' BOOT PROCESS

MS-DOS requires only three files to start your PC: IO.SYS, MSDOS.SYS, and COMMAND.COM. You use two additional files, CONFIG.SYS and AUTOEXEC.BAT, to configure your system and run startup programs. For MS-DOS, that's it. (I described the latter two files and how they fit with Windows in Chapter 1.)

Windows requires many more files to start. Yes, MS-DOS does set up file control, preliminary memory management, and a few device drivers for Windows. But that's nothing compared with the number of things Windows needs to set up before it can control your computer. In fact, Windows steals away many tasks from MS-DOS. Windows also provides your software with more resources and better access to your PC's hardware than

MS-DOS can. That's a big job, so Windows comes with a brood of files to pull it off.

In the Beginning, There Is WIN.COM

Everything begins with WIN.COM—the *win* command you use to start Windows. When you run WIN.COM, it checks the following things:

- The type of PC you have

- How much memory is available

- Whether to run Windows in standard or 386 enhanced mode (which will be called *enhanced mode* from now on)

- Whether Windows is already running

These are quick and dirty checks. If Windows is already running or if anything is awry—you have an 8088 PC or you don't have enough extended memory available—then Windows won't run, and WIN.COM displays an appropriate error message.

If everything checks out, WIN.COM displays Windows' startup logo and proceeds to load Windows in either standard mode or enhanced mode. Different files are used for each mode. The modes and their respective files are covered in the section titled "Loading Windows," later in this chapter.

The WIN.COM Program

The WIN.COM program file is a combination of three files: a configuration program that performs the bulk of WIN.COM's chores; a logo file, which contains the instructions for displaying the opening logo; and the logo graphic itself. These files were all welded together by Setup when you installed Windows. The reason for this metallurgy is that the startup logo is a graphic that is specific to the CGA, EGA, VGA, or Hercules video system. If all four graphics and the instructions for displaying them were stored in a single file, WIN.COM would be huge and take close to forever to load into memory.

You can use Windows' File Manager to see the remnants of the files used to create WIN.COM. They're scattered around your WINDOWS\SYSTEM directory like bomb fragments:

■ WIN.CNF is the configuration program, the core of WIN.COM's programming instructions. It's actually a COM program with the extension CNF. In fact, if you copy WIN.CNF to a new file called WIN1.COM and put the new file in your WINDOWS directory, you can enter *win1* to start Windows without seeing the startup logo.

■ The file with the LGO extension contains the instructions necessary to display the logo using your graphics adapter. The first part of the filename tells you which graphics adapter you have. For example, VGALOGO.LGO is used with VGA displays.

■ The file with the RLE extension is a bitmap file that contains the logo, sized properly for your graphics adapter. Like the LGO file, the first part of the RLE file's filename indicates the type of graphics adapter you have.

The filenames used for the LGO and RLE files are shown in Table 2-1. You have only one of these on your hard drive—the one that matches your video display. The rest are on the distribution disks that came with Windows.

Filename	Graphics Adapter Supported
CGALOGO	CGA (Color Graphics Adapter)
EGALOGO	EGA (Enhanced Graphics Adapter)
EGAMONO	EGA monochrome support
HERCLOGO	Hercules monochrome display
VGALOGO	VGA (Video Graphics Array) PS/2

Table 2-1. *LGO and RLE filenames.*

Note: RLE stands for run length encoded. The RLE files contain standard Windows bitmaps that have been compressed to occupy less space. Some programs recognize this format and automatically decompress the RLE file into bitmaps for viewing and editing. (Paintbrush, unfortunately, isn't one of them.)

If you're really fond of Windows' startup logo, you can use it as your desktop's wallpaper. First copy your RLE file to your WINDOWS directory, and rename the file, using the BMP extension. Then click the Desktop icon in the Control Panel to open the Desktop dialog box. Next in the Wallpaper area of the Desktop dialog box, select the logo file from the list. Click OK, and you have true Windows-zany wallpaper. (You might want to center the logo; the "tiled" effect is tacky.)

Windows' Startup Options

WIN.COM has a parade of optional switches, most of which you don't have to fiddle with because the program determines what you need to run

Creating a Startup Screen

If you have software that can store a graphic in the 4-bit RLE format, you can create and edit your own Windows startup screen. You can create a graphic in this format using Paintshop for Windows or the WinGIF shareware program.

After you've created the new startup logo, save it as a 4-bit RLE image in your WINDOWS\SYSTEM directory. In MS-DOS, change to that directory, and build a custom startup program using the Copy command, as follows:

```
copy win.cnf /b + vgalogo.lgo /b + newlogo.rle /b win2.com
```

Here, the Copy command is used with the /b (binary) switch to combine the three binary files WIN.CNF, VGALOGO.LGO, and NEWLOGO.RLE—your RLE logo file—to make a new startup file called WIN2.COM that uses your new logo. (If you're using a graphics adapter other than VGA, specify the proper LGO file from Table 2-1 in the above command.) The new startup file has a different name so as not to confuse it with the original WIN.COM.

Put the new WIN2.COM file in your WINDOWS directory, and try it. Chances are it won't look as good as Windows' traditional opening screen—in fact, it might look downright ugly. But as you can see, creating a new startup screen is possible, and it's a cool way to show off Windows to your friends.

Windows without any effort on your part. But in case you're curious, here is WIN.COM's full syntax line:

```
win [:] [/s:/2]:[/e:/3] [/b] [/d:[f][s][v][x]] [filename]
```

The colon (:) directs WIN.COM to start Windows without loading the startup screen. Many amateur Windows gurus claim that using the optional colon starts Windows "faster." But the truth is that WIN.COM simply skips over the startup screen; time-savings are minimal.

To force Windows to start in standard mode, you can specify the /s or /2 switches. Using these switches makes a difference only when Windows would otherwise start in enhanced mode, such as on a '386-based PC with plenty of extended memory.

To force Windows to start in enhanced mode, you can specify /e or /3. You need these switches only when Windows mistakenly thinks it cannot run in enhanced mode. Unfortunately, you can't use these switches on an 80286 computer to "fool" Windows into thinking that you have a '386-based PC.

The /b switch tells Windows to create a "boot log" record. Windows then maintains a file called BOOTLOG.TXT in your WINDOWS directory and appends information to the file each time Windows starts. The file lists the drivers and files Windows loads as it boots and whether each one was loaded successfully.

Note: The BOOTLOG.TXT file does not log startup and shutdown times. However, the Dr. Watson utility keeps track of when it's started and stopped. If you place Dr. Watson in the StartUp group window and keep the utility running during your session in Windows, you will have a record of when you started and stopped Windows. You can load the file named DRWATSON.LOG (it's in your WINDOWS directory) into Notepad and check there for startup and shutdown information.

The /d switch is used for debugging Windows. It lets you shut off some of Windows' more powerful features to check for hardware conflicts.

The *f* option shuts off 32-bit disk access; *s* directs Windows not to use ROM in bank F as a system break point; *v* instructs Windows to use ROM for disk access; and *x* tells Windows not to use any upper memory. Use these options only if you can't get Windows to run. (Microsoft Product Support technicians often ask you to use these switches when they're trying to discover why Windows won't run on your system.)

The *filename* option is used to start Windows and immediately load an application. *filename* must be the name of a Windows-based application.

Note: *Each of the* /d *(debug) options has a corresponding setting in the SYSTEM.INI file:*

/d:f *is equivalent to* 32BitDiskAccess=Off

/d:s *is equivalent to* SystemROMBreakPoint=Off

/d:v *is equivalent to* VirtualHDIrq=Off

/d:x *is equivalent to* EMMExclude=A000-FFFF

The idea behind using the /d *switch with the win command is that you can test one of these settings as Windows starts, without having to permanently change your SYSTEM.INI file.*

Loading Windows

The WIN.COM program checks your system hardware and determines whether you can run Windows in standard or enhanced mode. If you can't do either, WIN.COM displays an error message, explaining why Windows can't run.

After the mode is determined, several programs and drivers are loaded into memory. Windows' internal device drivers are installed, as well as any external drivers, network drivers, speed-up drivers or accelerators, and other special programs that give Windows control over your screen, keyboard, network, and other components of your PC. The sections that follow cover everything about loading Windows in detail, starting from the moment you type *win* and press Enter. Figure 2-1 shows the files that are executed as Windows boots in both standard and enhanced modes.

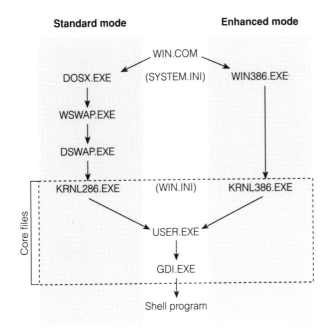

Figure 2-1. *How Windows boots.*

Standard or Enhanced Mode?

The minimum hardware requirements for running Windows in standard mode are as follows:

■ An 80286 or higher processor

■ 640 KB of conventional memory

■ At least 256 KB of extended memory

■ An XMS-compatible device driver, such as HIMEM.SYS

These are the bare minimum requirements—like saying ketchup qualifies as a "vegetable" in a school lunch program. To really make use of standard mode, you should have a PC with at least 512 KB of extended memory. The more extended memory you have, the better Windows will run.

To run Windows in enhanced mode, your PC must have at least the following:

■ An 80386 or higher processor

■ 640 KB of conventional memory

■ At least 1 MB of available extended memory

■ An XMS-compatible device driver, such as HIMEM.SYS

These requirements usually elicit the same knowing smirk as the standard mode requirements. Realistically speaking, 2 MB is the minimum required for Windows to run in enhanced mode. Windows really shines on a 4-MB system and, if you can afford the RAM chips, 8 MB puts a smile on Windows like the one on a hog belly-deep in mud.

Note: To run Windows for Workgroups in enhanced mode, you need at least 3 MB of memory. In enhanced mode, you can both share your printers and directories with other computers and connect to other computers. In standard mode, you're limited to connecting to other computers.

If you have less than the minimum requirements for standard mode, Windows won't run. If you have less than the minimum requirements for enhanced mode, Windows might start in standard mode. The only way to be certain which mode you're in is to run Windows. Then in Program Manager, pull down the Help menu, and choose About Program Manager. At the bottom of the dialog box that appears, you'll see either *386 Enhanced Mode* or *Standard Mode* displayed.

Note: Another way to find out which mode Windows will run in is to enter win /? at the MS-DOS prompt before you start Windows. WIN.COM then displays Windows' startup options, and the last line on the screen tells you in which mode Windows will start.

Loading the Core Files

After WIN.COM has decided which mode to run Windows in, it starts one of two programs: For standard mode, it runs DOSX.EXE, and for enhanced mode, it runs WIN386.EXE. Both are programs that finish the job of loading Windows. They shift the processor into high-gear protected mode and leave MS-DOS's real mode in the dust. In protected mode, your computer operates at top speed because the extended memory that is "useless" under MS-DOS becomes instantly accessible.

For standard mode, WIN.COM loads two additional programs after it runs DOSX.EXE: the WSWAP.EXE program, which swaps Windows-based programs in and out of memory; and the DSWAP.EXE program, which swaps MS-DOS programs. These programs are needed because the 80286 lacks the powerful multitasking capabilities built into '386-based processors. (Program swapping in enhanced mode is handled by WIN386.EXE.)

The next files to load are Windows' *core files*: the kernel, the user interface, and the graphics device interface. These three files carry out the following key functions:

■ The kernel file—called KRNL286.EXE for standard mode and KRNL386.EXE for enhanced mode—manages memory, loads applications, and controls multitasking.

■ The user interface file—USER.EXE—creates and destroys windows, and handles the icons, mouse, and menus, as well as the system timer, communications ports, and sound driver. It decides what must be done with your input, whether from the keyboard, the mouse, or some other input device.

■ The graphics device interface file—GDI.EXE—handles all drawing on the screen, as well as creating images on the printer and other graphical output devices.

All these files, except WIN.COM, are located in the WINDOWS\SYSTEM directory. They are the guts of Windows. In addition to these files, Windows requires various drivers, fonts, and support files to complete the operating system.

Drivers, Fonts, and Other Support Files

Windows controls everything in your computer. Everything. It maintains control through special programs, or *drivers*, which are loaded when Windows starts. These drivers are what makes the Windows environment so much more attractive than MS-DOS. Under Windows, you don't have to worry about setting up every program to work with your printer, monitor, or network. That's all handled by Windows' drivers.

The many different types of drivers installed by Windows can be classified as follows:

■ Communication drivers, which control the serial ports

■ Display drivers, which control the video system

- Keyboard drivers, which control the keyboard

- Mouse drivers, which control the mouse or a similar input device

- Multimedia drivers, which control sound, MIDI, CD-ROM drives, external video, and so on

- Network drivers, which control the network and integrate it with Windows

- Printer drivers, which control the printer or similar output device

- System drivers, which control the timer, disk drives, and other basic components of the computer

Windows Startup Batch File

Believe it or not, you can create a batch file that will run whenever Windows starts in enhanced mode. When WIN386.EXE starts, it looks for a file named WINSTART.BAT in the WINDOWS directory. If the file exists, it loads and runs it.

You can use WINSTART.BAT to load special TSRs that will be available for Windows but not for MS-DOS programs. For example, you can load a virus scanner, file protection software, and other memory resident programs that boost Windows' performance.

The idea here is that you load some TSRs for use with Windows only, and you don't want them taking away memory from the MS-DOS programs you run under Windows. By loading them with WINSTART.BAT, you make the programs available for Windows but not for your MS-DOS programs, so they don't decrease the amount of conventional memory available to MS-DOS.

You can load TSRs for use with MS-DOS programs running under Windows either by specifying them in AUTOEXEC.BAT or by using batch files to load the TSRs and then run the MS-DOS programs. That topic is covered in Chapter 5.

Windows comes with a host of different driver files to match the various hardware configurations of the more than 1000 computer systems it currently supports. That's what makes Windows' distribution disks so bulky. However, only the drivers required by your PC are copied to your hard disk. The drivers needed for your system are listed in the SYSTEM.INI file, located in your WINDOWS directory. (You'll find more information on SYSTEM.INI in "SYSTEM.INI Overview," later in this chapter.) The actual loading of the drivers is handled in standard mode by DOSX.EXE. In enhanced mode, the WIN386.EXE program takes care of this task.

Nearly all driver files have DRV extensions. Using File Manager, you can locate some of the ones used by your computer. For a PC that is fairly run-of-the-mill, you might find the drivers listed in Table 2-2 in your WINDOWS\SYSTEM directory. If your DRV files don't exactly match the ones listed, don't worry. Drivers can be very specific; for example, HPPCL.DRV is for Hewlett-Packard LaserJet Series II printers. If you have a different printer, Windows uses a different printer driver. The drivers your computer needs were all set up for you when Windows was installed.

Driver Name	Type of Driver
COMM.DRV	Communication driver
VGA.DRV	Display driver
KEYBOARD.DRV	Keyboard driver
MOUSE.DRV	Mouse driver
HPPCL.DRV	Printer driver
SYSTEM.DRV	System driver

Table 2-2. *Windows drivers used by most PCs.*

In addition to the DRV files, Windows loads font files and various dynamic link library (DLL) files when it starts. Font files have FON, FOT, or TTF extensions. Dynamic link library files have DLL extensions.

Note: The DLL files are "library" files. They contain programs that carry out specific tasks in Windows. For example, Windows uses the COM-MDLG.DLL library to create common dialog boxes such as the Open and Save dialog boxes. Unlike traditional programs, the DLL files are loaded into memory only when they are needed.

So that you can exchange information between MS-DOS applications and Windows, Windows loads a WinOldApp file, as well as a "grabber" file. For standard mode, the WinOldApp file is called WINOLDAP.MOD; for enhanced mode, it's called WINOA386.MOD. The grabber file is named after your graphics adapter and has the 2GR extension for standard mode or 3GR for enhanced mode. Together, these files lets you run MS-DOS programs under Windows, as well as share information between MS-DOS and programs for Windows. (The enhanced mode grabber also enables you to display an MS-DOS program in a window that isn't full screen and select information from it using the mouse.)

Windows might load even more files: various program files that come with Windows, their associated DLL files, other drivers for interesting hardware configurations, extra font files, and support files for specific printers and foreign languages—the Windows developers thought of everything. All this support makes up the majority of Windows' files on the distribution disks. The resulting operating system is complex, but it keeps us from having to constantly tweak applications to get them to work with our hardware.

How the INI Files Fit into the Picture

To load the device drivers, DLL files, and font files, enhanced mode's WIN386.EXE or its standard mode counterpart, DOSX.EXE, reads the SYSTEM.INI text file, located in your WINDOWS directory. This perplexing file controls much of how Windows works.

SYSTEM.INI is covered later in this chapter and throughout the rest of the book, so don't get huffy if I don't descibe it in detail here. What concerns us about SYSTEM.INI right now is that, as I mentioned earlier, it contains a list of the driver files your PC requires. Windows loads them, either from disk or from an internal library, according to the list in SYSTEM.INI.

Later in the startup process, the kernel file—either KRNL286.EXE or KRNL386.EXE—looks for and loads the WIN.INI text file. That file contains descriptive information about the Windows environment: how it looks and what settings you've made, both in Windows and in your Windows-based applications.

Note: Windows for Workgroups uses the PROTOCOL.INI initialization file when it loads the network drivers. You can change the values in this initialization file by using the Networks dialog box of the Control Panel.

You can think of the INI files as Windows' way of keeping track of various changeable settings. They're scratch pads—places where Windows can jot down information so that it knows what to do the next time it starts. The INI extension means "initialization," and that's exactly what Windows uses SYSTEM.INI and WIN.INI for.

Note: I pronounce INI as "innie," like a belly button. The tech gurus at Microsoft call them I-N-I files (eye-en-eye). Take your pick. (I think innie is cuter.)

Try not to think of the INI files as batch files. They were set up when you installed Windows, and they're updated as you use Windows, or if you change settings either in the Control Panel or by running the Windows Setup program again. But they aren't "run" at startup, and only rarely will you need to modify these files directly. (Don't panic; "Setting Up and Using the System Editor," later in this chapter, tells you how to edit the files if you need to.)

The Shell

Windows' final startup task is to run a *shell* program that allows you to use Windows. For MS-DOS, the standard shell is COMMAND.COM. For Windows, it's PROGMAN.EXE—Program Manager.

You can use different shells in Windows by loading the SYSTEM.INI file into a text editor, locating the Shell command in the [boot] section, and then specifying a program name after *shell=*. By default, Windows runs PROGMAN.EXE. To run a different shell, such as the Norton Desktop for Windows, Hewlett-Packard's NewWave, or one of the many other shell programs available, simply insert the program name.

THE BEFUDDLING INI FILES

One of the most confusing parts of Windows are those gosh-darn INI files. Ugh! They bug everyone. Most of this reaction is totally unwarranted.

From Windows version 3.0 on, you rarely need to edit an INI file, like you did with earlier versions of Windows. Windows updates these files as necessary, and you can make your own adjustments by using the Control Panel and the Windows Setup program. However, a certain curiosity remains, and a certain aura surrounds the daring Windows user who can understand an INI file enough to work its magic. In the following sections, I hope I can demystify these files for you.

How an INI File Works

As I've said, an INI file is an initialization file. It's like a scratch pad full of information Windows can read, modify, and save for later use. In a way, an INI file is like a permanent copy of MS-DOS's environment, in that it lists items (called *variables* in MS-DOS and *keywords* in Windows) that are set to certain values. The values can be changed, either by directly editing them in the file or, more commonly, by using Windows.

Can You Run Windows from a RAM Drive?

This isn't a silly question. Running a dreadfully slow program—for example, any MS-DOS batch file—from a RAM drive makes its execution seem almost instantaneous. But RAM drives aren't really a speed-boosting solution for Windows.

RAM drives work best with software that frequently accesses the hard disk. Windows' startup files are read only once, so putting them in a RAM drive produces no speed benefit. In fact, the time it would take MS-DOS to copy the files to the RAM drive would be longer than the time it takes them to load when Windows starts, netting a total speed savings of zero or less.

Another important point is that the amount of RAM required to pull off this stunt is best used for Windows itself. For example, creating a 4-MB RAM drive to contain the Windows files means that Windows doesn't have access to that 4 MB of memory, and its performance might suffer.

INI files aren't batch files. They're something like CONFIG.SYS, though they're sort of used all at once rather than read from top to bottom. And whereas you have only one CONFIG.SYS, you have a lot of INI files. A quick peek into your WINDOWS directory with File Manager reveals at least the five listed in Table 2-3.

INI File	Contents
CONTROL.INI	Control Panel settings
PROGMAN.INI	Program Manager settings
SYSTEM.INI	Windows' startup settings (Windows drivers, fonts, hardware support)
WIN.INI	Windows' environment settings
WINFILE.INI	File Manager settings

Table 2-3. *Windows' five basic INI files.*

You might have additional INI files in your WINDOWS directory, depending on the programs you've installed and used. For example, the Clock program has an INI file. All INI files serve the same purpose: to record configurations, files, and certain settings associated with each program— again, like scratch pads for remembering information.

The INI File Format

All INI files are text files that you can edit using a text editor. However, any changes you make don't take effect until you restart Windows or rerun the application associated with the INI file.

All INI files use a similar format for organizing and storing information. Each file is divided into *sections*, which contain various *keywords* and

Listing INI Files

To see how many INI files you have, change to your WINDOWS directory in File Manager. Choose the Select Files command from the File menu, type *.INI*, and press Enter. Then click the Close button. File Manager highlights every INI file. I counted 31 INI files in my directory.

values. The section names appear in square brackets on a line by themselves, like these examples:

```
[boot]
```

```
[Sounds]
```

```
[keyboard]
```

```
[Settings]
```

In each section, various keywords are set to values. Each section has its own set of keywords, though not all of them need to be included in the file. The format most often used is:

   keyword=value

keyword is a combination of letters and numbers. Sometimes it's descriptive, and sometimes it's not. It's usually, though not always, followed by an equal sign and the value, which determines the setting of the keyword. The value can be a filename, the name of an internal driver, or a "Boolean" value, such as *Yes* or *No, True* or *False, On* or *Off,* or 1 or 0. Positive Boolean values turn on the option represented by the keyword; that is,

---

For Solitaire Addicts

If you are one of the many people who find Solitaire addictive, you should know that Windows often creates an INI file called SOL.INI for the game. This INI file usually has two entries, *Options* and *Back. Options* specifies a number that expresses the various options you've set in Solitaire. *Back* contains the number of the card background you've selected. If you want Solitaire to randomly select a different background each time it starts, delete the *Back=number* line in SOL.INI.

Earlier versions of Windows stored information for Solitaire in the WIN.INI file. Look for the [Solitaire] section. If you want random backgrounds, delete the *Back=number* line there.

values of *Yes*, *True*, *On*, and 1 all turn on the option. Negative Boolean values turn off the option.

When a keyword isn't listed in an INI file (and a lot of them aren't), Windows assumes it is to use that option's standard, or default, value. So if you don't see a particular keyword that you think should be there, don't worry: Windows is simply using the default setting.

Case doesn't matter in an INI file. A mixed case style (for example, BorderWidth) is traditionally used when naming the keywords, but the program reading the INI file doesn't care. Sometimes text string values need to be in mixed case for readability. For example, if the text string in the entry

```
keyboard.typ=Enhanced 101 or 102 key US and Non US keyboards
```

were all lowercase, the US keyboard might be mistaken for an "us" keyboard.

Blank lines are okay in INI files. And any line starting with a semicolon (;) is taken to be a comment. So you can use the semicolon to annotate your changes to an INI file or to temporarily disable an option.

The order of the keywords doesn't really matter. Certain keywords must be in certain sections, but Windows isn't picky about the organization of

Boolean Formats

Generally, this book presents keywords requiring a Boolean value in this format:

keyword=Boolean

However, if a keyword requires either a 0 (off) or 1 (on) value, it is presented as follows:

*keyword=*0 ¦ 1

The pipe symbol (¦) lets you know that you should use either the value on its left or the value on its right.

the groups or the keywords within them. In fact, when Windows updates its INI files, it inserts any new items at the start of the appropriate section. This really jumbles things up, so don't be surprised if you go to edit an INI file and find things rearranged.

The Two Biggies: SYSTEM.INI and WIN.INI

The most mysterious of the INI files are Windows' key initialization files, SYSTEM.INI and WIN.INI. The former is read by the main Windows program—DOSX.EXE for standard mode and WIN386.EXE for enhanced mode—and the latter is read by Windows' kernel. (Refer to Figure 2-1 on page 39 to see where they fit into *The Big Picture*.)

Most of the settings in these two files are set and reset as you use Windows. Changing settings in the Control Panel, File Manager, and Program Manager and using the Windows Setup program automatically adjusts SYSTEM.INI or WIN.INI. You don't really need to mess with them. However, some tweaks can only be made to the files manually, and even if you never need to make these kinds of adjustments, it's good to know what's going on in the files.

Note: Changes made to SYSTEM.INI aren't read until you exit and restart Windows. Some changes made to WIN.INI are read as you use Windows; others take effect only when you exit and restart Windows.

Setting Up and Using the System Editor

You can use Notepad to edit any INI file. Simply choose Open from Notepad's File menu, specify *.INI* in the File Name text box, and click the OK button. When you see a list of the INI files stored in your WINDOWS directory, select the one you want, and click OK again.

A handier way to edit your SYSTEM.INI and WIN.INI files, as well as your CONFIG.SYS and AUTOEXEC.BAT files, is to install and use the System Editor (SysEdit) program included with Windows. Windows' Setup program does not install SysEdit when you first set up Windows, but it does copy the SysEdit program to your hard disk so that it is ready to use.

Installing SysEdit

To install SysEdit, select a group for it in Program Manager. I put it in my Utility group (a group I created specially for Windows utilities). After you select the group, choose New from the File menu, and check that the Program Item option button is selected. Click OK.

In the Program Item Properties dialog box, click the Browse button, and then change to your WINDOWS\SYSTEM directory. The file named SYSEDIT.EXE should be listed in the File Name list box. Next double-click SYSEDIT.EXE, and then click OK to close the Program Item Properties dialog box.

Using SysEdit

SysEdit is basically a custom version of Notepad, and using SysEdit is the quickest, easiest, and best way to customize your configuration files. When you start SysEdit, it automatically loads four files: CONFIG.SYS, AUTOEXEC.BAT, SYSTEM.INI, and WIN.INI. (See Figure 2-2.) Each appears in its own window, ready for viewing or editing.

SysEdit's commands are self-explanatory. It's missing a few of Notepad's fancier menu items, but the basic stuff is there. There's no Help file—I

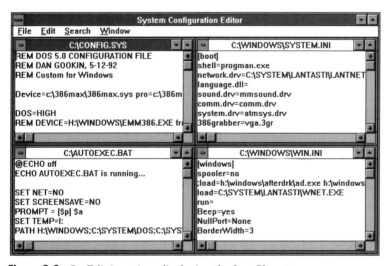

Figure 2-2. *SysEdit in action, displaying the four files at once.*

guess the developers figure that if you decide to edit these files, you're gutsy enough to dispense with Help.

Note: SysEdit automatically backs up the original INI, AUTOEXEC.BAT, and CONFIG.SYS files when you save your changes. The old files are saved with the extension SYD. If you use a different text editor, always create backup copies of your original files before making changes.

SYSTEM.INI OVERVIEW

The SYSTEM.INI file is used when Windows starts. The file contains information about setting up all aspects of Windows, configuring its operation, and loading device drivers. SYSTEM.INI is created by the Setup program when you install Windows. It's based on a file named SYSTEM.SRC, which is stored on one of Windows' distribution disks.

Note: The SYSTEM.SRC file is stored on Windows' distribution disks as SYSTEM.SR_. To see what the original SYSTEM.INI looks like, you can use MS-DOS's Expand command to expand SYSTEM.SR_ into SYSTEM.SRC. First copy SYSTEM.SR_ from Windows' distribution disks to your hard drive. Then use the following command at the MS-DOS command prompt:

```
expand system.sr_ system.src
```

You can now view SYSTEM.SRC in a text editor.

Everything in your SYSTEM.INI is either preset by the Setup program or created by running the Windows Setup or Control Panel programs. No additional tweaking of this file is necessary to run Windows, though some applications and utilities might modify its contents, especially when you add new hardware to your PC.

The Sections in SYSTEM.INI

SYSTEM.INI requires only the [boot], [keyboard], and [386Enh] sections to properly load Windows, but you might have other sections in your version of the file. Table 2-4 lists the eight sections documented by Microsoft. Any additional sections in your SYSTEM.INI file were probably put there by Windows-based applications such as multimedia kits or by external hardware attached to your computer.

Section	Contents
[386Enh]	Specifies device drivers, fonts, and settings required by enhanced mode
[boot]	Specifies device drivers, fonts, startup modules, shell, and files needed by Windows when it starts
[boot.description]	Describes the devices that can be changed with the Windows Setup program and other system startup information
[drivers]	Identifies names or "aliases" assigned to installable driver files
[keyboard]	Gives information about the keyboard
[mci]	Specifies media Control Interface (MCI) drivers
[NonWindowsApp]	Gives information used by non–Windows-based applications
[standard]	Specifies device drivers, fonts, and settings used in standard mode

Table 2-4. *The sections in SYSTEM.INI.*

Note: Windows for Workgroups adds a few sections to its SYSTEM.INI file. The [network] section contains settings for the network. [Password Lists] tells Windows for Workgroups where to find its list of passwords for each user that has logged on. Three other sections, [DDEShares], [ClipShares], and [DDEItemShares], keep track of information that is shared between computers.

Many keywords are available for use within each section, and not all the keywords will be present in any given SYSTEM.INI file. Many of the sections and their contents are discussed at length later in this book. Chapter 5 discusses various settings in the [386Enh], [standard], and [NonWindowsApp] sections. And this chapter looks at some of the settings in the [boot] section, plus the important *EMMExclude* setting in the [386Enh] section.

Checking Out the [boot] Section

The [boot] section in SYSTEM.INI contains information about device drivers, fonts, and all sorts of other vital stuff that Windows needs to know before it can start. All the keywords that might wend their way into this section are listed in alphabetic order in Table 2-5 on the next page.

Entry Format	Typical Value	Description
286grabber=*filename*	VGACOLOR.2GR	Specifies the device driver required to run an MS-DOS window in standard mode
386grabber=*filename*	VGA.3GR	Specifies the device driver required to run an MS-DOS window in enhanced mode
CachedFileHandles=*n*	Not specified	Controls the number of most-recently accessed EXE and DLL files that Windows can cache. Values for *n* range from 2 through 12.
comm.drv=*filename*	COMM.DRV	Identifies Windows' serial communications driver
display.drv=*filename*	VGA.DRV	Identifies Windows' display driver
drivers=*filename/alias*	MMSYSTEM.DLL	Specifies any installable drivers to be loaded when Windows starts. Never mess with this entry.
fixedfon.fon=*filename*	VGAFIX.FON	Specifies the fixed system font to be used with Windows 2.x applications
fonts.fon=*filename*	VGASYS.FON	Tells Windows which font to use as its system font
keyboard.drv=*filename*	KEYBOARD.DRV	Identifies Windows' keyboard driver
language.dll=*library*	Blank	Specifies the file that contains language-specific information used by Windows
mouse.drv=*filename*	MOUSE.DRV	Identifies Windows' mouse driver
network.drv=*filename*	Blank	Identifies your network driver. If blank, no network is installed.
oemfonts.fon=*filename*	VGAOEM.FON	Specifies the font for the OEM character set

Table 2-5. *Entries for SYSTEM.INI's [boot] section.*

Table 2-5. *continued*

Entry Format	Typical Value	Description
shell=*filename*	PROGMAN.EXE	Identifies Windows' startup program or shell
sound.drv=*filename*	MMSOUND.DRV	Identifies Windows' sound driver
system.drv=*filename*	SYSTEM.DRV	Identifies the system hardware driver for your PC
TaskMan.Exe=*filename*	TASKMAN.EXE	Identifies the task switching program activated by Ctrl-Esc

How these keywords appear in your SYSTEM.INI file will vary; each time the section is updated, the order of the keywords might change.

The majority of the keywords are assigned values during installation; you should never mess with these items. If you must, the majority of the items in the [boot] section can (and should) be changed either by using the Windows Setup program or by running the Setup program at the command prompt outside of Windows. The *language.dll* item can be changed by double-clicking the International icon in the Control Panel and selecting a new language from the Language drop-down list in the International dialog box. The following items can be changed only by editing SYSTEM.INI: *CachedFileHandles*, *comm.drv*, *shell*, *sound.drv*, and *TaskMan.Exe*. (You'll need to change the *CachedFileHandles* item only if you are running Windows on a file server and only if the server can't handle all the files you want to open.)

You'll probably see a bunch of blank items in your SYSTEM.INI file, which means that Windows loads the default driver. Default drivers for a VGA Windows system were listed in Table 2-2 on page 43. As I've said, your SYSTEM.INI file might include items that aren't listed in Table 2-5. (My file includes an item that specifies the screen saver file.) If so, great; don't mess with them.

One item you might want to change in the [boot] section is *shell*. That keyword identifies the shell program that Windows runs when it first

starts. Under most circumstances, *shell* will be set to PROGMAN.EXE—
Program Manager—but you can specify other shells, like this:

```
shell=c:\ndw\ndw.exe
```

This setting causes Windows to use the NDW.EXE shell—Norton Desktop
for Windows—in place of Program Manager.

Your shell program is important because it's the last program run when
Windows starts up (refer to Figure 2-1 on page 39). When the program
identified as Windows' shell quits, so does Windows. More information
on Program Manager and how it fits into Windows' startup scheme is covered in "Program Manager," later in this chapter.

The *EMMExclude* Setting

One item you might find yourself adjusting in the [386Enh] section is
EMMExclude. This item forbids Windows to use a specific chunk of upper
memory. It avoids conflicts between hardware devices and Windows,
which might try to use the same memory locations.

Most often, your *EMMExclude* setting will be identical to any *x* (exclude)
settings specified by EMM386.EXE or a similar memory manager in
CONFIG.SYS. (EMM386.EXE's role in CONFIG.SYS is covered in Chapter 1; refer to "Including and Excluding Memory.") For example, if your
network driver sits in memory locations D800 through DFFF, you may
have the following command in CONFIG.SYS:

```
device=c:\windows\emm386.exe x=d800-dfff noems
```

Here, the exclude range is set to D800–DFFF, and a corresponding
EMMExclude item must appear in SYSTEM.INI's [386Enh] section,
like this:

```
EMMExclude=d800-dfff
```

Windows is then clued into the fact that your PC might have something
sitting in the D800–DFFF range in upper memory. If you exclude more
than one range, then you need multiple *EMMExclude* entries; you cannot
list the ranges one after the other on the same line, as you do with
EMM386.EXE in CONFIG.SYS.

WIN.INI OVERVIEW

The second of Windows' two big, bewildering INI files is WIN.INI. This initialization file is read before Windows actually appears on the screen because many of Windows' visible attributes are controlled in WIN.INI: The desktop colors, window attributes, fonts, and even system sounds are specified in this file. Other applications might add information to WIN.INI as well, making it appear somewhat chaotic. However, the chaos doesn't matter because it's nothing you need to grapple with on a regular basis.

WIN.INI is maintained by Windows and the applications that put their settings in it. Unlike SYSTEM.INI, WIN.INI holds a treasure of interesting and oddball settings that you can manipulate to tweak Windows' look, feel, and performance. You start out with the basic WIN.INI file created by Setup when you installed Windows. This file is based on a file called WIN.SRC, which can be expanded from the file called WIN.SR_ that is stored on Windows' distribution disks. (Follow the instructions in the note about SYSTEM.SRC on page 52 to expand this file. Be sure to use the filenames WIN.SR_ and WIN.SRC instead of SYSTEM.SR_ and SYSTEM.SRC.)

As with SYSTEM.INI, you can control many of the settings in WIN.INI from Windows (mostly by using the Control Panel). However, unlike SYSTEM.INI, the WIN.INI file contains many settings you can change manually to customize Windows' environment. And because many of WIN.INI's options aren't listed in the dialog boxes accessed through the Control Panel, your file may be a true treasure of hidden Windows nuggets.

The Major Sections in WIN.INI

WIN.INI contains many sections, 17 of which are listed in alphabetic order in Table 2-6 on the next page. Your WIN.INI file might have fewer or many more sections, depending on how long you've been using Windows and how many third party programs have clumped their own information in WIN.INI. (Windows for Workgroups adds a few sections that keep track of the resources to which you have connected.) As long as Windows starts, the number of sections is probably correct for your computer.

Section	Contents
[colors]	Sets the colors used to display Windows' desktop. Change this item only by using the Control Panel's Color dialog box.
[Compatibility]	Provides information for running older Windows applications that relied on bugs fixed in Windows 3.1
[Desktop]	Controls the appearance of the desktop, icons, background pattern, and wallpaper
[devices]	Basically an echo of the [PrinterPorts] section, but without the timeout values. This section is included for compatibility with Windows 2.x applications.
[embedding]	Provides information for object linking and embedding (OLE) support. This section includes the objects' descriptions, creators, and file formats. Use REGEDIT.EXE—the Registration Info Editor application—to make changes to this section.
[Extensions]	Associates filename extensions with programs
[fonts]	Specifies the screen fonts to load when Windows starts. Change this item only by using the Control Panel's Fonts dialog box.
[FontSubstitutes]	Specifies fonts that replaced the fonts in earlier versions of Windows. (Helv, Tms Rmn, Times, and Helvetica were all replaced in Windows 3.1.)
[intl]	Specifies the date, time, and currency formats and other international and foreign language support settings
[mci extensions]	Associates filename extensions with various media control interface (MCI) devices, primarily multimedia devices such as sound cards and MIDI sequencers
[network]	Describes network settings and drive and printer connections. (Your network driver may not need this section to be in WIN.INI.)
[ports]	Describes your parallel (printer) and serial ports
[PrinterPorts]	Specifies printer settings and connection information. Change this item only by using the Control Panel's Printers dialog box.
[programs]	Lists the full pathnames of programs Windows needs in order to run. This section lists programs that are not on the search path (which you set in AUTOEXEC.BAT).

Table 2-6. *Major sections in WIN.INI.*

Table 2-6. *continued*

Section	Contents
[Sounds]	Describes system events and the sounds associated with them. Change this item only by using the Control Panel's Sound dialog box.
[TrueType]	Controls TrueType font support
[windows]	Specifies various settings for Windows, such as startup programs, window appearance, printer control, keyboard and mouse response rates, the beep, and document and program definitions
[Windows Help]	Provides settings for Windows' Help, such as Help window position and colors

In the olden days, every application and its uncle put information in WIN.INI. The file was a mess! In a sudden twist of sanity, developers started giving their applications their own INI files (which is why you'll find so many INI files in your WINDOWS directory). You may still see some settings for third party applications in your WIN.INI file. For the programs that you are still using, this is fine. However, if you spy some information in WIN.INI that belongs to programs you've deleted from your hard drive, feel free to delete the information.

Note: Always make a backup of WIN.INI before you edit it. The SysEdit program backs up the file automatically, creating a backup file called WIN.SYD.

Additional details about the settings in each of WIN.INI's sections is given throughout the rest of this book. Specific information about loading startup programs is covered in "Automatic Program Startup," later in this chapter.

The [Compatability] section

The [Compatibility] section was included in Windows 3.1 to fix some problems with Windows' programs that were "customized" for version 3.0. These programs rely on parts of Windows that were optimized or debugged during the upgrade to version 3.1. They are listed in the [Compatibility] section, along with hexadecimal "flags" that will allow them to run under future versions of Windows.

PROGRAM MANAGER

Unless you've installed a different shell, Program Manager is where you do your work under Windows. Working in conjunction with File Manager, Program Manager gives you most of what you need from an operating system.

Unlike other graphical operating systems, such as the Macintosh Finder or the OS/2 Workplace Shell, Program Manager does not represent your disk's organization directly. There is no relationship between Program Manager's icons and groups and the way your files and directories are stored on your hard disk. Although you may find the lack of a relationship strange at first, it does have its benefits: You can move and delete icons in Program Manager without affecting any files on your hard disk. (Moving and deleting the files themselves can be done neatly in File Manager.) On the other hand, deleting a file from disk doesn't affect the icons in Program Manager. If you delete a file, you must remember to also delete its icon.

The following sections give an overview of Program Manager and its INI file, PROGMAN.INI. If you want more detailed information, a tutorial, or information about the applets that come with Windows, then I suggest you read the Cobb Group's *Windows 3.1 Companion*, as well as Craig Stinson's *Running Windows 3.1*, both from Microsoft Press.

Windows Control Central

Program Manager is a system of groups and icons. The groups are windows within the Program Manager window. (These are called *child windows* in Windows programmer lingo). Within the groups are icons that represent programs or data files stored on your hard disk. Figure 2-3 shows how Program Manager looks on my screen.

Program Manager's groups are created in three different ways: The Setup program creates groups when you install Windows; the Windows-based applications you install may create their own groups; and you can create groups by choosing the New command from Program Manager's File menu.

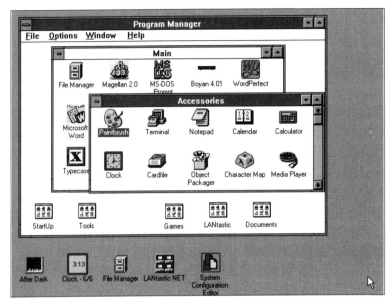

Figure 2-3. *Group windows and icons in Program Manager.*

You can put programs or data files into each group by choosing New from the File menu or by dragging the files you want from File Manager and dropping them into the group in Program Manager. Using either method, you can create groups that suit your needs. For example, you might use the Main group to hold your main applications, a Utility group to hold utility programs, and a Projects group to hold all files related to a particular project.

Note: Setting up a group for use by several people on a network is covered in "Network Groups for Program Manager" in Chapter 8.

If you put files into Program Manager groups, they are represented by a special icon only if they are associated with an application that is stored on disk. Otherwise, they are represented by a standard icon. You can assign different icons to these files, as described in Chapter 7.

A quick way to access the programs and data files you use most often is to put them in a single group and maximize the group's window. The icons then look like a control panel. To run a program, double-click its icon.

The PROGMAN.INI File

Program Manager maintains an initialization file called PROGMAN.INI, which helps Program Manager set itself up and remember any changes you've made since the last time you started Windows. You can use Notepad to edit PROGMAN.INI, which you'll find in the WINDOWS directory.

Unless you've messed with PROGMAN.INI before, it should have only two sections: [Settings] and [Groups]. A third section, [restrictions], is added to PROGMAN.INI when Windows is set up to run on network workstations or in other situations when you don't want someone changing your Program Manager settings.

The [Settings] Section

The [Settings] section controls the way Program Manager looks as well as keeps track of the options set in the Options menu. This section can have anywhere from three to seven items, which are listed in Table 2-7. None of these items should be modified directly. They are controlled from within Program Manager. A typical [Settings] section is shown in Figure 2-4.

Entry Format	Description
Window=a b c d 0¦1	Sets the size and location of Program Manager's window. The first four values shouldn't be edited; otherwise, the next time Windows starts, Program Manager won't appear the way you left it. To change the values, move the window. The last setting controls whether the window is maximized (1) or not (0).
SaveSettings=0¦1	Indicates whether you've turned on the Save Settings On Exit option on Program Manager's Options menu (1) or turned it off (0)
MinOnRun=0¦1	Indicates whether you've turned on the Minimize On Use option on the Options menu (1) or turned it off (0)
AutoArrange=0¦1	Indicates whether you've turned on the Auto Arrange option on the Options menu (1) or turned it off (0)
Startup=$group$ $name$	Identifies the name of Program Manager's startup group. If blank, the group is StartUp. You can use this item to specify any group in Program Manager for automatic loading and executing of applications. (For more information, see "Automatic Program Startup," later in this chapter.)

Table 2-7. *Entries for PROGMAN.INI'S [Settings] section.*

Table 2-7. *continued*

Entry Format	Description
display.drv=	Specifies your system's display driver. This item, which is also specified in SYSTEM.INI, isn't documented in the manual, but don't mess with it anyway.
Order=	Indicates the order in which Program Manager draws each of the group (child) windows. Also shows how Program Manager will "cycle" through its child windows when you press Ctrl-Tab.

The [Groups] Section

The [Groups] section identifies the groups in the Program Manager window. Each group is assigned a number as it's created by Program Manager and is represented by the keyword *Group* followed by that number. Each keyword is set equal to the full pathname of the group's file in your WINDOWS directory. (Group files have GRP extensions.) By the way, the number is also used in the *Order* item in the [Settings] section. The group numbers may not be in sequence in the [Groups] section; as you delete and create groups, the numbers can get quite random. A sample [Groups] section is shown in Figure 2-5; what you see in your PROGMAN.INI file will undoubtedly be different.

```
[Settings]
Window=20 4 585 394 1
SaveSettings=1
MinOnRun=0
AutoArrange=0
display.drv=VGA.DRV
Order= 2 10 1 3 4 9 5
```

Figure 2-4. *A typical [Settings] section.*

```
[Groups]
Group1=C:\WINDOWS\MAIN.GRP
Group2=C:\WINDOWS\ACCESSOR.GRP
Group3=C:\WINDOWS\GAMES.GRP
Group4=C:\WINDOWS\STARTUP.GRP
Group10=C:\WINDOWS\TOOLS.GRP
Group9=C:\WINDOWS\LANTASTI.GRP
Group5=C:\WINDOWS\APPLICAT.GRP
```

Figure 2-5. *A typical [Groups] section.*

Adding Custom Groups During Installation

You can have Windows Setup add groups to Program Manager by creating them in the SETUP.INF file. Edit this file only if you're performing multiple installations of Windows and you want everyone to use the custom groups—for example, on a network.

Start by adding your custom group to both the [new.groups] and [progman.groups] sections in SETUP.INF, using this format:

groups#=*name*

is a number greater than those already specified in the SETUP.INF file, and *name* is the name of the new group window. (If you want the group window to be maximized when Windows starts, add a comma followed by 1. By default, the window is minimized.) Here's an example:

```
group8=Tools
```

You must then add a [group#] section to SETUP.INF that contains information about the programs in the group. The section title should be identical to the *group#* keyword you created. Here is the format for adding programs to the group:

[group#]
"icon_title" ,*program,icon_filename,index,profile*

"icon_title" is the name that will appear below the program's icon in the group window. It can be as many as 40 characters and must be enclosed in quotation marks.

program is the name of the program associated with the icon. If the program's file isn't in the WINDOWS directory, specify a full pathname. You can specify COM, EXE, BAT, or PIF files. (If you're updating a Windows installation, you can leave this item blank to delete the corresponding icon from the group.)

icon_filename is the name of the file that contains the icon graphic. Specify this item only if the program doesn't supply its own icon or if you want to use a different icon.

index is a value that indicates the location (starting with 0) in *icon_filename* of the icon you want to use. (See the example below.)

profile allows you to tag the file for installation using the Add/Remove Files dialog box (in the Windows Setup program) after Windows is set up. If *profile* is blank, the icon is always added to the group during setup. If the filename (not the extension) is specified, the icon is not added.

Here is an example of an entry in a [group#] section in SETUP.INF. This entry is for the MS-DOS Prompt icon that Windows first sets up in Program Manager's Main group:

```
"MS-DOS Prompt",DOSPRMPT.PIF,PROGMAN.EXE,9
```

Each item is separated by a comma. DOSPRMPT.PIF is the name of the program information file (PIF) that specifies the program's filename (COMMAND.COM) and other information needed to run the MS-DOS shell in Windows. Its icon is the ninth one listed in PROGMAN.EXE. If you omit an item but want to specify subsequent items (such as *profile*), you must use commas as placeholders, like this:

```
"Solitaire",SOL.EXE,,,sol
```

Here, *icon_filename* and *index* are missing, indicating that Solitaire will use its own icons. However, *profile* is present so commas have been inserted as placeholders for the missing items.

Don't bother with editing the [Groups] section. You create and destroy groups by using Program Manager's interface.

The [restrictions] Section

Your PROGMAN.INI file probably won't have a [restrictions] section, which limits access to Program Manager's commands. You can add items to this section only by editing PROGMAN.INI and manually inserting the section. This section usually comes last and includes the five optional keywords listed in Table 2-8.

Entry Format	Description
NoRun=0 ¦ 1	Indicates whether the Run command on the File menu is disabled (1) or enabled (0). With Run dimmed, you're restricted to using only those programs that appear as icons in Program Manager.
NoClose=0 ¦ 1	Indicates whether the Exit Windows command on the File menu and the Close command on the Control menu are disabled (1) or enabled (0). Yes, with *NoClose* turned on, there's no way to exit Windows— not even with Alt-F4.
NoSaveSettings=0 ¦ 1	Indicates whether the Save Settings On Exit command on the Options menu is disabled (1) or enabled (0). Program Manager will not remember its window arrangement or size when you set this keyword to 1. (Turning it on here even overrides the SaveSettings item in the [Settings] section of PROGMAN.INI.)
NoFileMenu=0 ¦ 1	Indicates whether the entire File menu is disabled so that none of its options can be selected (1) or whether the File menu is enabled (0). When the File menu is disabled, you can still start a program by double-clicking its icon or by selecting the icon and pressing Enter. And the user can still quit with Alt-F4, unless *NoClose* is set to 1.
EditLevel=n	Sets the edit level: 0 allows full editing, adding, and rearranging of icons and groups in Program Manager; 1 restricts the creating, moving, copying, and deleting of groups, and disables the corresponding items on the File Menu; 2 applies the restrictions of 1 to both groups and icons in the groups; 3 includes all the restrictions of 2, plus prevents the user from changing the command line in an icon's Properties dialog box; and 4 includes all the restrictions of the other settings and also restricts the user from changing anything in an icon's Properties dialog box.

Table 2-8. *Entries for PROGMAN.INI's [restrictions] section.*

Editing or adding any of the [restrictions] items would really cramp an advanced user's style. These items should be set only when you're working in controlled situations—or when you're feeling mean and think it would be fun to turn on *NoClose* and watch a coworker struggle to exit Windows.

Using the Task Manager

The task manager pops up when you press Ctrl-Esc or when you double-click an empty area of the desktop. By default Windows' task manager is TASKMAN.EXE, but you can designate any program as the task manager by following the *TaskMan.Exe* keyword in SYSTEM.INI's [boot] section with the name of the task manager.

There's nothing special about this. The program you specify simply pops up whenever you press Ctrl-Esc or double-click the desktop. You could, for example, specify SOL.EXE if you are a Solitaire freak by adding the line

```
TaskMan.Exe=SOL.EXE
```

but then you'd undermine the usefulness of the task manager included with Windows.

The default task manager program (Task List) displays a list of the programs currently open in Windows, as shown in Figure 2-6. If you have a document or file loaded in an application, its name is shown with the application's. To switch to an application, highlight it in the list, and click Switch To, or simply double-click the name you want. To close an open application, highlight it, and click End Task. (This is the equivalent of closing the application's window by pressing Alt-F4.)

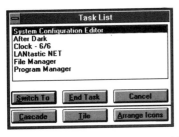

Figure 2-6. *The task manager, which lists open applications.*

The buttons at the bottom of the Task List window allow you to control the appearance of your desktop. You can tile or cascade the open windows or use the Arrange Icons button to clean up the unsightly clot of icons at the bottom of the desktop.

AUTOMATIC PROGRAM STARTUP

Just as AUTOEXEC.BAT can start programs for you in MS-DOS, Windows can lock-and-load applications for you when it starts. On the surface, directing Windows to automatically load certain programs involves adding icons to Program Manager's StartUp group and setting the properties of the icons. Beneath the surface, you can accomplish the same thing by manually editing the WIN.INI file. However, starting with version 3.1, Program Manager's StartUp group has made the second option archaic.

The difference between *loading* and *running* a program is superficial: Either way, the program is started by Windows. The program that's *loaded* is started and then minimized to an icon. The program that's *run* is started and remains on the screen as a window.

As an example of how you might want to load and run applications, consider a typical Windows session: You start Program Manager; then you start File Manager, the Clock, and the Calculator and minimize them for later use; then you start Word for Windows, and—some time later—you start Solitaire. The following sections describe how you can start all these programs automatically in Windows.

Automatically Loading or Running a Program

Windows scans the StartUp grou each time you start Program Manager. Any programs represented by icons in the StartUp group window are automatically started. Whether they're loaded or run depends on the program's properties. If the Run Minimized check box in the Properties dialog box is selected, then the program is loaded; otherwise, the program is run.

Going back to the example from the previous section, to automatically load File Manager, the Clock, and the Calculator, you must first copy their icons one at a time to the StartUp group by highlighting each icon in its current group, holding down the Ctrl key, and dragging the icon to the StartUp group's icon (or window). With the icons in the StartUp group, you need to modify their properties one at a time, so that they start minimized. Highlight an icon, and then choose Properties from the File menu. (As a shortcut, click the icon once, and press Alt-Enter.) In the Properties dialog box, select the Run Minimized check box to tell Program Manager to start the application and then shrink it down to an icon. Repeat these steps for each of the icons in the StartUp group that you want to load.

Continuing the example, to automatically run Word for Windows and Solitaire, copy their icons one at a time to the StartUp group by highlighting an icon, holding down the Ctrl key, and dragging the icon to the Startup group's icon. Then for each icon, choose Properties from the File menu, and, in each item's Properties dialog box, be sure that the Run Minimized check box is not selected so that Program Manager will run the program in a window, not as an icon.

Note: You can load or run documents associated with programs. Simply copy the document's icon to the StartUp group just as you would a program icon. You can also drag document icons from File Manager to the StartUp group.

You can add as many programs as you like to the StartUp group. You can even create new items specifically for the StartUp group. Just remember

Other Groups as Startup

If you don't have a group named StartUp, you can designate any other group in Program Manager as the startup group. Simply load PROGMAN.INI into a text editor, and in the [Settings] section, add the group name after the *Startup* keyword. For example,

```
Startup=Main
```

designates the Main group as the startup group. All of the programs represented by icons in the Main group window will automatically be started each time Windows runs.

to select their Run Minimized option if you want to load them, and de-select it if you want to run them. Don't get too carried away, though. You don't want to waste memory by loading programs you won't be using.

Editing WIN.INI to Load
or Run a Program at Startup

Before Program Manager had a StartUp group, you could automatically load or run programs or documents by specifying their names after the *load* or *run* keyword in the [windows] section of WIN.INI. This method still works, but working with the StartUp group in Program Manager is much easier.

To load a program using WIN.INI's *load* keyword, specify the program's full pathname after *load*. If you want to load more than one program, you can list them all on one line, separated by spaces, like this:

```
load=c:\afterdrk\ad.exe c:\afterdrk\adinit.exe c:\wnet.exe
```

Here, three programs are loaded into memory: the After Dark screen saver, its initialization program, and the LANtastic for Windows network interface utility. Their full pathnames are specified because none of them are located in the WINDOWS directory.

To run a program using WIN.INI's *run* keyword, specify the program's full pathname after *run*. If you want to run more than one program list them on the same line, separated by spaces, like this:

```
run=c:\winword\winword.exe sol
```

This entry tells Windows to run Word for Windows and Solitaire automat-ically. Because SOL.EXE is stored in the WINDOWS directory, its full pathname need not be specified.

Some applications may install their startup programs using WIN.INI in-stead of the StartUp group. Either way, the programs will load or run. However, changes made to WIN.INI are not reflected in the StartUp group, and icons you put in the StartUp group do not magically appear as *load* or *run* items in WIN.INI.

Chapter 3

Windows and
Your Hardware

One of the shortcomings of MS-DOS is its inability to deal with nonstandard computer hardware. For the basics, MS-DOS is fine: It knows about your keyboard and display, and it knows a wee bit about your printer. But MS-DOS doesn't care which type of display you have or about the special things your printer can do. It leaves the chore of figuring those things out to your applications. So for each MS-DOS application, you must make individual adjustments to get the most from your hardware, which is part of the reason MS-DOS is not such a joy to use.

Windows offers a solution to MS-DOS's limited ability to master your hardware. It marries itself with your PC's configuration and is quite agreeable when it encounters new and unusual hardware devices. This flexibility is all made possible thanks to Windows' device drivers—the special programs designed to integrate your hardware with Windows' software. This chapter discusses how that integration works. Also covered is information about getting the most from your printer under Windows, upgrading your hardware, running Windows on a laptop, and other important hardware issues.

DEVICES AND DRIVERS

Life would be so much easier if everyone used the same make and model of computer, and if there were no options. Thankfully, that's not the case. To deal with the differences that make life interesting—but not easy— MS-DOS uses *device drivers*, programs that control devices (hardware) in or attached to your computer. Device drivers allow the operating system to take advantage of the hardware by controlling the device in a manner that can be understood by your software.

71

Like MS-DOS, Windows uses device drivers, but Windows goes beyond MS-DOS's feeble ability to control hardware devices. With Windows, device drivers control everything in your PC with one goal in mind: to make all Windows computers—no matter who made them, no matter what peripherals are attached, and no matter what options you've set—work the same way. This enormous task is handled by the Setup program when Windows is installed and is maintained through the Control Panel and the Windows Setup program, as well as by means of tune-ups and tweaks to the SYSTEM.INI and WIN.INI files. (Refer to Chapter 2 for more information about those two initialization files.)

MS-DOS's Device Drivers

MS-DOS uses device drivers on two levels. First, low-level *system device drivers* (sometimes called *resident device drivers*) connect MS-DOS directly with the basic elements of your PC: the keyboard, screen, printer, serial port, system clock, and disk drives. On top of them are *installable device drivers*, the SYS files you see in CONFIG.SYS. They slap on a layer of control for special external devices, as well as provide additional control over devices MS-DOS already knows about.

The System Device Drivers

The system device drivers control how MS-DOS integrates itself with your hardware. When you boot MS-DOS, the system device drivers are loaded into memory as part of the hidden IO.SYS file, the first of MS-DOS's boot files loaded from disk (see Table 1-1 on page 2). The original theory behind MS-DOS was that each PC manufacturer would create their own IO.SYS file to contain the system device drivers specific to that PC. In reality, the differences between the various PC makes and models isn't that great on a low level, so everyone's IO.SYS file is more or less identical.

The system device drivers might seem scary, but they aren't really all that alien. In fact, their names might be familiar to you. To prove it, you can use the Mem command in conjunction with the Find command to see the names of the system device drivers in your computer's memory. Type the following command at the MS-DOS prompt:

```
C:\>mem /d : find /i "system device driver"
```

The *mem /d* command outputs the status of all device drivers, programs, and more. The *find /i "system device driver"* command finds all instances of the string *"system device driver"*. (The */i* switch makes Find ignore the case of letters as it looks for the string.)

After pressing Enter, you'll see a list of system device drivers with names like CON, PRN, COM1, and so on—MS-DOS's standard device names.

The Installable Device Drivers

The installable device drivers are the ones MS-DOS loads in response to the Device commands in CONFIG.SYS. The drivers' files are stored on disk, and they typically have SYS extensions. Their job is to control extra hardware devices attached to your PC or to offer extended control over any hardware you may already have.

Note: Not all installable device drivers have SYS extensions. For example, EMM386.EXE and SETVER.EXE are device drivers that double as MS-DOS commands. And some device drivers, such as network drivers, are loaded as TSR programs at the MS-DOS prompt or from within AUTOEXEC.BAT. But the end result is the same: The drivers provide extra control for your hardware, usually devices that MS-DOS itself doesn't recognize.

Overall, MS-DOS's device drivers provide only superficial support. They can establish standards for using hardware unknown to MS-DOS, but these standards are external; there's no solid integration between MS-DOS and the device drivers. Your software must still make extra efforts to communicate with the external devices. The result is no organization, few rules, no unity, and a certain lack of sanity.

With MS-DOS, device drivers are a haphazard way to integrate hardware with the operating system. Face it: MS-DOS is boring. It uses text to display information and accepts input from the keyboard. Ho hum. Nothing else is needed, so it doesn't really care about external devices. Therein lies the rub: MS-DOS ignores the devices for which you install device drivers, so it's up to your applications to do the integration work.

Windows' Device Drivers

Windows doesn't operate like MS-DOS, which is one of the things that makes it so attractive. Windows is built around device drivers. Peel back Windows' skin, and you'll find dozens of device drivers, each connected to and controlling a different part of your PC. The drivers all work together to give you a smooth, integrated operating system. Even though two PCs may have different displays, keyboards, sound cards, or networks, everything in the two machines works the same in Windows thanks to the many device drivers.

Windows also addresses your PC's expansion needs. New hardware can be integrated into every Windows-based application simply by installing the proper device drivers in Windows. This integration is usually accomplished through modifications to SYSTEM.INI that are made when you set up the new hardware, though additional modifications to MS-DOS in CONFIG.SYS may also be required.

Like MS-DOS's SYS files, Windows' drivers are files stored on disk. They're generally located in the WINDOWS\SYSTEM directory. Some third party driver files, such as display drivers or network drivers, may be located in their own directories elsewhere on your hard disk. Under Windows, drivers can have three extensions:

- DRV identifies the typical Windows driver.
- 386 identifies drivers used for enhanced mode. (They are usually virtual device drivers.)
- DLL identifies a dynamic link library.

The drivers loaded from within the SYSTEM.INI file are listed in four of its sections: [boot], [drivers], [mci], and [386Enh]. Other sections may load drivers as well, but those sections are specific to the driver and are not standard SYSTEM.INI sections.

Some driver information may be stored in WIN.INI, but that information tends to be specific to a driver loaded from within SYSTEM.INI, such as details about the driver's settings, options, and so on.

Changing Windows' Device Drivers

When you first install Windows, its Setup program examines your PC and determines which drivers it needs. These drivers are then copied to your WINDOWS\SYSTEM directory and assigned their place in SYSTEM.INI.

After installation, the Setup program copies itself to your WINDOWS directory, ready to be used to reconfigure your PC as necessary. (Reconfiguration must be done before or after you run Windows.) Under most circumstances, however, you'll never need to use Setup again. Setup handles only one thing that can't be dealt with from within Windows: the type of PC you own. And if you don't have that set up properly, Windows won't run.

Some programs insist that you run Setup to modify Windows and install their device drivers. Others allow you to reconfigure your hardware and load their device drivers from within Windows. Table 3-1 lists several hardware-related elements of Windows and the various places you would visit to change their drivers.

Element	How to Change the Driver
Code page	Run Setup at the command prompt or edit the *codepage* entry in SYSTEM.INI.
Display	Use Windows Setup from within Windows.
Keyboard	Use Windows Setup from within Windows.
Keyboard layout	Use the Control Panel's International dialog box.
Language	Use the Control Panel's International dialog box.
Mouse	Use Windows Setup from within Windows.
Network	Use Windows Setup from within Windows (use the Control Panel's Network dialog box in Windows for Workgroups).
PC type	Run Setup at the MS-DOS command prompt.
Printer	Use the Control Panel's Printers dialog box.
Sound/MIDI	Use the Control Panel's Drivers dialog box.
Other devices	Use the Control Panel's Drivers dialog box or edit SYSTEM.INI.

Table 3-1. *How to change drivers for your hardware.*

The Control Panel and the Windows Setup program are basically cheery fronts for the dirty work done to SYSTEM.INI. That's where Windows looks to find the names of the drivers. In all cases, when you change a driver, you must quit and restart Windows (and, therefore, reload SYSTEM.INI) for the new drivers to take effect.

Using the Windows Setup program is the primary method for adding or changing drivers. It handles the display, keyboard, network, and mouse drivers. (Because the network is built into Windows for Workgroups, the Windows Setup program in Windows for Workgroups doesn't let you change the network driver. Instead, you must use the Networks dialog box in the Control Panel.) The first step in updating or adding a new driver is making any hardware additions to the PC. The next step is installing the corresponding software. If you're lucky, the installation program will modify CONFIG.SYS or SYSTEM.INI or both for you. Otherwise, you need to move to the proper area of Windows and update the driver yourself.

Note: It's best to follow whatever instructions are included with your new hardware if they're different from the instructions given here. These directions are generic and intended only to give you an idea of how to install drivers under Windows.

To install a driver using the Windows Setup program (see Figure 3-1), you choose the Change System Settings command from the Options menu to bring up a dialog box where you can select from any of a number of device drivers for your display, keyboard, mouse, or network. Windows supports quite a few popular drivers, so the one you want may be on the list. If it isn't, select the option titled Other *name* (Requires Disk From OEM), where *name* is either Display, Keyboard, Mouse, or Network. After selecting the option, slip the disk containing the driver into drive A, and click OK to install the driver. No sweat.

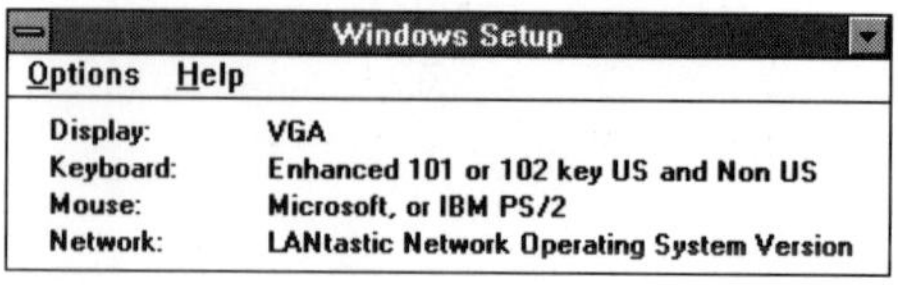

Figure 3-1. *The Windows Setup program, run from within Windows.*

To install a driver using the Control Panel (see Figure 3-2), you use one of three dialog boxes: Printers, International, or Drivers.

Figure 3-2. *The Control Panel.*

Use the Printers dialog box to install and set up your printer for use under Windows. After double-clicking the Printers icon to open the dialog box, you install a new printer driver by clicking the Add button. Windows supports more than 250 printers. If your printer is listed, locate it in the list, double-click it, and you're done. (Windows may ask you to insert a Windows distribution disk in drive A.) If your printer isn't listed but came with its own driver, select the Install Uninstalled Or Updated Printer option, and then click the Install button. You'll be asked to insert the disk containing the printer driver into drive A. Then follow the directions on the screen, and your printer will be ready to use in no time.

Unusual Printer?

If your printer isn't on Windows' list (and that's a pretty rare circumstance), and if your printer didn't come with a printer driver, select the Generic/Text Only option. This type of printer doesn't print graphics, but Windows will send text to it. Also, consider contacting your printer manufacturer to see whether an updated driver is available. Windows' Product Support at Microsoft can give you the phone number (providing the manufacturer is still in business).

The International dialog box lets you set up your computer's keyboard layout, date, and time, for use in a different country and language. Different device drivers and settings in SYSTEM.INI are used for different aspects of international support. They're all comfortably set and reset by the Control Panel and typically require no extra software other than the drivers that come with Windows.

The Drivers dialog box is used primarily when you add sound equipment to Windows, such as a sound card, MIDI mixer, or sequencer. Simply click the Add button in the dialog box, select your hardware driver from the list, and click OK. If the driver isn't listed, select the Unlisted Or Updated Driver option, and click OK. You'll be instructed to insert the disk on which the driver is stored in drive A. Then click OK to add the driver.

Additional information about adding and updating drivers is provided in "Installing New Drivers," later in this chapter.

Examining the Drivers in SYSTEM.INI

Four of SYSTEM.INI's standard eight sections contain information about Windows' device drivers. You can use SysEdit to display SYSTEM.INI so that you can see which drivers you have installed on your PC. But don't edit the driver items directly! Always use the programs discussed in the previous section to make modifications or updates to your drivers.

It all starts with SYSTEM.INI's [boot] section, which describes the nine basic hardware drivers used to boot Windows. These are listed in Table 3-2. You might want to venture into SYSTEM.INI territory to see which drivers are installed for your system. Most of them will be fairly standard (see Table 2-2 on page 43). Your network and printer drivers will reflect the devices attached to your computer, and you might find a nonstandard display or mouse driver as well. For example, I have a high speed display driver installed on my system, so my *display.drv* is set to WINSPEED.DRV.

The [drivers] section of SYSTEM.INI contains drivers you might have installed using the Control Panel's Drivers icon. By default, this section contains the *timer* and *midimapper* item, so don't mess with 'em.

Keyword	Type of Driver	Where You Install
comm.drv	Communication driver	SYSTEM.INI (The only time you would ever need to change this is if a substitute communications driver became available.)
display.drv	Display driver	Windows Setup
drivers	Installable system driver	Control Panel's Drivers dialog box
keyboard.drv	Keyboard driver	Windows Setup
language.dll	Language support software	Control Panel's International dialog box
mouse.drv	Mouse driver	Windows Setup
network.drv	Network driver	Windows Setup
sound.drv	Sound driver	Control Panel's Drivers dialog box
system.drv	System driver	Setup at the command prompt

Table 3-2. *The drivers listed in SYSTEM.INI'S [boot] section.*

The [mci] section contains drivers used for multimedia, which were set up using the Control Panel's Drivers dialog box. You'll find entries for compact disc audio, sound cards, MIDI, and so on. Usually you'll see Windows' standard drivers, as shown in Figure 3-3.

```
[mci]
CDAudio=mcicda.drv
WaveAudio=mciwave.drv
Sequencer=mciseq.drv
```

Figure 3-3. *Default drivers found in SYSTEM.INI's [mci] section.*

Additional information on media control interface (MCI) files might wind up in various sections of your WIN.INI file. Again, these files are installed using the Drivers dialog box in the Control Panel.

The [386Enh] section contains virtual device drivers used for enhanced mode. This section is the biggy. A typical SYSTEM.INI's [386Enh] section could contain over 50 entries, three-fifths of which will be device drivers. They're easy to recognize because they all have this format:

*device=*device* ¦ *filename*.386

If the driver is stored as a separate file, the file has a 386 extension. The full pathname is given if the file isn't in the WINDOWS directory. If the driver is internal—actually a part of the WIN386.EXE file—it has no 386 extension, and it's identified by a leading asterisk, like this:

```
device=*vfd
```

Not all drivers are identified by the *device* keyword. Some use keywords that are specific to their type of driver, as in:

```
mouse=*vmd
```

If you're curious, a list of the internal drivers that may be listed in the [386Enh] section is provided in Table 3-3, and the external virtual driver files (of which only a few may be listed in the [386Enh] section) are listed in Table 3-4. Many of them have names that contain V*x*D, where V is for *virtual*, D is for *device*, and *x* is for one or more characters that offer some meaning as to what the driver does. For example, *vmd* stands for *virtual mouse driver*. As usual, don't bother messing with any of these drivers.

Name in [386Enh]	Driver Name
apm	Power management device
bioshook	BIOS interrupt hooker
biosxlat	BIOS translation device
blockdev	32-bit disk access block device
debug	WIN386 debug device
dosmgr	MS-DOS translation device
dosnet	MS-DOS networks translation device
ebios	Extended BIOS device
int13	Interrupt 13h 32-bit disk access client
mca_pos	Microchannel architecture device
pagefile	Paging FastDisk client
pageswap	Page swapping device
parity	Parity detection device
qemmfix	QEMM compatibility driver
reboot	Reboot handling device
scsifd	SCSI 32-bit disk access device
shell	WIN386 shell interface device
v86mmgr	Virtual machine manager device
vadlibd	Virtual Adlib device

Table 3-3. *Internal device drivers.*

Table 3-3. *continued*

Name in [386Enh]	Driver Name
vcd	Virtual communications device
vdd	Virtual display device
vdmad	Virtual DMA device
vfd	Virtual floppy disk device
vhd	Virtual hard disk device
vkd	Virtual keyboard device
vmcpd	Virtual math coprocessor device
vmd	Virtual mouse device
vmm	Virtual machine manager
vmpoll	Virtual machine polling device
vnetbios	Virtual netBIOS device
vpd	Virtual printer device
vpend	Virtual pen device
vpicd	Virtual PIC device
vprod	Virtual profiling device
vsbd	Virtual Sound Blaster device
vsd	Virtual sound device
vtd	Virtual timer device
wdctrl	Western Digital WD1003 FastDisk controller

Virtual Driver	Device Supported
BANINST.386	Banyan VINES 4.0 instancing virtual device
DECNB.386	DEC Pathworks
DECNET.386	DEC networks
LANMAN10.386	LAN Manager version 1.0 support
HPEBIOS.386	EBIOS virtual device for Hewlett-Packard computers
LVMD.386	Logitech virtual mouse device
MONOUMB2.386	UMB in monochrome address range support
MSCVMD.386	Mouse Systems virtual mouse device
V7VDD.386	Video Seven virtual display device
VADLIBD.386	Virtual DMA device for Adlib
VDD8514.386	8514/a virtual display device
VDDCGA.386	CGA virtual display device
VDDCT441.386	82C441 VGA virtual display device

Table 3-4. *External virtual drivers and the hardware they support.* *(continued)*

Table 3-4. *continued*

Virtual Driver	Device Supported
VDDEGA.386	EGA virtual display device
VDDHERC.386	Hercules monochrome virtual display device
VDDTIGA.386	TIGA virtual display device
VDDVGA30.386	VGA virtual display device (version 3.0)
VDDXGA.386	XGA virtual display device
VIPX.386	Novell NetWare virtual IPX support
VNETWARE.386	NetWare virtual support
VPOWERD.386	Advanced Power Management virtual device
VSBD.386	Sound Blaster virtual device
VTDAPI.386	Multimedia virtual timer device
WIN386.PS2	PS/2 architecture

What Are Virtual Device Drivers?

MS-DOS allows only one application to run at any given time. This makes deciding which application gets the use of hardware very easy. The only one running gets the hardware! However, Windows in enhanced mode lets you run Windows-based applications and any number of MS-DOS applications simultaneously. What happens if a Windows-based application and an MS-DOS application want to use a piece of hardware, like the hard disk, at the same time? How can Windows be sure that information goes to the correct application? That's where virtual device drivers come in.

The virtual device driver (in this case, the one for the hard disk) simulates the hardware, forming a cushion between the application and the hardware. It keeps track of the application's input and output and makes sure that the data doesn't get confused with data that doesn't belong to it. The virtual device driver makes it possible for multiple applications to access the hardware at once. The application doesn't realize that it's not working with the real McCoy, so it can work with hardware the same as it always does. It's all part of the beauty of Windows.

You may find additional 386 files in SYSTEM.INI. These files are third party drivers that provide support for enhanced mode. For example, LANTASTI.386 provides LANtastic network support under Windows, but the file itself comes with the LANtastic network package; the files in Table 3-4 are shipped with Windows.

Where Is the Printer Driver?

This is weird: The printer driver is set up in WIN.INI—and it's the only driver mentioned there. Under the [windows] section in WIN.INI, you'll find this sole device driver entry:

> device=*printer,driver,port*

printer is the name of your printer, *driver* is the name of the device driver without the DRV extension, and *port* is the printer port. Two other items in the [windows] section of WIN.INI, *DeviceNotSelectedTimeout* and *TransmissionRetryTimeout*, also deal with the printer. Both list values in seconds, like this:

```
DeviceNotSelectedTimeout=15
TransmissionRetryTimeout=45
```

WIN.INI's [PrinterPorts] section duplicates the value of the printer driver's *device* entry but adds the other two values in the following format:

> *printer=driver,port,DeviceNotSelectedTimeout,TransmissionRetryTimeout*

In addition to these two sections, you may find a specific section in WIN.INI for your printer that contains information about your printer that Windows needs to know. These sections vary from printer to printer, and it's fairly common to see more than one section dedicated to your printer.

Installing New Drivers

Whenever you add some interesting bit of hardware to your computer or you receive an updated driver for the hardware you already have, you'll need to install a new Windows device driver. The installation process under Windows isn't the chore that it is under MS-DOS (unless you count any modifications the hardware may require you to make in CONFIG.SYS or AUTOEXEC.BAT).

When adding to your system, you should always install the hardware first. Then let the software install itself in MS-DOS, setting up its own directory and, optionally, making modifications to CONFIG.SYS or AUTO-EXEC.BAT. If you're an MS-DOS wizard, you may want to make modifications yourself. (Any edits can be made from within Windows using SysEdit; see "Setting Up and Using the System Editor," in Chapter 2.) Then test the hardware, rebooting your computer if necessary. If you've installed a sound card, run its test program to make sure it squawks properly. For a CD-ROM drive, try accessing one of the disks or running a demo. For any other type of hardware, test drive it to make sure it works. When you know the hardware is functioning "within known tolerances," you can install its drivers for Windows.

You install a new driver or update a driver for existing hardware in one of three ways:

■ Run a special installation program that sets up the drivers in SYSTEM.INI.

■ Use the Control Panel or the Windows Setup program to install the driver from within Windows.

■ Modify SYSTEM.INI directly.

Most Windows-based software—the cool software at least—takes the first road: Everything will be set up for you. If it isn't, you'll need to set up your hardware using the Control Panel or Windows Setup. (Refer to Table 3-1 on page 75 to see which method to use for various types of hardware.) Hopefully, the third option will never be necessary.

Some installation programs are "Windows-aware." They can seek out Windows and make any necessary adjustments to it. If an installation program offers that option, use it. Otherwise, look for information about using that device under Windows in the device's installation program, READ.ME files, or documentation.

Note: Windows provides third party support information in three files: README.WRI, PRINTERS.WRI, and NETWORKS.WRI. Load the appropriate file into Windows' Write program, and use the Find command to search out information about your hardware or its device driver.

The following sections demonstrate how you might add or update a driver for your printer and sound card. These examples apply to most of the situations you'll run into when you install or update drivers in Windows.

Example: Adding a New Printer Driver

Installation of a printer driver is as painless as it can be. Open the Control Panel's Printers dialog box, click the Add button, and find your printer in the list. Double-click the printer's name. Windows may ask you to insert one of its distribution disks, and if it does, follow the directions on the screen. If your printer isn't on the list but came with its own driver disk, select the Install Unlisted Or Updated Printer option from the list, and follow the directions on the screen.

Example: Installing the Generic PC Speaker Driver

The PC Speaker driver allows you to hear Windows' system sounds with a typical internal speaker. We're not talking high fidelity here, but the sounds are audible. You'll be able to hear the chimes, chord, ding, and tada sounds in place of the plain beep. If you don't already have the driver, contact Microsoft or use your modem to download the file from either a national online network or the Microsoft Download Service. (For more information, refer to the section titled "Secrets You Can Download" in Chapter 4.)

The driver, SPEAKER.DRV, is accompanied by four other files, only one of which you really need: OEMSETUP.INF, the file that tells Windows how to install the driver.

To set up the driver, double-click the Control Panel's Drivers icon, and click the Add button. Select the Unlisted Or Updated Driver option from the list, and then specify the drive and directory where SPEAKER.DRV and—more importantly—the OEMSETUP.INF files are located. Windows relies heavily on the INF files to tell it how and where to set up special drivers. (INF means *installation information*.) Now follow the directions on the screen to set up the driver. When setup is complete, you'll be asked whether you want to restart Windows or continue. You need to restart Windows so that your updated SYSTEM.INI or WIN.INI file can be read into memory and you can start using the new driver.

Optimizing Drivers

Under Windows, optimizing drivers doesn't involve using command line switches or secret options that no one else knows about. Instead, it's more of a treasure hunt. Some device drivers are controlled by dialog boxes, and the secret to optimizing a particular driver is often lurking way down under several levels of these boxes. That's where you can set special options and really control your hardware. But these options are available for only a few drivers, and only the cleverest Windows users can ferret out all the secrets.

As an example, exploring the various options and advanced settings for the PostScript printer driver can really be a journey of discovery. After opening the Control Panel's Printers dialog box, highlight the PostScript driver if you have one, and click the Setup button. Then click the Options button. Next try the Advanced button. Here, four dialog boxes deep, you are presented with a slate of options for controlling your PostScript printer. Figure 3-4 shows the Advanced Options dialog box. The settings you select for your PostScript printer—or whichever device you are tin-

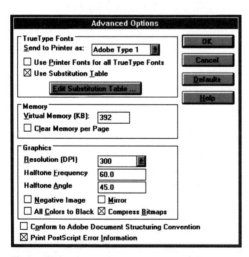

Figure 3-4. *The Advanced Options dialog box for a PostScript printer.*

kering with—are up to you. Experimentation is usually the name of the game when optimizing a device driver, and with so many options available, it would be meaningless to list them all here.

USING YOUR PRINTER

With the proper printer drivers installed and the proper network connections made (if any are necessary), printing in Windows is a snap: Choose the Print command from the File menu, click OK in the dialog box, and you have your hard copy. However, several elements of Windows have to work pretty hard to make printing seem so effortless.

Your printer is controlled from two places in Windows: the Control Panel's Printers dialog box and Print Manager. The Printers dialog box is where you install and configure your printer. Print Manager is what prints your documents, holding them in memory while they wait for the printer. (In Windows for Workgroups, you can also use Print Manager to share your printer with other users on your network.)

The Printers Dialog Box in the Control Panel

When you double-click the Printers icon in the Control Panel, Windows displays a dialog box similar to the one shown in Figure 3-5. The default printer is the printer Windows currently uses. The Installed Printers box lists the printers available to your computer, either through a printer port or somewhere out on the network.

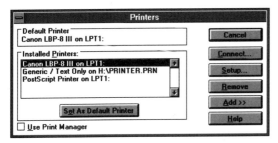

Figure 3-5. *The Printers dialog box accessed from the Control Panel.*

Two buttons in the Printers dialog box allow you to modify the setup of your printer. Click the Connect button to change how your computer communicates with the printer—through a port or over a network. Click the Setup button to configure your printer's operation. (Use the other buttons, Remove and Add, to manage the Installed Printers list.)

Printer Connections

If you click the Connect button in the Printers dialog box, you can describe for Windows how your printer is connected to your PC. A dialog box, similar to the one shown in Figure 3-6, appears. The Ports box contains a list of the available ports; you select the one to which your printer is connected or to which you want the printer's output sent.

Most printers are connected to LPT1, the first printer port on your computer. Windows lets you select any of a number of ports for printer output: Up to three printer ports named LPT1 through LPT3; up to four serial ports named COM1 through COM4; the EPT port (actually a special expansion card for the IBM Personal Pageprinter); FILE, which directs output to a file on disk; and entries such as LPT1.DOS for printing directly to MS-DOS's ports.

Selecting a Printer

If you can access more than one printer in Windows, you switch between them using the Control Panel's Printers dialog box. Simply highlight the printer you want to use, and click the Set As Default Printer button.

Most programs in Windows also allow you to switch printers on the fly using the Print Setup command on the File menu. If more than one printer is available, you can select the one you want there, as well as adjust its options.

In some cases, changing printers can affect the fonts you see on the screen as well as the fonts available to Windows. Refer to "Working with Fonts" in Chapter 7 for more information about fonts.

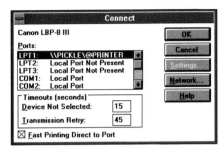

Figure 3-6. *The Connect dialog box.*

Note: On some systems, the LPT1.DOS and LPT2.DOS entries appear as LPT1.OS2 and LPT2.OS2. These are carryovers from Windows 3.0, which offered support for people running Windows on OS/2 1.1 and 1.2. Essentially, these entries designate the same ports as LPT1.DOS and LPT2.DOS.

When you select a COM port, the Settings button becomes available. Clicking Settings allows you to set the port's communications settings to match those of your printer. By default, Windows uses the settings shown in Table 3-5. They should be okay for most serial printers.

Setting	Value
Baud	9600
Data Bits	8
Parity	None
Stop Bits	1
Flow Control	Xon/Xoff

Table 3-5. *Windows' default serial port settings.*

Note: The Advanced button in the Settings For COM dialog box displays another dialog box in which you can set the base address and IRQ (interrupt request) values for the serial port. These settings will be correct for most serial ports. However, if you're using COM3 or COM4 and have nonstandard serial port settings, this is the place to enter the correct values. Refer to your hardware manual for the correct base address and IRQ numbers. For additional information about troubleshooting these values, see "Setting Up for Communications" in Chapter 8.

The Device Not Selected and Transmission Retry boxes allow you to enter timeout values. Device Not Selected determines how often Print Manager checks your printer to see if it's ready to print. For example, a value of 15 means that Print Manager waits 15 seconds before assuming your printer isn't connected or ready to print.

The Transmission Retry box tells Print Manager how long to wait before sending another batch of information to the printer. Some printers take a while to print, so specifying a value of 45 means Print Manager waits 45 seconds before resending a batch of information to a busy printer.

All the information from the Connect dialog box is stuffed into your WIN.INI file in various sections. To see a summary of the printer information, scan the file for the [PrinterPorts] section. The information is stored in a format described earlier in this chapter; see "Where Is the Printer Driver?" Each installed printer has one line in that section.

Printing to a Designated File

You can set up any printer to save its output to a file on disk, by selecting FILE: in the Ports box instead of an LPT or COM port. You'll then be prompted for a filename each time you "print" from Windows. But here's a cool shortcut.

In WIN.INI, look for the [ports] section, where all the ports are listed just as they appear in the Printer Connections dialog box (except that each is followed by an equal sign and its optional settings). Figure 3-7 shows what this section might look like in your WIN.INI file. The *FILE:=* entry directs Windows to ask you for a filename each time you print. However, you can add to the list the names of the files you want the output stored in simply by adding the filenames to the [ports] section of WIN.INI. Use the following format:

   pathname.PRN=

Note: *You should set the value in the Transmission Retry box to 90 seconds for PostScript printers. Set the value higher if you experience timeouts when printing complex graphics or text (even on non-PostScript printers).*

Here, *pathname* is the full name of the file to which you want to send your output. You can add as many filenames as you want. Be sure to specify the full pathname, as I did with C:\PRINTER.PRN in Figure 3-7. Then save

WIN.INI on disk, and reboot your computer so that the modified WIN.INI takes effect.

```
[ports]
LPT1:=
LPT2:=
LPT3:=
COM1:=2400,e,7,1
COM2:=9600,n,8,1
COM3:=9600,n,8,1
COM4:=9600,n,8,1
EPT:=
FILE:=
LPT1.DOS=
LPT2.DOS=
C:\PRINTER.PRN=
```

Figure 3-7. *A sample [ports] section in WIN.INI.*

To select a file to store your printer output, highlight your printer's name in the Control Panel's Printers dialog box, click the Connect button, and then select the name of the file from the Ports box. All output will be sent to that file whenever that printer is selected; you won't be prompted to enter a filename when you print. Each new batch of output will overwrite the previous batch, so if you want to keep it, be sure to save the file with a different name (or do whatever with it) before you print again.

Note: The format of the output depends on your printer. The output you save in a file is guaranteed to be readable if you use the Generic/Text Only printer driver.

Here's another secret: The LPT1.DOS and LPT2.DOS entries in the Ports box are actually *filenames*. Windows sees the LPT1.DOS filename and sends printed output to MS-DOS to be saved to that file. However, MS-DOS sees only LPT1 and recognizes it as the name of the printer port. So instead of sending the output to the file on disk, MS-DOS reroutes it to the LPT1 printer port. This is why you can use the LPT1.DOS and LPT2.DOS entries in the Ports box to avoid printing from Windows and print directly to MS-DOS's printer ports. (The *.OS2 entries serve the same function.)

Network Connections

When your PC is connected to a network, you usually print on a network printer. If your PC is designated as a server or printer server, you have to print on a network printer even when that printer is connected to your own PC. This rule was devised to avoid conflicts with the other computers on the network that are trying to use your printer. To be fair, you must print through the network like everyone else. (If you have Windows for Workgroups, you can share your printer with everyone on your network, and you can print to your printer locally.)

The section titled "Network Printing" in Chapter 8 gives details about network printers, as well as scriptures on networking in general. Refer there for additional information.

Printer Settings

After you highlight a printer in the Control Panel's Printers dialog box, you can use the Setup button to control how that printer behaves. The dialog box you see when you click the Setup button is customized for each printer. For example, the dialog box for PostScript printers lets you set options such as page orientation and number of copies. It also has an Options button that opens a dialog box for sending output directly to an Encapsulated PostScript (EPS) file instead of to the printer itself. The HP LaserJet's dialog box contains options for selecting a font cartridge, as well as a Fonts button that opens a dialog box for downloading fonts to your printer.

The dialog boxes for some printers might also have an Advanced button that allows you to set advanced options for your printer. This is truly a blessing: You can choose all these options and settings in one location, instead of having to mess with them in every application.

The changes you make in the Control Panel's Printers dialog box aren't cast in stone. The settings you make there will be in effect every time you print, but you can still make small adjustments on the fly from within your applications. For example, nearly all applications in Windows that support printing have a Print Setup command on their File menu. Choosing this command displays a list of available printers, and all you have to do to change your printer setup for that one program is click the Setup button and make your modifications. But keep in mind that the changes will effect printing in that one program only.

Using Print Manager

Print Manager is activated using the Control Panel's Printers icon. At the bottom of the Printers dialog box is the Use Print Manager check box. If the box is checked, Print Manager is activated and will control your printing. (If Print Manager isn't activated, one document must finish printing before you can print another.)

Figure 3-8 on the next page shows what Print Manager looks like. Printers available or attached to your PC are listed by name and connection, including a network pathname, in the main part of the window. Also given is the printer's status in square brackets. The message box to the right of the Delete button tells you what Print Manager is currently doing.

Below each printer name (or below the only printer name if you have only one) are lists of documents that are waiting to be printed. Print Manager lines them up and feeds them to the printer one at a time. The top document in the list, or queue, is the one that's currently printing; any other documents appear below the current one in the list.

EPS Files

Here's a handy way to use the generic PostScript Printer driver to create an EPS file: Choose Printer Setup from the File menu, select the PostScript Printer driver from the list, click the Settings button, and then click the Options button. Click the Encapsulated PostScript File option to turn it on, and then type the name of the EPS file in the text box. Finally, click OK a few times to back your way out of the dialog boxes.

If the EPS file you're creating is going to be used in a program that accepts a PostScript header, then click the Send Header button to prefix the file with the PostScript header.

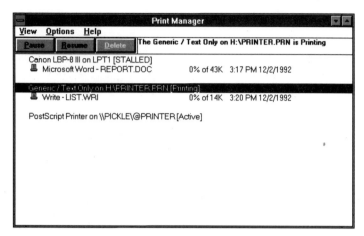

Figure 3-8. *The Print Manager window.*

You can pause and resume printing by clicking the buttons with those names, and you can remove documents from the waiting list by highlighting them and clicking the Delete button. In this way, Print Manager gives you control over the printing of documents long after you've chosen the Print command from a File menu.

To keep Print Manager handy, I recommend starting it and then minimizing. To print a document from File Manager, you can then drag its icon to the Print Manager icon. Print Manager starts that file's application and immediately print it.

Note: Some networks, such as LANtastic, handle their own printing chores. If you're using such a network, you should have Windows bypass Print Manager when you print to a network printer. Choose the Network Settings command from Print Manager's Options menu, and select the Print Net Jobs Direct check box. With this option set, you can print to both local and network printers as quickly as possible.

From Print Manager's menus, you can control other aspects of printing. The Printer Setup command on the Options menu allows you to reconfigure your printer without having to use the Control Panel. You can also use menu commands to check the network printing queue and make network connections.

My main beef with Print Manager is that it's too fast. On a network, a file prints so quickly that it barely has time to visit Print Manager for a quick cup of coffee. Rarely have I seen a queue build up. If you're not on a network, you might notice files sitting in Print Manager's queue if you switch to Print Manager while an application is printing. For example, Word for Windows might spin off a document to the printer in "real time"; you'll

Windows for Workgroups' Print Manager

As you can see here, Windows for Workgroups has a modified Print Manager:

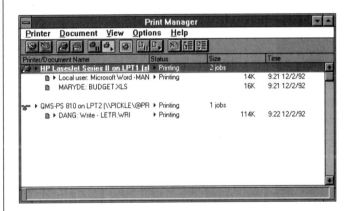

With the buttons on the toolbar beneath the menu bar, using Print Manager couldn't be easier. A click of a button connects you to a network printer, disconnects you from one, shares or unshares your own printer, selects the default printer, deletes documents from a printer queue, and more.

The Print Manager in Windows for Workgroups also gives you plenty of information about the printers. For example, the icon to the left of the printer description tells you whether a printer is yours or a network printer. You can also see exactly whose documents are printing on each printer.

see the file in Print Manager only if you press Ctrl-Esc and switch to Print Manager while Word is printing. At other times, you might see a print queue only if you print a whole bunch of files at once and then switch to Print Manager.

Of course, on slower impact (dot matrix) printers, a formidable queue can build up. If you have one of these printers, bend a knee toward Redmond, Washington, and thank the Windows gurus that you're not sitting around waiting for your printer to finish before you can get back to work.

HARDWARE UPGRADES WORTH MAKING

An old saying goes, "Never ride a motorcycle bigger than your own." Hardware envy is the same as motorcycle envy. If you're content with Windows now, wait until you run it on your neighbor's next-generation PC. The bottom line is that Windows just loves hardware muscle, and it takes a big, fast hard drive and lots of RAM to satisfy Windows.

Most of us can't afford to buy a new computer every six months. In the meantime, while you're whittling down your Visa bill or crawling to your boss's office with a P.O. in your teeth, you can inexpensively add hardware muscle to your existing PC. Listed below are six hardware upgrades that are designed to make Windows run more comfortably or to give it an extra boost:

■ Buy a larger hard-disk drive or a second hard-disk drive.

■ Add more memory.

■ Purchase a math coprocessor.

■ Upgrade your processor.

■ Buy a printer accelerator.

■ Buy a faster video card or video accelerator.

The following sections elaborate on these worthy ways to upgrade your PC. These upgrades will make Windows run faster, but you can squeeze more performance by optimizing Windows, which is covered in Chapter 4.

Maxing Out the Hard Disk

Running out of disk space is easy to do these days. Programs for Windows offer more features than before, but they also require more disk space. For example, any time you deal with a graphics program, you're going to kiss a lot of disk storage space good-bye. And now that Windows supports a throng of installable fonts, hard disk space dwindles away quicker than you'd ever think possible. There are several solutions to this problem:

■ Adding a second hard disk drive

■ Replacing your hard disk drive with a larger, faster model

■ Expanding the drive with a disk doubler or disk compression utility

The old option of deleting files and moving seldom-used programs to a floppy disk simply doesn't cut it any more. Although you might be able to scrounge a couple of megabytes that way, it doesn't give you the large chunks of permanent storage space necessary for Windows-based applications. If you're really desperate, consider deleting tutorial, sample, and help (*.HLP) files first, and then refer to "Creating the 'Minimum Windows Footprint'" at the end of this chapter to see which of Windows' other files you can safely delete.

Note: Dan Gookin's PC Hotline, *also from Microsoft Press, goes into detail on selecting, installing, and configuring hard-disk drives for your computer.*

Adding a Second Hard-Disk Drive

Most PCs have room for two hard-disk drives but come with only one. The hard-disk drive controller—the device that connects the hard drive to the computer's motherboard—can also handle two drives at a time. If your system has an "only child" hard drive, it's a snap to buy and install a second one. Here are my suggestions:

■ Buy a drive that's compatible with your hard-disk drive controller: ESDI, SCSI, and so on. (This "suggestion" is actually mandatory.)

■ Buy the fastest drive you can afford.

■ Buy the largest capacity disk you can afford.

You can install the drive yourself, if you like. There's really nothing to it, as long as you ordered the drive as your second hard drive and you're sure the dealer configured it as such. Installation is fairly straightforward and takes about a half hour. If the thought sits uneasy with you, then most dealers will install the hard drive for a small fee.

Replacing Your Hard Drive

If your hard drive is full and your computer has no room for another one (such as in a laptop), you have the option of replacing the hard drive outright with a newer, faster, larger model. Replacement requires three more steps than simply adding a second drive to your system: First you must backup your entire hard drive (to be safe, I recommend doing it twice); second you must make sure you have a bootable copy of MS-DOS and your backup program handy on floppy disks; and third, after installing the replacement drive, you must restore all your files and programs to the new hard drive. This way, you have the same information on your new disk, but with much more room available.

Expanding Your Hard Drive

A better option than replacing your hard drive—and a cheaper one—is to buy a disk doubling program, such as STAC Electronics' Stacker, which doubles the storage capacity of your hard drive. For example, if you have a 40-MB hard drive, you'll have 80 MB of storage after installing Stacker. This trick works without any intervention on your part, thanks to an ingenious installation program, and it's an ideal and inexpensive option for users with crowded hard drives. If you have a laptop, you'd be foolish not to use Stacker.

SCSI Hard Drive Limits

If you have a SCSI hard drive controller, you aren't limited to only two hard drives. Each SCSI controller can handle seven SCSI devices, so you can add up to seven hard drives to your system using one controller (providing, of course, that you don't have any other SCSI devices).

What Stacker does is to create a "Stacker" drive using your current hard drive. Special device drivers in CONFIG.SYS create the Stacker drive and monitor all disk activity, automatically compressing information saved on the Stacker drive and decompressing information retrieved from it. It's amazing stuff and deserves a much more detailed description than I have room for here.

If you buy Stacker, I have a few suggestions for setting it up:

■ My personal experience is that it's best not to "stack" drive C. If possible, create a 10-MB drive C—just enough to boot the computer, plus space for a permanent swap file for Windows. (Of course, this adjustment involves repartitioning your hard drive, which is a mondo pain.) Then stack the remaining drives in your system.

■ If you have a lot of free space on your drive, create an Empty Stacker Volume, which builds a second "hard drive" with immense storage potential on your system. Use that drive for your Windows-based applications.

■ You must keep the swap file for Windows' enhanced mode on an un-stacked drive (the uncompressed portion of drive C or the "host" drive).

■ Stack your RAM drives to double their storage.

The Stacker manual has other advice and suggestions for running the soft-ware with Windows. Other programs are similar to Stacker but lack its clever installation program. Check your favorite software store for more information.

Adding More Memory

Here is the rule for adding memory to your computer: Pack your PC full of RAM—as much as you can afford. For Windows, all the RAM should be extended memory. Don't bother with expanded memory cards, options, or switches. If you have a memory expansion card, such as Intel's AboveBoard or AST's RAMpage, configure all its memory as extended. On '386-based PCs, add all your memory to the motherboard or the mem-ory expansion card.

How much memory is enough? I recommend 4 MB minimum extended memory to run Windows in enhanced mode. But, hey, 8 MB doesn't hurt, either. And if you're upgrading and you have the slots for extra memory, why not bring the total up to 10 MB, 12 MB, or 16 MB in one computer.

The Advantages of a Math Coprocessor

A math coprocessor is available only for 80286, 80386, or 386SX computers. For the 80286 chips, you can get an 80287 math coprocessor. The 386 chips take an 80387. The 486 chips—and beyond—all have built-in math coprocessors, except that the 486SX has a companion 487 math coprocessor.

The main advantage of the math coprocessor is, obviously, the speed with which you can do mathematical computations. For monster spreadsheets, CAD, and graphing, the extra power comes in handy. For everything else: Naaa. Windows experiences a minor speed boost with a math coprocessor installed, but at several hundred dollars each, I recommend upgrading your hard drive or adding memory before considering this option.

A Better, Faster Processor

Some of the newer PCs have processor upgrade options. Use them if you can afford them. After adding all the RAM you can pack in the box and giving yourself a bigger hard drive, a newer processor is the next step in making Windows run faster.

Which processor should you upgrade to? Either the latest one or the one you can just barely afford. A word of advice: Grab the fastest, hottest chip available. Don't waste time taking "baby steps."

Accelerating the Printer

The slowest part of any computer system is the printer. This is one area where software can't help too much: Printers can produce only so many pages of information per minute. For text, you might not have a long wait, but for complex graphics images, you can expect to have an image of Solitaire burned into your retina while your application first creates the image and then prints it. When Print Manager is turned on, Windows sends the information to it instead of directly to the printer. (You turn on Print Manager using the Control Panel's Printers dialog box; the Use Print Manager option must be selected.)

Once your file is in Print Manager, you can continue working. Meanwhile, Print Manager concerns itself with sending your file to the printer, spoon-feeding it a bit at a time. This is known as *spooling*. Print Manager spools at three speeds: low, medium, and high. The high priority sends information to the printer faster, but slows down the rest of Windows. Low priority lets Windows run faster, but slows down printing. You can set the priority by choosing commands on Print Manager's Options menu.

Another way to speed up printing is to turn on the Fast Printing Direct To Port option. In the Control Panel's Printers dialog box, select your printer, and click the Connect button. At the bottom of the Connect dialog box, check Fast Printing Direct To Port, and click OK. Windows then zips information directly out the printer port, avoiding MS-DOS, which is slow. (Incidentally, when you use MS-DOS applications under Windows, they print without Print Manager; you'll have to wait for those programs to finish printing before you can continue working.)

On the hardware side, you can improve your printer's speed only by spending money. One of the best ways is to add more printer memory. For example, a laser printer with only 512 KB of RAM prints painfully slowly. Boost that memory up to 3 MB or 4 MB and you'll notice an instant performance improvement. Your printer can then handle larger amounts of information at one time.

Money Saving Tip

When upgrading printer memory, buy the memory upgrade card "unpopulated," or without any RAM chips on it. If the dealer quibbles, order the least amount of RAM you can. Then, after you're clear of the place, buy the extra RAM chips and plug them in yourself. This strategy saves you money because you're not paying for all the RAM to be installed at the factory.

It's also possible to expand your printer's capabilities by installing a different engine. For example, you can upgrade a Hewlett-Packard LaserJet IID with a PostScript engine. Your printer can then render PostScript images and use PostScript fonts that would otherwise be unavailable. (Make sure you install the proper PostScript driver in Windows after you upgrade.)

Accelerator cards are also available to improve printing speed and the quality of the printed output. Some of these cards actually double the resolution of the printer, but not without a cost.

Upgrading Video Performance

The CGA, EGA, and Hercules monochrome video standards are etched in glass. But for VGA and SuperVGA, you have options galore. VGA manufacturers often include secret bonus graphics modes that are exploitable under Windows. You need to install special drivers to enable these modes, which are usually included on the disk that came with the video adapter.

On the upgrade path, some video adapters are designed to be speed demons under Windows. Most of them have special graphics coprocessors; the Texas Instruments Graphics Architecture (TIGA) chip is an example. Like a math coprocessor, the graphics coprocessor takes over the complex math and other aspects of drawing graphics, leaving the main processor more time to work with the programs that present the graphics. If you're looking for a video accelerator, make sure it contains its own graphics coprocessor and at least 1 MB of onboard video memory. (2 MB is better.)

For software, the most popular solution is the WinSpeed device driver from Panacea, Inc. WinSpeed supports most VGA and SuperVGA video systems and offers improved performance over the VGA drivers included with Windows. I use WinSpeed in my system, and the graphics really cook. Highly recommended.

Using Big Monitors

With a high resolution VGA card, you can get very high graphics resolution under Windows. The problem is that the image gets smaller as you add more detail to it; what used to fill the entire screen now takes up a fraction of the available space. More information can be displayed, but the tiny image will make you cross-eyed.

The solution is to buy a larger monitor. A 19-inch monitor displays an 800-by-600 pixel image much more cleanly than a 12-inch or 14-inch monitor. Most of these monitors can be plugged directly into compatible VGA adapters without having to install additional drivers.

Running More than One Monitor

If you have really exotic taste, consider running Windows on more than one monitor. Dual monitors are made possible with the proper video hardware, such as the Colorgraphic Super Dual VGA card.

Each Super Dual VGA card supports two VGA monitors. Using two cards in a single PC gives you an extended Windows desktop display of four VGA monitors. You can have up to four cards and a total of eight monitors. Special driver software allows Windows to run with the multiple monitors. You can slide windows from one screen to another, run two programs "full screen" and see both at once, and so on. Macintosh owners have had the same luxury for years, and it's now available on PC's with Windows—but only with the proper hardware.

Note: It's possible, though rare, to use both a monochrome and color monitor on a PC. At Microsoft, that's the setup used by many programmers: They run programs on the color screen and debug them on the monochrome screen. Windows handles this situation just fine, but without special hardware it will run only on your primary monitor, not both.

USING WINDOWS ON A LAPTOP

You can never think too small for Windows. Today's laptops have the storage and fancy graphics that make running Windows more than possible. Combine them with the cutest li'l mouse that clips on to the edge of your keyboard, and just about any laptop that meets the minimum hardware requirements can be a Windows machine. (I personally favor a color laptop system—but my preference stems from greed.)

Laptop Hardware Requirements

To run Windows on your laptop, you'll need an 80286 or '386-based processor, a minimum of 1 MB of RAM, and at least 10 MB of hard disk space. The typical Windows laptop system is a 4-MB 386SX system. Anything faster or with more memory is going to cut down on your battery life, though if you can afford a better machine, don't let me stop you from buying it.

You should concern yourself with three issues that are particular to a laptop computer:

■ Hard disk space

■ Memory

■ A portable mouse

Hard disk space is going to be tight, so I recommend a disk doubler such as Stacker. Install it right away or upgrade your system, converting your entire hard drive into a "Stacker drive" to double its size. You can install the disk doubler before or after you install Windows.

Note: Windows is going to take up quite a bit of space on the hard disk, especially when you toss in a few programs. The section titled "Creating the 'Minimum Windows Footprint'," later in this chapter, offers some tips on paring down Windows' size for your laptop system.

As far as memory is concerned: Make sure it's all extended. And don't waste any room on a RAM drive—even for temporary files—unless you really have a lot of memory. Try to load as many device drivers and TSRs "high" as possible; refer to "Memory Management Issues" in Chapter 1 for more information.

Finally the issue of the mouse rolls into play. A laptop doesn't really fit on your lap. More likely, it sits on an airplane tray, on the bed in the hotel, or on the chair beside you. And if you do put it on your lap, where are you going to roll the mouse? While laptops get smaller and lighter, the mouse remains the same size. Rolling a mouse on one's thigh is a popular laptop user's pastime. Most thighs (at least mine) are wide and smooth (okay, and hairy), offering a usable but limited place to maneuver the mouse.

The solution is to purchase one of those cute thumb mice. Figure 3-9 shows the Microsoft BallPoint mouse in use on a laptop. A similar type of mouse is Logitech's Trackman Portable. These devices parasitically clip onto the side of your keyboard and give you access to a "thumb ball" that moves the mouse pointer. It's a space conscious way to use a laptop with a mouse without the required desk surface (and custom mouse pad).

Figure 3-9. *The Microsoft BallPoint mouse.*

Note: When you install Windows, you install the BallPoint mouse as the standard Microsoft or IBM PS/2 mouse. However, this standard installation doesn't give you access to some of the cool features available with the BallPoint. You must load the Point utility (in the file POINT.EXE), which gives you custom control over the BallPoint and allows you to make settings that don't apply to your standard mouse. For example, you can specify which way you want to move the ball to make the mouse pointer move up on the screen. If you prefer, you can move the thumb ball left to right to make the pointer go up!

Making Windows Look Good on Your Laptop

Although most laptop screens are VGA compatible, their display is a muddled gray-on-gray. And some early VGA screens have an annoying tendency to flicker, particularly when some "colors" are displayed. Finding the proper color scheme on such a computer is important. You need to balance the darks with the lights to enable you to see Windows properly.

The Control Panel's Color dialog box has four settings suitable for laptops:

- LCD Default Screen Settings
- LCD Reversed - Dark
- LCD Reversed - Light
- Plasma Power Saver

The Monochrome setting may also work with some laptops, though the setting is designed for monochrome VGA systems, not the monochrome laptop. The Plasma Power Saver setting is designed for portables that use gas plasma displays (and looks severely funky on a VGA screen). My personal preference is the LCD Reversed-Light option. It allows text to show up well in Windows and avoids the color blue, which tends to flicker (well, at least on my laptop's VGA screen).

If you have trouble seeing the mouse on your laptop, consider turning on the Mouse Trails option. (This option is cool, even on non-laptop computers.) In the Control Panel, bring up the Mouse dialog box. Select the Mouse Trails check box, and then move the mouse around. Instead of one pointer, you'll see several trailing the lead mouse pointer as it floats around the desktop. This mouse trail makes your mouse more visible on an LCD screen. The trails might not appear when the insertion pointer is active (which makes the mouse pointer even harder to find), but the standard pointer and hourglass will dance conga lines around your screen.

Creating the "Minimum Windows Footprint"

It is possible to whittle down Windows so that it sits on less than 3 MB of disk space. You accomplish this feat by running Windows only in standard mode after deleting a whole horde of files. But is this sacrifice worth it? In this section, you'll find lists and descriptions of the Windows files you can delete. Ax these files with extreme caution, and only after reading the following note.

Note: Deleting Windows files is a touchy issue. Delete these files only when you're very low on disk space and only after first considering using a disk doubler utility, such as Stacker.

Start deleting "excess" Windows files by running the Windows Setup program in Windows. From the Options menu, choose the Add/Remove Windows Components command. Then use the dialog box to pluck out the sections of Windows you don't use. This is the best and most efficient way to remove unwanted files.

In the Control Panel, use the Drivers dialog box to remove unneeded drivers from Windows. Select the drivers you don't use and click the Remove button. Note that removing a driver from Windows doesn't remove the driver from disk. You need to delete the file later using File Manager.

Also in the Control Panel, open the Fonts dialog box. Select any fonts you don't really need and click the Remove button. In the Remove Font dialog box, select the Delete Font File From Disk check box, and then click Yes (or Yes To All). The fonts and their files will be removed.

Your next step is to delete files associated with various accessories. Delete only those you don't need. Table 3-6 lists the accessories and their associated files. When you delete these files, you'll no longer have access to them in Windows; do this only if space is tight and you don't really use the files to begin with. (The other accessories and games can be removed using Windows Setup.)

Windows' Accessory	Associated File(s)
Clipboard Viewer	CLIPBRD.EXE
Microsoft Diagnostics	MSD.EXE, MSD.INI
PIF Editor	PIFEDIT.EXE
Print Manager (spooler)	PRINTMAN.EXE
System Editor (SysEdit)	SYSEDIT.EXE
Task Manager	TASKMAN.EXE
Windows Write	WRITE.EXE, WRITE.HLP

Table 3-6. *Windows' accessories you can delete.*

Windows help files are a ripe candidate for deletion: Remove all the files with HLP extensions you can find. Also delete the Help program, WINHELP.EXE, because without the HLP files it has nothing to do.

If you want to run Windows only in one mode or another, you can remove the other mode's files. These files are listed in Table 3-7 on the next page;

delete the files from one column only. The files can be found in the WIN-
DOWS\SYSTEM directory.

For Standard Mode Only, Delete...	For Enhanced Mode Only, Delete...
CGA40WOA.FON	DOSX.EXE
CGA80WOA.FON	DSWAP.EXE
CPWIN386.CPL	KRNL286.EXE
DOSAPP.FON	*.2GR
EGA40WOA.FON	WINOLDAP.MOD
EGA80WOA.FON	WSWAP.EXE
KRNL386.EXE	
*.3GR	
*.386	
WIN386.EXE	
WIN386.PS2	
WINOA386.MOD	

Table 3-7. *Files you can delete when running Windows in one mode only.*

Additional files that you might want to delete are MORICONS.DLL,
EMM386.EXE, RAMDRIVE.SYS, and the mouse files with the extensions
SYS, COM, and INI. Delete these files only if they're not being used by
CONFIG.SYS, AUTOEXEC.BAT, or something else on your system. For
example, delete the mouse, RAMDRIVE.SYS, or EMM386.EXE driver
files only if they're not listed in AUTOEXEC.BAT or CONFIG.SYS. All
these files are found in the WINDOWS directory, though some might be
stashed in subdirectories of that directory.

You can also remove all support files for running MS-DOS programs under
Windows. These files are listed in Table 3-8.

And while we're at it, Table 3-9 lists MS-DOS files you can do without.
The list contains MS-DOS files you can freely delete; however, be careful
to read the notes associated with each file. If you delete all of them, it's
possible to slim MS-DOS down by as much as 1.5 MB of disk space. (The
MS-DOS Shell program takes up about 500 KB by itself; QBasic and its
associated files—including EDIT.*—occupy another 500 KB.)

*.2GR

APPS.INF

CGA40WOA.FON

DOSAPP.FON

EGA80WOA.FON

WINOLDAP.MOD

*.3GR

CGA80WOA.FON

DSWAP.EXE

Table 3-8. *Windows' MS-DOS support files you can delete.*

Filename	Notes
4201.CPI	Not required under Windows
4208.CPI	Not required under Windows
5202.CPI	Not required under Windows
APPEND.EXE	Delete; do not use this command with Windows
APPNOTES.TXT	MS-DOS 5 release notes; read then destroy
ASSIGN.COM	Delete; do not use this command with Windows
COUNTRY.SYS	Delete if not used in CONFIG.SYS
DISKCOMP.COM	Okay to delete
DISKCOPY.COM	Okay to delete; use the Copy command from File Manager's Disk menu
DISPLAY.SYS	Delete if not used in CONFIG.SYS
DOSHELP.HLP	MS-DOS's online help information; delete if you've deleted HELP.EXE
DOSSHELL.COM	Do not use this program with Windows; delete its associated files
DOSSHELL.EXE	Associated with MS-DOS Shell
DOSSHELL.GRB	
DOSSHELL.GRB (table)	Associated with MS-DOS Shell
DOSSHELL.HLP	Associated with MS-DOS Shell
DOSSHELL.INI	Associated with MS-DOS Shell
DOSSHELL.VID	
DOSSHELL.VID (table)	Associated with MS-DOS Shell
DOSSWAP.EXE	Associated with MS-DOS Shell
EDIT.COM	MS-DOS Editor; delete if not used
EDIT.HLP	MS-DOS Editor help file; delete if you've deleted EDIT.COM

Table 3-9. *MS-DOS programs and files you can delete.*   *(continued)*

Table 3-9. *continued*

Filename	Notes
EGA.CPI	Not required under Windows
EGA.SYS	Delete if not used in CONFIG.SYS; okay to delete on any non-EGA system
EMM386.EXE	Delete; use Windows' EMM386.EXE instead
EMM386.SYS	Older Windows EMM386 driver; delete
EXE2BIN.EXE	Delete if you're not doing MS-DOS programming
FASTOPEN.EXE	Delete; do not use this command with Windows
GORILLA.BAS	Delete if you've deleted the QBasic program
GRAFTABL.COM	Not required under Windows
GRAPHICS.COM	Not required under Windows
GWBASIC.EXE	Delete if you're not doing BASIC programming
HELP.EXE	
HELP.EXE (table)	MS-DOS's online help; delete DOSHELP.HLP if you delete this file
HIMEM.SYS	Delete; use Windows' HIMEM.SYS instead
KEYB.COM	Not required under Windows
KEYBOARD.SYS	Delete if not used in CONFIG.SYS
LCD.CPI	Not required under Windows
MONEY.BAS	Delete if you've deleted the QBasic program
MSHERC.COM	Okay to delete on non-Hercules graphics PCs
NIBBLES.BAS	Delete if you've deleted the QBasic program
NLSFUNC.EXE	Not required under Windows
PACKING.LST	Disk/program list; delete
PRINT.EXE	Delete; do not use this command with Windows
PRINTER.SYS	Delete if not used in CONFIG.SYS
QBASIC.EXE	Delete if you're not doing QBasic programming
QBASIC.HLP	Delete if you've deleted the QBasic program
RAMDRIVE.SYS	Delete; use Windows' RAMDRIVE.SYS instead
README.TXT	Delete after reading
RECOVER.EXE	Delete; do not use this command with Windows
REMLINE.BAS	Delete if you've deleted the QBasic program
SMARTDRV.SYS	Delete; use Windows' SMARTDRV.EXE instead
XMA2EMS.SYS	Delete; do not use this command with Windows

Chapter 4

Optimizing Windows' Performance

Making Windows perform at its peak is a hot issue. Here's the big secret: Buy a fast computer. Even then, the basic optimization chores exist: To make Windows run best on any computer you need to properly configure your system. This chapter attacks that issue on three fronts: resources, memory management, and disk management. Also covered here are several techniques for making Windows run faster, as well as the usual interesting and curious things—buried treasures within Windows that you may not know about.

WINDOWS' RESOURCES

Just as a long car trip demands a lot from your car, Windows requires a lot from your PC. In both cases, being prepared is important. Having enough gas, oil, air, and water is essential for a car. For Windows, the gas, oil, air, and water come from your PC's processor, memory, and hard disk—the basic resources. But having the resources isn't enough. They must each be properly configured, or Windows' performance suffers.

You can prepare for a long car trip by giving your car a tune-up. For Windows, the tune-up is done by optimizing resources. Then, once you get going, it's important to keep an eye on those resources, just as you would the gas gauge in your car. When the resources get low, you need to make more available. Of course, you can't fill up a PC with a tank of RAM. Instead, you'll have to rely on some resource-boosting techniques.

Checking Windows' Gas Gauge

Former New York mayor Ed Koch, who once declined the privilege of jumping out of an airplane with me, used to walk around and ask New

Yorkers "How am I doing?" Windows has a "How am I doing?" feature
that displays the mode of operation and two values: amount of free memory and percentage of free system resources. This feature is the informa-
tive About Program Manager dialog box, shown in Figure 4-1.

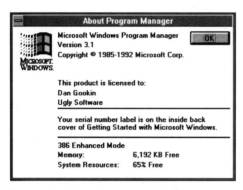

Figure 4-1. *The About Program Manager dialog box.*

The information you're interested in appears in the last three lines of the
dialog box. Windows' mode appears first. It will be either standard or enhanced, though for older versions of Windows, you might see real mode,
instead. The mode depends on your processor and the amount of memory
in your PC. (Refer to "Standard or Enhanced Mode?" in Chapter 2.)

The Memory value in the dialog box is a total of the amount of conventional and extended memory in your system plus any virtual memory supplied by a swap file. For example, a 386 system with 3 MB of extended

Shutting Down Inactive Programs

It's always a good idea to shut down programs you're no longer
using. They reduce the system resources available to those programs
you are using, making the system's response slower. Examples of
programs you can shut down when they're not being used are games
(old Sol is always active on too many computers), Dr. Watson, the
Clock, Print Manager, and File Manager.

memory and a 2-MB swap file puts nearly 6 MB of memory at Windows' disposal. In the About Program Manager dialog box, the Memory value shows what's left over after deducting the memory MS-DOS uses, any RAM drives and disk caches, and the memory Windows itself uses for device drivers, libraries, and any open applications.

Windows sets aside a certain amount of system resources (special sections of memory) for managing windows, menus, icons, fonts, and more. The System Resources value lets you see the percentage of available system resources. Of the two values in the dialog box, the percentage of free system resources is more important. You can be swimming in an ocean of memory, but open one more application or one more "child" window and—*slam!*—you're out of resources. This is why it's a good idea to keep an eye on that percentage indicator. If it slips below 40, you should close some windows and shut down some applications you aren't using. When resources do get too low, you see an *Out of Memory* error message (or something similar).

Optimizing Resources

Keeping an eye on the System Resources gauge is important, but more important is making sure your hard disk and memory resources are available and optimized when you start Windows. This section covers some basic software techniques for configuring your PC to meet that end. These are software suggestions only; hardware upgrades are discussed in Chapter 3. Additional ideas and techniques are provided in the remaining sections of this chapter.

■ Use a disk optimization program to test—and fix, if necessary—your hard disk's interleave (the physical ordering of the disk's sectors). The interleave may not be a problem on newer SCSI, IDE, or ESDI-type drives. However, if the disk was formatted with the wrong interleave, running a utility to optimize the interleave can drastically improve disk performance. Such programs include PC Tools' DiskFix, DTC's Disk Technician Advanced, and Gibson Research's SpinRite II. Interleave optimization needs to be done only once, but the utilities do come in handy for other types of maintenance.

- Ensure that you have a lot of extended memory in your computer and keep it all as extended memory. If you have a memory expansion card that can be configured as either extended or expanded memory, switch it over to 100 percent extended memory. The sole exception here is if you run MS-DOS programs that *really need* expanded memory. Then you should configure your card so that it gives enough expanded memory for those MS-DOS programs, but only if you're running Windows in standard mode. In enhanced mode, Windows can use extended memory to emulate expanded memory. (Refer to "Giving MS-DOS Programs Expanded Memory" in Chapter 5 for additional information.)

- Use the most recent version of your software, including MS-DOS. MS-DOS version 5 is very Windows friendly and is a much better operating system than 3.3—which a surprising majority of people are still using. Also, keep up to date with your device drivers, such as HIMEM.SYS, EMM386.EXE, and the SMARTDrive and RAMDrive drivers. Always use the most recent version of each.

- Install an XMS memory device driver in CONFIG.SYS. Windows runs best under the XMS (Extended Memory Specification), and HIMEM.SYS is the XMS-compatible device driver shipped with Windows. Be sure any third party memory manager you are using is also compatible with the XMS standard.

- Load MS-DOS high. Putting the command *dos=high* in CONFIG.SYS frees up 40 KB to 50 KB of conventional memory. Not only is that good for Windows, but MS-DOS programs can use the memory as well.

- Properly configure CONFIG.SYS and AUTOEXEC.BAT. Don't over-complicate these files. Set up MS-DOS, configure your system, load necessary device drivers and TSRs, connect to your network, and then run Windows. Additional information about these files is offered throughout Chapter 1.

- Create UMBs, and load device drivers and TSRs high. Create UMBs in CONFIG.SYS with the EMM386.EXE device driver and its *noems* option. HIMEM.SYS must be loaded first, and the command *dos=high, umb* must appear in CONFIG.SYS. (Third party memory managers can also be used, though each will have its own set of commands.) After that, you can use the Devicehigh configuration command to load device drivers high in CONFIG.SYS, and the Loadhigh command to load TSRs high in AUTOEXEC.BAT. See Chapter 1 for a complete explanation.

■ Don't load any TSRs and device drivers that you don't need. For example, you don't need to load a mouse driver to run Windows. A mouse driver is necessary only if you're running MS-DOS programs that use a mouse. Also avoid ANSI.SYS and any TSRs that Windows absolutely doesn't use.

Three Ways to Load TSRs

There are actually three ways to load TSRs for Windows, depending on which program needs the TSR: Windows, MS-DOS programs running in enhanced mode, or both.

■ For Windows only—not for MS-DOS programs running under Windows—load the TSR in WINSTART.BAT in the WINDOWS directory. (See "TSRs in Windows" in Chapter 5.) Advantage: Uses only Windows memory, not MS-DOS memory. Disadvantage: TSRs are unavailable to MS-DOS programs running in Windows.

■ For an MS-DOS program running in enhanced mode, specify the TSR in a batch file that runs the program, or run the TSR from an MS-DOS command prompt in Windows. The TSR is available only in that window. Advantage: Saves memory. Disadvantage: The TSR is unavailable to Windows or to other MS-DOS programs running under Windows.

■ For both Windows and MS-DOS programs, load the TSR from within AUTOEXEC.BAT. Advantage: TSRs are available to both Windows and MS-DOS programs. Disadvantage: Takes up vital memory.

■ Use a disk cache. Windows comes with the SMARTDrive disk cache, which speeds up reading from and writing to your hard disk. Starting with Windows version 3.1, this driver is supplied as SMARTDRV.EXE. The best way to run the driver is without any options; SMARTDrive automatically configures itself to suit your system. (Refer to Appendix A for SMARTDrive's full command format.)

Other disk caches can also be used with Windows. Be careful not to devote too much memory to the cache. The increased speed in disk access won't do you much good if you don't have enough memory to run your programs. As a suggestion, use a 256-KB cache on machines with 1 MB or 2 MB of RAM, a 1-MB cache on machines with 4 MB or less of RAM, and a 2-MB cache on machines with 8 MB and more.

■ Create a RAM drive. With Windows, memory is often best used for Windows itself or for a disk cache, not a RAM drive. But if you have memory to spare, consider using a RAM drive to store temporary files. A 512-KB RAM drive on a 4-MB system is okay; 1 MB on an 8-MB system is workable if you really need the full megabyte, but may consume too much memory.

Note: If you have the Stacker disk doubling program, use the SCREATE.SYS command to double the size of your RAM drive, as discussed in "Creating a Windows RAM Drive" in Chapter 1.

Use as many of these suggestions as possible to give Windows a nice, dry runway and a strong head wind for takeoff. Overall, memory is going to be the biggest issue. Even though this chapter is about software, I can't say enough about adding as much RAM to your PC as it will hold. Make all the RAM extended, and Windows will be very happy.

MEMORY MANAGEMENT FOR WINDOWS

The idea of memory management on a PC does not create a mental image of calm blue waters. Windows must weather a lot of storms, primarily because MS-DOS loads first and because Windows must be able to run

MS-DOS programs. As long as you've set up memory management properly in CONFIG.SYS, this task shouldn't be a hassle for Windows.

To understand memory management, you must know the terms associated with it, which device drivers control it, how Windows and MS-DOS deal with it, and how to make special settings within Windows to fine-tune your control.

Note: More detailed information about memory conditions under MS-DOS can be found in the Microsoft Guide to Managing Memory with DOS 5. *And I promise that this is the last time I'll plug one of my own books.*

The Four Types of Memory

Windows inherits four types of memory from MS-DOS:

■ Conventional memory

■ Upper memory

■ Extended memory

■ Expanded memory

A fifth type of memory, *virtual memory*, is exclusive to Windows. It's covered in its own section later in this chapter.

Conventional Memory

Conventional memory is the basic 640 KB available to applications under MS-DOS. MS-DOS programs expect to run in conventional memory, and most of them expect much of the full 640 KB to be at their disposal. All '386-based systems come with 640 KB of conventional memory. 80286 systems sometimes have only 256 KB or 512 KB installed. To run Windows, you must upgrade to 640 KB.

Upper Memory

Upper memory, also called *reserved memory*, is the 384-KB chunk of RAM between the 640-KB and 1-MB marks. It's set aside for use by your video display, hard drive controller, network adapter, system BIOS, and other hardware you might add to your system. Using memory management software, you can create special upper memory blocks (UMBs) in upper memory for storing device drivers and TSRs.

Together, conventional and upper memory total 1 MB of RAM. This is the same 1 MB that was available in the first IBM PC over a decade ago. To stay compatible with MS-DOS, all machines follow the same pattern—even though today's PCs are capable of accessing a lot more memory.

Extended Memory

The 80286 and '386-based PCs can access more than 1 MB of RAM. All memory over 1 MB is called *extended memory*. You can have up to 16 MB of extended memory in an 80286 system and 4096 MB, or 4 gigabytes (GB), of memory in a '386-based system. This is the memory Windows wants and needs. Conventional and upper memory are also put to use, but the real power lies in extended memory because there's so much of it.

Extended memory is controlled according to the XMS (Extended Memory Specification)—a set of rules and regulations for accessing extended memory. For MS-DOS and Windows, the XMS is set up by loading HIMEM.SYS in CONFIG.SYS. Third party memory managers should also implement the XMS standard.

How much extended memory is enough? You'll need at least 350 KB on an 80286 system to load HIMEM.SYS, which is required to run Windows. The '386-based systems come with at least 1 MB of RAM, 384 KB of which can be configured as extended memory—provided you turn off your PC's "shadow RAM" option. After that, '386-based PCs are upgraded in full megabyte increments. I recommend at least 4 MB of RAM for running Windows in enhanced mode.

Expanded Memory

Most MS-DOS programs can't use extended memory. For them, a solution known as the EMS (Expanded Memory Specification) was devised. It allows MS-DOS programs to access more than 640 KB of memory no matter which processor the computer has. The EMS makes lots of memory available by setting aside blocks of upper memory called *page frames*. When you want to access a portion of expanded memory, the EMS swaps the portion from the expanded memory "pool" into the page frame. For 8088/8086 and 80286 PCs, you need both hardware and software to use expanded memory. On '386-based PCs, expanded memory can be simulated and managed with software.

Windows doesn't like expanded memory, but it tolerates it. The only time you need expanded memory under Windows is when the MS-DOS programs you're running want it. Even then, Windows can simulate expanded memory for them in enhanced mode. In standard mode, you should configure expanded memory as necessary before you start Windows.

Taking a Look at Your PC's Memory Situation

Windows comes with the Microsoft Diagnostics utility, which allows you to see how Windows is using memory. Use File Manager to look for a file named MSD.EXE in your WINDOWS directory. When you find it, double-click it to start MSD. Because you're running the diagnostic program in Windows, you'll see a warning message; click OK. To view Windows' use of memory, select the Memory option by pressing the M key. You'll see something similar to Figure 1-4 in Chapter 1. (Turn back to page 30 and take a look now; I have to take a break myself and will rejoin you shortly.)

A "map" of upper memory is displayed on the left side of the window that appears. The right side of the window contains information about all the types of memory on your machine, including the total amounts and available amounts of each type. Be sure to click the down arrow of the scroll bar to display additional information about expanded memory, as well as DPMI information.

Note: DPMI stands for DOS Protected Mode Interface. *It's the standard by which Windows runs MS-DOS programs and multitasks without causing a major train wreck.*

The memory totals, especially those for conventional and expanded memory, can be manipulated from within Windows. For example, if you've directed Windows to simulate expanded memory, that memory shows up in the Memory window. The memory totals are then screwy; because the expanded memory is simulated, adding it to the extended and conventional memory produces a total of more RAM than really exists in your PC. Weird stuff.

How Windows Uses Memory

Windows has to contend with MS-DOS's memory management and all the rules related to it. Before you run Windows, some of your PC's memory is already being used. Conventional memory and upper memory contain MS-DOS and any TSRs or device drivers you've loaded. Extended memory can be used by a disk cache or RAM drive. The rest of both conventional and extended memory is then combined by Windows and treated as one large piece of RAM directly under its control.

By itself, Windows ignores expanded memory. In fact, expanded memory is sluggish and awkward to use, which is why Windows much prefers the smoother extended memory. In both standard and enhanced modes, the expanded memory you create before running Windows can be used only by MS-DOS programs running under Windows. In enhanced mode, you can simulate expanded memory if you need it, so you don't have to waste memory by setting aside expanded memory. The section "Giving MS-DOS Programs Expanded Memory" in Chapter 5 tells you how to set up expanded memory.

SYSTEM.INI Memory Settings

For the curious, the following sections describe various SYSTEM.INI settings that control memory in Windows' enhanced mode. These settings all belong to the [386Enh] section, and none of them affect operations in standard mode. If you run Windows only in standard mode, or you feel comfortable with Windows' preset memory values, skip ahead to the section titled "Virtual Memory."

Conventional Memory Settings

In enhanced mode, conventional memory is controlled by the following settings in SYSTEM.INI's [386Enh] section:

PerformBackfill=*Boolean* "Backfilling" is the process by which extended or expanded memory is used to supplement conventional memory. For example, if your PC has only 512 KB of conventional memory, Windows can backfill it to get the full 640 KB. *PerformBackfill* by default is *On*, so

Windows backfills automatically, and there is no reason to change this entry to *Off*.

ReservePageFrame=*Boolean* When Windows needs more memory for MS-DOS programs, it has the option of either destroying an expanded memory page frame in upper memory (*Off*) or stealing conventional memory (*On*). In the latter case, the conventional memory is no longer available to MS-DOS programs running under Windows. The default *ReservePageFrame* setting is *On*. When you set *ReservePageFrame* to *Off*, Windows uses the page frame's memory instead of conventional memory, which saves that memory for MS-DOS programs.

WindowKBRequired=*kilobytes* This entry tells Windows how much memory it needs to start. The default value is 256; Windows starts only when at least 256 KB of conventional memory are free. There is no need to mess with this setting.

WindowMemSize=*kilobytes* Use this entry to put a cap on the amount of conventional memory Windows uses to run. Normally, *WindowMemSize* is set to −1, meaning Windows can use as much conventional memory as it wants. By setting the value to something between 256 and 640 KB, you can limit the amount of conventional memory Windows uses, making more memory available to MS-DOS programs running under Windows.

Upper Memory Settings

Upper memory blocks can be created and used before Windows starts. Still, Windows peers into that 384-KB chunk of memory to see if anything's left over. When it does, it uses the following items in the [386Enh] section of SYSTEM.INI:

LocalLoadHigh=*Boolean* This entry is normally set to *Off*, meaning that Windows grabs as much upper memory as it can, leaving no UMBs for MS-DOS programs running under Windows. By setting *LocalLoadHigh* to *On*, you can preserve some UMBs for MS-DOS programs in Windows. Do this only if you need to load TSRs high in an MS-DOS window.

ReservedHighArea=*num1−num2* The numbers specified in this setting use hexadecimal values to describe a block of upper memory. Windows does not scan the specified range when it looks for usable high memory. This entry can be used to protect adapters in upper memory that may get fouled up when scanned by Windows. For example, an entry of

```
ReservedHighArea=C000-DFFF
```

excludes a 128-KB block of memory from Windows' search for unused memory. Additional chunks of upper memory can be reserved by specifying multiple *ReservedHighArea* entries in SYSTEM.INI. By default, there are no reserved chunks.

UsableHighArea=*num1-num2* This entry is the opposite of *Reserved-HighArea*. It uses hexadecimal values to specify a block of upper memory that Windows can peer into when it looks for available UMBs. For example, an entry of

```
UsableHighArea=C800-EFFF
```

tells Windows to scan from address C800 through EFFF for usable memory. This entry overrides any *ReservedHighArea* settings that would otherwise block the scanning of the same memory areas.

Expanded Memory Settings

The [386Enh] section of SYSTEM.INI contains the following enhanced mode expanded memory settings:

AllEMSLocked=*Boolean* This entry prevents expanded memory from being swapped to disk. If set to *Off*, the default, Windows swaps the expanded memory to disk as necessary. Set this entry to *On* if you're using an expanded memory disk cache. The *AllEMSLocked* setting overrides an EMS Locked setting in an MS-DOS program's PIF. (See "Building Program Information Files" in Chapter 5 for information about PIFs.)

EMMExclude=*num1-num2* Use this entry to block out a region of upper memory, just as you would use the *x* (exclude) option with EMM386.EXE. Follow *EMMExclude* with the address range—in hexadecimal—of the region of upper memory you don't want Windows to use. For example, the entry

```
EMMExclude=D800-DFFF
```

protects a ROM adapter on my machine that is located between addresses D800 and DFFF.

EMMInclude=*num1–num2* This entry directs Windows to scan a block of memory and use it, if its available. The entry overrides the settings of *EMMExclude*. The block of memory is described in hexadecimal. For example, an entry of

```
EMMInclude=E000-EFFF
```

directs Windows to scan the block of memory between addresses E000 and EFFF. On most PCs, this entry gives Windows an extra 64 KB of memory.

EMMPageFrame=*paragraph* Windows uses this entry when it can't find the space to create a page frame for expanded memory. *paragraph* is a hexadecimal address that marks the beginning of a 64-KB block of memory that Windows can use even though the block might contain some unused ROM or RAM. Preferably, *paragraph* should be in upper memory.

EMMSize=*kilobytes* This entry directs Windows to simulate expanded memory. Provided an MS-DOS program specifies expanded memory in its PIF, Windows creates expanded memory and makes it available to the program. Windows will create the amount of expanded memory specified by the PIF as long as it's less than or equal to the amount specified by *EMMSize*. (See Chapter 5 for information about PIFs.) Windows can simulate expanded memory only if *NoEMMDriver=Off* also appears in the [386Enh] section of SYSTEM.INI.

IgnoreInstalledEMM=*Boolean* This entry forces Windows to ignore an unrecognized expanded memory manager that manages the physical expanded memory installed in your system. *Physical expanded memory* is EMS memory on an expansion card, not memory created using a software driver. Set this entry to *On* only if you are certain your physical expanded memory will not conflict with Windows' operation. The default setting is *Off*.

NoEMMDriver=*Boolean* Setting this entry to *On* prevents Windows from using its expanded memory simulator. The default value is *Off*, which means that the expanded memory driver is available and is able to provide the amount of expanded memory specified by the *EMMSize* entry.

ReservePageFrame=*Boolean* Refer to the discussion of this item in "Conventional Memory Settings," earlier in this chapter.

Extended Memory Settings

Only one entry in SYSTEM.INI's [386Enh] section deals with extended memory:

AllXMSLocked=*Boolean* When set to *On*, this entry directs Windows not to swap extended memory to disk. This setting overrides the XMS Memory Locked setting in an MS-DOS program's PIF. The default value is *Off*, and normally there's no reason to set this value to *On*.

VIRTUAL MEMORY

To augment real memory—the RAM in your computer—Windows borrows space from your hard disk by "roping off" a section of RAM and copying the contents of that section to disk. That section of RAM is then made available to other programs. When a program wants to access the original contents, they are quickly copied back into memory from disk. The disk space that supplements the real RAM in your PC is called *virtual memory*.

Virtual memory is nothing for you to worry about; Windows manages everything. Occasionally you may notice your PC's hard drive light flashing, but that's about all there is to the "look" of virtual memory in action. On the "feel" side, activating virtual memory is slow because the PC must stop and swap between memory and disk. But that's a minor drawback, considering that virtual memory takes care of any amount of memory requirements for software running under Windows.

The Swap Files

To make virtual memory work, Windows swaps a swath of RAM out to disk, saving its contents in a swap file. Windows offers two different types of swap files: permanent and temporary. The permanent swap file is available only if you have enough disk space for it. Otherwise, Windows uses a temporary swap file.

The permanent swap file is a hidden file called 386PART.PAR and is located in the root directory of a specific drive on your system. A second file called SPART.PAR is located in the WINDOWS subdirectory and tells Windows where to locate 386PART.PAR and how big it is.

Swap Files in Standard Mode

I can summarize virtual memory in standard mode with two words: It's unavailable! However, standard mode does use swap files. When Windows runs in standard mode, it uses the DSWAP.EXE and WSWAP.EXE programs to swap MS-DOS and Windows applications to disk, but using these programs is not the same as using virtual memory. With virtual memory, you never know what information is being swapped to disk to make room. In standard mode, you know what's being swapped and when.

Windows creates a special file for the information it swaps to disk. The file is located in the directory specified by the TEMP environment variable. If you didn't set a TEMP variable in AUTO-EXEC.BAT, then Windows uses the root directory on your boot drive. To boost performance, you can specify another location by modifying your AUTOEXEC.BAT file or by using the *SwapDisk* entry in SYSTEM.INI's [NonWindowsApp] section. Here's the format of the entry:

SwapDisk=*drive:directory*

To best optimize standard mode's disk swapping, specify a fast drive and roomy subdirectory for this option. Try to avoid using slower Bernoulli drives, optical drives, and floppy drives for the swap disk. Instead, consider a RAM drive or fast hard drive.

Windows creates the temporary swap file called WIN386.SWP each time it starts. This file can grow or shrink in size, depending on Windows' needs. When you quit Windows, WIN386.SWP is removed from disk.

Of the two types, the permanent swap file is better, because it can be accessed more quickly than a temporary one.

Creating a Permanent Swap File

To create a swap file for Windows, double-click the 386 Enhanced icon in the Control Panel. In the 386 Enhanced dialog box, click the Virtual Memory button to display a dialog box that lists your swap file's current status, drive letter, size, and type (permanent, temporary, or none).

Your best option is to create a permanent swap file, if one doesn't exist already. To create the file, or to get more information about an existing swap file, click the Change button. The dialog box extends to look like the one in Figure 4-2.

Using the Drive drop-down list box, you can select each hard drive in your system, and then check the Space Available and Recommended Maximum Size settings to determine whether that drive has enough space to be a home for a swap file. It's best to select a fast hard drive. Selecting a large RAM drive isn't a good idea because the memory used by the RAM drive is best used by Windows. You cannot stick a permanent swap

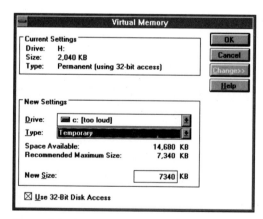

Figure 4-2. *The Virtual Memory dialog box, which you use to create swap files.*

file on a network drive; if you do, Windows claims that the drive is *Not an Int 13 device*. Stacker drives are also verboten for swap files; use only the uncompressed or "host" drive if you're running Windows from a Stacker drive.

Note: If your system is a file server, log off the network before you create your permanent swap file. You can create temporary swap files on a file server drive, but the permanent swap file gives you better performance.

Next you need to designate the type of swap file and its size. Select Permanent from the Type drop-down list box. As far as size is concerned, my advice is not to go by the Maximum Size setting, which is usually about half the available space on the drive. Instead, the Recommended Size value offers a good suggestion. A permanent swap file size of 2048 KB seems to be adequate for most PCs. If your applications produce large files, such as huge graphic images, then consider a swap file of 4096 KB.

If a permanent swap file cannot be created, only the Temporary and None options are available. Use at least 1.5 MB for a temporary swap file. If you don't have enough room, select the None option. On some systems that have little available disk space, that's the best option. Otherwise, Windows would spend all of its time swapping little bits of memory back and forth from this hard drive.

After you've properly set everything, click OK. A few confirmation dialog boxes might appear, and you may need to restart Windows for the new settings to take effect. Restarting reads the updated SYSTEM.INI file into memory so that Windows can start using the new swap file.

Swap Files Must Be Contiguous

The permanent swap file must be contiguous—one big, endless chunk of disk space. If the Virtual Memory dialog box reports small values for your permanent swap file even though you have lots of space available, consider exiting Windows and running a hard disk compaction or defragmentation utility.

32-Bit Disk Access

The lower left corner of the Virtual Memory dialog box contains the interesting Use 32-Bit Disk Access option. Selecting this check box directs Windows to skip over MS-DOS's 8-bit and 16-bit disk access and greedily use the hard drive in full 32-bit mode. This option produces excellent results on many '386-based PCs, and I recommend using it.

Selecting the Use 32-Bit Disk Access check box can greatly improve disk performance. However, some systems can't deal with 32-bit access. For example, some laptops have "sleep" features that will interfere with the 32-bit access. If you experience problems, simply deselect the Use 32-Bit Disk Access check box.

Virtual Memory Settings in SYSTEM.INI

Most of the information that can be set in the Virtual Memory dialog box is echoed in Windows' SYSTEM.INI file. Here, I'll describe eight settings that you can find in the [386Enh] section. Most of these settings should not be edited directly in SYSTEM.INI; use the Control Panel instead.

32BitDiskAccess=*Boolean* This setting turns 32-bit disk access on or off. The default is *Off.*

MaxPagingFileSize=*kilobytes* This entry tells Windows the maximum amount of disk space it can use for the temporary swap file. Normally, Windows calculates the value as 50 percent of the available disk space. If you specify a value here, the value appears as the maximum allowable size for a swap file in the Control Panel's Virtual Memory dialog box.

MinUserDiskSpace=*kilobytes* This entry sets the amount of free disk space that should remain after a temporary swap file is created. The default value is 500. If disk space is tight and you need a temporary swap file, you can edit SYSTEM.INI to specify a smaller value.

Paging=*Boolean* This entry specifies whether Windows uses virtual memory. The default is *On.* Edit SYSTEM.INI to change the value.

PagingDrive=*drive* This entry specifies the drive where Windows should attempt to create a temporary swap file.

PagingFile=*pathname* This entry specifies the name of the file Windows uses as a temporary swap file. Windows creates a WIN386.SWP file in the WINDOWS directory unless another drive, directory, or filename is specified in SYSTEM.INI.

PermSwapDOSDrive=*drive* *drive* specifies the letter (no colon) of the drive where a permanent swap file is located.

PermSwapSizeK=*kilobytes* This entry specifies the size of the permanent swap file.

HARD DISK MANAGEMENT ISSUES

Hard disk management is the art of organizing files on a hard drive. MS-DOS gives you three simple organizing tools: Mkdir, to make new directories; Chdir, to change to them; and Rmdir, to remove the directories. You then use MS-DOS's file commands to copy, delete, rename, and backup the files on a regular basis. Together, these operations are called *housekeeping*, and their goal is to keep your PC's hard disk neat and organized.

Great tomes have been written about how hard disk management works and which strategies you should use. You can gleefully toss all that information when you run Windows; it obeys few of the organizational rules of hard disk management. Windows needs only its own directory plus a SYSTEM directory. Theoretically, you could put everything in either directory, and Windows would still run in spite of the big mess. New applications are installed in their own directories, but they too add files to the WINDOWS and SYSTEM directories. This blurring of organizational lines really makes the hard disk neatnicks cringe.

The organizational rules of hard disk management shouldn't be ignored. Instead, treat them like the speed limit: Obey when necessary. Of all the other rules, backup and disk maintenance are the only two that should be practiced regularly. I'm not going to bore you with details about backing up. But the disk maintenance is important because most of it should be done outside of Windows—before or after it starts.

Organizing Windows Directories

As far as hard disks are concerned, *organization* means putting similar files into the same subdirectories. For example, you should store MS-DOS in its own DOS directory, with all of its files, commands, and whatnot. Likewise, you can create a TEMP directory for temporary files and a PROJECTS or WORK directory for work in progress. For example, on my computer I have a PROJECTS directory, and in that directory are other subdirectories for the various projects I'm currently working on. That's organized enough for my needs.

Windows-based applications are mostly self-organizing. Each of them wants to install itself in its own directory but lets you select another drive and directory if you want. For example, by default Microsoft Excel puts itself in its own directory and then creates subdirectories for its data. The result is nice and neat and representative of the excellent hard disk organization followed by most Windows-based applications.

Although most Windows-based applications are good organizers, Windows itself is not. Windows simply piles a lot of "stuff" into the WINDOWS directory. You can organize this stuff into neat little subdirectories, but after moving files to the proper places, you have to contend with the major hassle of reworking the icons in Program Manager to reflect the moves. If you don't feel the results will be worth the effort, skip ahead to the section titled "Disk Maintenance," later in this chapter.

For those of you who are still with me, I'll discuss some small steps you can take toward organizing the WINDOWS directory. A well-structured directory won't make Windows more efficient, but it will help you stay organized. Start by creating the directories listed in Table 4-1 and moving some independent files to them.

You can start with the easy stuff. If you create your own icons, consider putting them into a WINDOWS\ICONS directory. You can even toss in an icon editor for convenience.

One directory you'll definitely want to create is WINDOWS\GAMES. Windows comes with two games: Solitaire and Minesweeper. Two files,

Directory Name	Contents
WINDOWS\ICONS	Icon (ICO) files and maybe an icon editor
WINDOWS\GAMES	Games and such
WINDOWS\BITMAP	Bitmap and wallpaper (BMP) files
WINDOWS\WAVES	Sound and MIDI files
WINDOWS\APPLETS	Windows applets (accessories)
WINDOWS\APPLETS\TERMINAL	Settings files from Terminal

Table 4-1. *Examples of organizational directories under Windows.*

SOL.EXE and SOL.HLP, are associated with Solitaire, and another two, WINMINE.EXE and WINMINE.HLP, are associated with Minesweeper. You may also have two more files, SOL.INI and WINMINE.INI, in your WINDOWS directory. Move all these files to WINDOWS\GAMES by selecting them in File Manager and then dragging them to their new directory. After moving the files, bring up Program Manager, and select each game's icon. Press Alt-Enter to display the icon's Properties dialog box, and insert *GAMES* before the filename in the Command Line text box. Do this for every game you move, and then test run the games to make sure they work. As you acquire additional games, stick them in the GAMES directory. Some games might have associated DLL files; move them as well. If a game has a DLL file and you don't move it to the same directory as the game's program file, you'll be alerted that the game's program file is missing when you start the game. Run File Manager, and move the DLL file from the WINDOWS directory to the WINDOWS\GAMES directory.

If you're not using the wallpaper feature (for the desktop), you can move all the BMP files to their own WINDOWS\BITMAP directory. If you are using wallpaper, you must either keep the current bitmap file in the WINDOWS directory or specify its new pathname in the Desktop dialog box. And if you want to change your wallpaper, you need to move the files back to the WINDOWS directory if you want the Control Panel's Desktop dialog box to display their names.

You can use the same strategy with sound files, which all have a WAV or MID extension. Create a WINDOWS\WAVES directory, and move all the WAV and MID files there. If your PC has a sound card, leave the system sounds in the WINDOWS directory, but sounds you use to impress your friends can be stuffed into WINDOWS\WAVES.

The applets—the mini-applications that come with Windows—are the most cumbersome things to move. They comprise close to a third of the files and half the bulk of your WINDOWS directory. Moving them isn't the problem; it's rewiring Program Manager after the move that takes time and effort.

If you're in the mood to tackle this task, start by creating a WINDOWS\ APPLETS directory. Then copy the files associated with the applets (see Table 4-2) to this directory. Don't move the files for Program Manager, File Manager, and the Windows Tutorial; these files are central to Windows' operations. You could move them, but you would then have to edit SYSTEM.INI and WIN.INI, and there's no reason to go through that hassle for so few files. One application you definitely should not move is the WINHELP.EXE file. This is the Windows Help engine, used by every program that has a Help menu and a corresponding HLP file. If you move this file out of the WINDOWS directory, you'll be unable to use your applications' help systems.

Application	Associated Files
Calculator	CALC.EXE, CALC.HLP
Calendar	CALENDAR.EXE, CALENDAR.HLP
Cardfile	CARDFILE.EXE, CARDFILE.HLP
Character Map	CHARMAP.EXE, CHARMAP.HLP
Clipboard Viewer	CLIPBRD.EXE, CLIPBRD.HLP
Clock	CLOCK.EXE, CLOCK.INI
Dr. Watson	DRWATSON.EXE
Media Player	MPLAYER.EXE, MPLAYER.HLP
Microsoft Diagnostics	MSD.EXE, MSD.INI
Notepad	NOTEPAD.EXE, NOTEPAD.HLP
Object Packager	PACKAGER.EXE, PACKAGER.HLP
Paintbrush	PBRUSH.EXE, PBRUSH.HLP, PBRUSH.DLL
PIF Editor	PIFEDIT.EXE, PIFEDIT.HLP
Print Manager	PRINTMAN.EXE, PRINTMAN.HLP

Table 4-2. *Windows' applets and their associated files.*

Table 4-2. *continued*

Application	Associated Files
Recorder	RECORDER.EXE, RECORDER.HLP, RECORDER.DLL
Registration Editor	REGEDIT.EXE, REGEDIT.HLP, REDEDITV.HLP
Sound Recorder	SOUNDREC.EXE, SOUNDREC.HLP
System Editor	SYSTEM\SYSEDIT.EXE
Terminal	TERMINAL.EXE, TERMINAL.HLP
Windows Version	WINVER.EXE
Write	WRITE.EXE, WRITE.HLP

Note: Windows for Workgroups includes three other accessories: Chat, NetWatcher, and WinMeter. You can move the files associated with these accessories to the APPLETS directory as well.

After moving these files, you'll need to update their icons in Program Manager. Select each one, press Alt-Enter to bring up its Properties dialog box, and then insert *APPLETS* before the program name in the Command Line text box. This step takes some time.

Note: When you load a document that is associated with a moved applet, Windows asks for its new location. Enter the APPLET directory's path, and click OK. Windows saves the program's new location in WIN.INI's [programs] section for future reference.

If you're feeling really compulsive about cleaning up the WINDOWS directory, you can delete files you don't need. Start by removing the files not used for the mode in which you run Windows; for enhanced mode, remove standard mode files and vice-versa. A complete list of the files you can hack away is presented in "Creating the 'Minimum Windows Footprint'" in Chapter 3. But don't go crazy with the scissors; my mom did once, and I had a terrible haircut for the first day of school. Fortunately, hair grows back. The only way you can rectify overzealous file cutting is if you have a recent backup handy.

The suggestions I've made so far will pare down your WINDOWS directory by over 50 files and 2 megabytes. You'll still have a hefty number of files in the WINDOWS directory, but most of them are vital to Windows' operation and should remain where they are.

Dealing with Font Files

As your system grows, you'll doubtlessly add font files—especially the interesting TrueType fonts, bazillions of which are appearing on the market and on various shareware disks and national networks. (The subject of fonts is covered in Chapter 7.)

Font files are fairly large. Windows, and all the third party font utilities, expect you to stow these files in your WINDOWS\SYSTEM directory. A better approach is to move the TrueType font files to another directory, preferably one on a Stacker drive where they won't gobble up as much

The WINA20.386 File

Are you using Windows version 3.1 or later? If so, you can gleefully delete the WINA20.386 file from the root directory of your hard drive. Remove its read-only status using the *attrib -r wina20.386* command, and then zap it!

Only Windows 3.0 needs WINA20.386 to run its enhanced mode with MS-DOS 5.0. If you still have Windows 3.0, you can't delete the file, but you can move it to another location. This move requires three steps:

1. Copy the file to a different directory—say your WINDOWS\ SYSTEM directory. Then delete the original.

2. Use the System Editor to make changes to CONFIG.SYS and SYSTEM.INI. In CONFIG.SYS, add the following command, and then save the file:

```
switches=/W
```

In SYSTEM.INI's [386Enh] section, add a Device command that specifies the new location of WINA20.386. Here's an example:

```
device=c:\windows\system\wina20.386
```

Save the new SYSTEM.INI to disk, and exit Windows.

3. Reboot your PC so that the changes take effect.

)

disk space. You must move two files for each font: one with an FOT extension and one with a TTF extension. The first part of each filename has something to do with the name of the font: ARIAL for Arial, TIMESBI for Times New Roman Bold Italic, and so on. You'll see other font files that have an FON extension; these are Windows' screen font files, and you shouldn't move them from WINDOWS\SYSTEM.

The first step is to copy (not move) the TrueType files to their new directory; remember to copy both the FOT and TTF files. Then double-click the Control Panel's Fonts icon to display the Fonts dialog box. Select the names associated with the fonts you've moved. The tricky part is knowing the connection between a font's name and its filename. If you've moved all the FOT and TTF files, then you can select all the files in the list that have the (*TrueType*) description.

When you have selected all the files, click the Remove button. In the Remove Font dialog box, make sure the Delete Font File From Disk check box is selected. Then click the Yes To All button to zap all the font files in your WINDOWS\SYSTEM directory.

To install the fonts from the new directory, click the Add button in the Fonts dialog box. Select the drive and directory in which you stashed the copies of your font files, and then select the files from the list, or click Select All. Click OK to install the fonts from their new location.

Although this technique doesn't reduce the amount of disk space taken up by the fonts (unless you move them to a Stacker drive), it does pull them out of WINDOWS\SYSTEM, making that directory a lot less cluttered. Unfortunately, most font installation programs install TrueType fonts in the WINDOWS\SYSTEM directory, and you'll have to repeat the preceding steps to move them elsewhere.

Fonts on a Network

If you're on a network, consider moving the font files to a directory on the network server. Before you move them, check with your network administrator to see if stashing them on the server is kosher.

Disk Maintenance

The disk maintenance part of hard disk management involves three basic tasks, but you can add other tasks if you have the utilities to carry them out or if your computer or network requires that certain tasks be done. The basic three are:

- Deleting temporary or "junk" files

- Checking the disk with Chkdsk

- Defragmenting (optimizing) the hard drive

One way to carry out these tasks is from within AUTOEXEC.BAT, before or after running Windows. You can use the Ask utility to ask whether you want to perform disk maintenance or the OnDay utility to carry out disk maintenance chores automatically. (Both of these utilities are covered later in this section.) Either way, this type of housekeeping must be done outside of Windows; some of these utilities can really spin Windows dizzy if used improperly.

A second way to perform these housekeeping chores is to write a separate batch file—perhaps calling it MAID.BAT. Whereas sticking the commands in AUTOEXEC.BAT runs them automatically, you would need to remember to run MAID.BAT every so often, after you quit Windows.

Routine Housekeeping

However you choose to perform your housekeeping, some tasks should be carried out routinely—at least once a week. In this section, I give batch file command formats for some of the most popular tasks. If you like, you can use these suggestions to build your own MAID.BAT batch file.

First you'll want to clean up any temporary files Windows may have left around and delete any other temporary or "junk" files from your hard drive. Because you know where these files are placed on your system, you are the best person to decide how to delete them. For example, my computer puts junk files in C:\TEMP. Here's how I delete them:

```
REM Remove temporary files
if exist c:\temp\*.* del c:\temp
```

This batch file command removes all the files from the C:\TEMP directory. The test for existance checks whether there are any files to delete. Without it, you'll see a *File not found* error message if the directory is empty.

Note: *If you've set up a RAM drive for Windows' temporary files, those files will automatically be deleted. The contents of a RAM drive are erased each time you boot your PC.*

Once a week, you should run the Chkdsk command with its */f* switch. Using *chkdsk /f* cleans up any lost files or "allocation units" on your hard disk. These accumulate when a program crashes or when you have to reboot suddenly, and they occasionally appear for no apparent reason.

You should run *chkdsk /f* on each of your hard drives and then optionally test for and delete any FILE*.CHK files Chkdsk might create. These recovery files never contain anything really worth recovering. Here are the two commands you can use in a batch file to run Chkdsk and optionally remove any lost files it finds:

```
REM Run Chkdsk for drive C
chkdsk c: /f
if exist c:\file*.chk del c:\file*.chk
```

Remember to repeat these two commands for each hard drive in your system, substituting the proper drive letter for c: each time.

Another worthy housekeeping chore is optimizing, or defragmenting, your hard drive. Files fragment as your disk gets full and contiguous space for your files gets harder to find. To avoid getting a "disk full" message when megabytes are available (albeit not contiguously), MS-DOS splits up files and stores them on disk as best it can. Fragmented files work just fine, and MS-DOS (and Windows) loads them without any problem, but your system works harder to put all the pieces together. Periodically, you should run an optimization utility to rewrite the files to disk in contiguous chunks.

Three rules apply with optimization utilities. The first is that you should not bother running the utility until total disk fragmentation rises above 10 percent. (Optimizing a drive with fewer than 10 percent of its files fragmented just spins your wheels.) The second rule is that you should disable any disk caches you have set up before running the utility. You cannot disable SMARTDrive, so you must run the disk optimizer before SMART-Drive is enabled, by putting the command to run the utility in AUTO-EXEC.BAT before the command that sets up the disk cache. The third rule is that you should reboot after running the utility. The following example shows how this works:

```
echo Optimize hard drive?
c:\dos\ask
if errorlevel 1 goto no_optimize
<Disable disk cache here (if applicable)>
<Defragment your hard disk>
echo Reboot your PC now.
pause
:no_optimize
```

If you're using SMARTDrive, plop these commands into your AUTO-EXEC.BAT file (or call a MAID.BAT batch file that includes these commands before SMARTDrive runs). These commands start with an Echo command that asks the yes/no question *Optimize the hard drive?* If you type N, optimization is skipped. If you type Y, an optional command disables your disk cache—if that's possible for the disk cache you're using. Next the command that optimizes your hard disk is run. The Echo command directs you to *Reboot your PC now* after optimization. Then the Pause command halts everything while you whack the reset button or reboot your system.

MS-DOS doesn't come with an optimization utility, so you'll have to run a third party program. Popular programs include Golden Bow System's VOpt, Mace Utilities' Unfrag by Fifth Generation Systems, Norton Utilities' SpeedDisk by Symantec, and PC Tools' Compress by Central Point Software. The following examples provide suggestions for using each utility.

For VOpt

```
echo Optimize hard drive?
c:\dos\ask
if errorlevel 1 goto no_optimize
<Disable disk cache here (if applicable)>
c:\v\vrun 1 c:\v\vopt c: /F
echo Reboot your PC now.
pause
:no_optimize
```

The VRun program is used to run VOpt once every day. You can specify a different number after VRun to ensure that VOpt runs once in that many days. A manual reboot is required after running VOpt.

For the Mace Utilities

```
echo Optimize hard disk?
c:\dos\ask
if errorlevel 1 goto no_optimize
<Disable disk cache here (if applicable)>
c:\mace\sqzd
c:\mace\sortd EN
c:\mace\unfrag c:
echo Reboot your PC now.
pause
:no_optimize
```

If you have more than one drive to optimize, follow the Sqzd, Sortd, and Unfrag commands with a drive letter. The Unfrag command automatically runs the Fragchk utility and reports whether the drive needs to be optimized.

For SpeedDisk

```
echo Optimize hard disk?
c:\dos\ask
if errorlevel 1 goto no_optimize
<Disable disk cache here (if applicable)>
c:\norton\speedisk c: /sen /b
:no_optimize
```

SpeedDisk automatically reboots your computer when the */b* switch is specified, as it is here.

For PC Tools' Compress

```
echo Optimize hard disk?
c:\dos\ask
if errorlevel 1 goto no_optimize
<Disable disk cache here (if applicable)>
c:\pctools\compress c: /cu /nm /oo /se
echo Reboot your PC now.
pause
:no_optimize
```

Whichever utility you use will work fine, but never run any of them from within Windows.

Note: For Stacker drives, use the Sdefrag utility that comes with Stacker. Sdefrag tells you whether the drive needs to be optimized.

Putting all the routine housekeeping commands together in one MAID.BAT batch file requires a real Erector-set mentality. Figure 4-3 shows how MAID.BAT looks with all the housekeeping chores I've discussed included. This example uses the Mace Utilities for optimizing the hard drive. Creating the Ask utility called by the batch file is covered in the next section.

Create the batch file using Notepad or the MS-DOS Editor, and save it to disk as MAID.BAT. If you don't have a BATCH or UTILITY directory, save the file in the DOS directory.

You must run MAID.BAT independently, before or after you run Windows. If you're going to optimize your hard drive, then MAID.BAT must be called from AUTOEXEC.BAT before SMARTDrive is run. For example, you can use the commands on the next page in AUTOEXEC.BAT:

```
@echo off
REM Batch file housekeeping program
echo Housekeeping batch file running...

REM Delete temporary files.
if exist c:\temp\*.* del c:\temp

REM Check the disk.
chkdsk c: /f
if exist c:\file*.chk del c:\file*.chk

REM Optimize the disk
echo Optimize hard drive?
c:\dos\ask
if errorlevel 1 goto END
<Disable disk cache here (if applicable)>
c:\mace\sqzd
c:\mace\sortd EN
c:\mace\unfrag c:

echo Reset your PC now.
pause
:END
```

Figure 4-3. *A sample MAID.BAT housekeeping batch file.*

```
echo Perform housekeeping now?
c:\dos\ask
if errorlevel 1 goto SKIP
call c:\dos\maid.bat
:SKIP
```

You'll be asked the question *Perform housekeeping now?* each time you start your computer. If you press Y, MAID.BAT will go to work. Otherwise, AUTOEXEC.BAT will skip MAID.BAT and carry out the commands following *:SKIP*.

The next two sections describe how to write the Ask and OnDay utilities. Ask is used in MAID.BAT; OnDay can be used in AUTOEXEC.BAT to automatically run the housekeeping batch file on a specific day of the week. If you don't need these utilities, feel free to skip ahead to the section titled "Making Windows Run Faster."

Writing the Ask Utility

The Ask utility is a small program that allows you to press Y or N and then communicates which key you pressed to your batch file as an Errorlevel value. To create Ask, first create the text file shown in Figure 4-4. Double-check your work. In particular, make sure you entered lines 2 through 4 exactly as shown in Figure 4-4. Save the file in the DOS directory as ASK.SCR.

```
n ask.com
e100 B4 08 CD 21 24 5F 3C 59
e108 74 08 3C 4E 75 F2 B0 01
e110 EB 02 B0 00 B4 4C CD 21
rcx
18
w
q
```

Figure 4-4. *The contents of ASK.SCR.*

Next type the following at an MS-DOS command prompt. (You can do this outside Windows or in an MS-DOS shell running under Windows.)

```
C:\DOS>debug < ask.scr
```

This Debug command creates the ASK.COM program. You can then use the program to ask a yes or no (Y/N) question in a batch file. ASK.COM waits for either the Y key or the N key to be pressed. Pressing Y returns an Errorlevel value of 0; pressing N returns an Errorlevel value of 1.

Writing the OnDay Utility

A second, more automatic approach to doing housekeeping is with the OnDay utility. OnDay returns an Errorlevel value equal to a specific day of the week, allowing you to automatically run your housekeeping programs without having to press Y or N during AUTOEXEC.BAT.

To create OnDay, first create the text file shown in Figure 4-5. This program is ingeniously shorter than ASK.COM (and I recommend it in place of Ask for routine housekeeping). Check the second line to make sure you have typed it exactly as shown in Figure 4-5. Save it to your DOS directory as ONDAY.SCR.

```
n onday.com
e100 B4 2A CD 21 B4 4C CD 21
rcx
8
w
q
```

Figure 4-5. *The contents of ONDAY.SCR.*

Now type the following at an MS-DOS command prompt:

```
C:\DOS>debug < onday.scr
```

This command creates the ONDAY.COM program. OnDay returns an Errorlevel value based on the day of the week: Sunday returns 0, Monday 1, Tuesday 2, and so on through Saturday, which returns 6.

Suppose you want to perform routine maintenance every Friday (Errorlevel 5). All you have to do is put the following commands in your AUTOEXEC.BAT file:

```
REM Perform housekeeping on Friday
c:\dos\onday
if errorlevel 6 goto SKIP
if not errorlevel 5 goto SKIP
call c:\dos\maid.bat
:SKIP
```

This batch file is a bit trickier to figure out than the ones that use ASK.COM. You must use two If Errorlevel commands to narrow down the day of the week because MS-DOS's If command returns True if the Errorlevel value is *greater than or equal to* the specified value. So the first If Errorlevel command tests to see if today is Saturday (6)—the only day that is "greater than" Friday. If it is, housekeeping is skipped. The second If Errorlevel command then tests to see if today is not Friday (5). If it isn't, housekeeping is skipped. Otherwise, MAID.BAT is executed.

As I said, these commands are tricky to set up, so copy them carefully, adjusting the numbers for your preferred day of the week. (Always add 1 to your chosen day for the first If Errorlevel command. That way, you'll narrow down the day precisely.)

MAKING WINDOWS RUN FASTER

This whole chapter is about making Windows run faster. Other than buying a faster computer, most of the suggestions so far have been along the lines of optimization. Alas, no secret switch exists to boost Windows into turbo mode (unless your PC's "turbo" switch is turned off, in which case I strongly suggest turning it on). However, the next two sections offer additional suggestions for activating Windows' warp engines.

More Optimization Tips

Central to optimizing Windows is properly setting up your PC, as described earlier in this chapter. You should also be sure to create a swap file in Windows—preferably a permanent one. Beyond that, try the following techniques:

■ Select a plain color or pattern desktop background instead of wallpaper. Using wallpaper requires extra memory to store the desktop's image and takes extra time to redraw the desktop. By using a color or pattern, you make more memory available to other programs and cut down on redraw time. Select a background pattern using the Control Panel's Desktop dialog box. Use the Color dialog box to change the background color; click the Color Palette button, select Desktop from the drop-down list, and click the color you want for your background.

■ Use lower resolution graphics. Selecting the lowest resolution available for your video card improves speed because Windows then has to manage and update fewer pixels. For example, select plain VGA (640 x 480 pixels) over SuperVGA (800 x 600 pixels).

■ If you're running Windows in enhanced mode, turn off the Monitor Ports options in your PIFs, including _DEFAULT.PIF. Disable all the options (deselect their check boxes) in the Monitor Ports area of the Advanced Options dialog box. (See "Building Program Information Files" in Chapter 5 for more information.) Only if an MS-DOS program's screen fouls up when you run the program in text mode should you consider checking the option that corresponds to the application's screen mode. (These options are not available in standard mode.)

■ Disable updating File Manager when an MS-DOS program is running. File Manager tries to sense all the changes you make to your hard disk and updates its display accordingly. If updating slows down MS-DOS programs that are running under Windows, add the following entry to SYSTEM.INI's [386Enh] section:

```
FileSysChange=No
```

■ Disable expanded memory use if you don't need it. If you don't plan to run any MS-DOS programs, or if your MS-DOS programs don't need expanded memory, disable it by adding the following entry to the [386Enh] section of SYSTEM.INI:

```
NoEMMDriver=Yes
```

■ Enable faster mode switching when running in standard mode. To direct Windows to switch more quickly from protected mode to real mode, add this entry to the [standard] section of SYSTEM.INI:

```
FasterModeSwitch=1
```

This entry has no effect on '386-based PCs, even when they are running in standard mode.

General Usage Tips

Here are some suggestions that make Windows run faster as you use it:

■ Maximize your windows. After starting a Windows-based application, click the Maximize button in the upper right corner of its window to make the window fill the screen. Windows-based applications behave much better when run full screen. In addition, you can see all the application's options, and other icons—especially the blinking ones—don't pester you from the background. (Use the Alt-Tab "cool switch" to switch to the hidden windows of other open applications.)

■ Shut down programs you're not using. There's no sense in keeping an application in memory when you're not using it. Even minimized applications take up memory and resources. Shutting down idle programs makes more resources available for the active ones. Similarly, if you have many windows open for a single application, such as Microsoft Excel or Word for Windows, closing the windows you're not using makes more resources available.

■ Switch Print Manager to low priority. If you're doing something else while Print Manager is printing, choose the Low Priority command from the Print Manager's Options menu. Your printer jobs then take longer to complete, but more time is available to your Windows-based applications. On the other hand, you can accelerate graphics printing by switching Print Manager to High Priority.

■ Print to a networked printer. Even faster than using Print Manager is printing to a networked printer. Your file quickly zips off down the network pipe, and the network printer server then fusses with the printing, leaving your PC 100 percent free to do something else.

■ Use standard mode. I know it's hard to believe, but using standard mode can sometimes save you time. Standard mode takes less time to start than enhanced mode, and single Windows-based applications running in standard mode have total control over your PC's resources. For example, if you're going to run only Word for Windows, consider starting Windows with the following command:

```
win /s winword
```

This command starts Windows and runs WINWORD.EXE as the foreground application; Program Manager is minimized, and Word for Windows fills the screen. Because standard mode does not incur the multitasking overhead of enhanced mode, your system operates more efficiently. This setup is ideal for PCs that have only enough memory to run one Windows-based application.

HIDDEN GEMS WITHIN WINDOWS

Windows is just bursting with hidden treasures—and I'm not talking here about cryptic SYSTEM.INI settings. Windows provides many programs and utilities, some of which aren't even installed in Program Manager, that can perform all sorts of useful functions and interesting tricks. The System Editor is an example (see "Setting Up and Using the System Editor" in Chapter 2). I've discovered several others—some documented; some not—and have organized them into two groups in this section.

Not covered here is the wealth of applications that are available as shareware and public domain programs. If you're curious about them, you can obtain them from national online services, such as CompuServe and GEnie, from local bulletin boards (BBSs), or from software "warehouses," such as the PC-SIG Library.

Forgotten Programs

Here I list several programs that are included with Windows, but which may not be installed in Program Manager when you set up Windows.

Character Map

The Character Map program is installed when you set up Windows. Its icon, which can be found in the Accessories group window, looks like a key from a multilingual keyboard. Running the Character Map displays the character set for the font selected in its Font box. An example is shown in Figure 4-6.

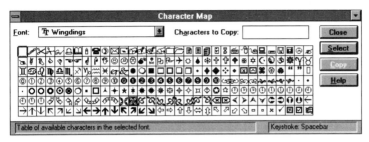

Figure 4-6. *The Character Map program, displaying the Wingdings font.*

You can use the Character Map to see which characters are available in that particular font, as well as to copy individual characters or groups of characters to the Clipboard. For example, you can copy the interesting ✈ Wingding by double-clicking the Character Map window and then clicking the Copy button. Use the Paste command in your Windows-based application to stick the airplane in your document.

Dr. Watson

Dr. Watson is a *debugging tool*—a program designed to help Windows programmers find out why their programs don't work the way they should. By itself, Dr. Watson doesn't do much. Most users stick him (actually his icon) in Program Manager's StartUp group and forget about him (or his icon). If an error occurs while you are running a program, Dr. Watson

---

ANSI vs. ASCII

Windows' fonts use an ANSI character set, not the extended ASCII set used by MS-DOS. The "upper set" of ANSI characters consists mostly of foreign symbols, not the traditional text-based line drawing characters of the ASCII set. The System font, however, does contain those line drawing characters, as you'll see if you run the Character Map program for the System font. If you use Terminal to call a BBS that uses those characters, set the Terminal Font option in the Terminal Preferences dialog box to the system font (Fixedsys) so that you can see the fancy graphics they create.

records pertinent information in a file named DRWATSON.LOG in your WINDOWS directory. He also displays a dialog box that allows you to describe what you were doing when the error occurred. That information and the log file can help you (and anyone from whom you elicit help) track down errors.

Microsoft Diagnostics

The Microsoft Diagnostics program (MSD) is a handy tool that tells you what's going on inside your PC. It's used primarily to provide information to Microsoft Product Support personnel. When you call them, they may have you run MSD to determine exactly what type of hardware you have and to make sure your PC is properly configured. As I mentioned earlier in this chapter, you can also use MSD to check out your memory configuration.

Registration Editor

The Registration Editor program (RegEdit) is used with object linking and embedding (OLE) to keep track of applications and the type of objects they can create. You don't have to run RegEdit to use OLE because most applications that support OLE provide their own information for Windows. However, this program is interesting and has a really cool ice cube icon you can steal for your other applications. For more information about RegEdit, read the program's online help.

System Editor

The System Editor (SysEdit) is hidden in the WINDOWS\SYSTEM directory; don't miss it. It offers quick editing for the system files: CONFIG.SYS, AUTOEXEC.BAT, SYSTEM.INI, and WIN.INI. Incidentally, similar editing is also possible in the Microsoft Diagnostics program.

WinHelp

The Windows Help engine is an application that runs all files with an HLP extension. Any Windows application that has a Help menu uses WinHelp to display the application's help information. This file must be located in your WINDOWS directory.

WinVer

This silly little program displays the Windows version, logo, and copyright. It's sole function is to reassure you that you're using Windows. Suggestion: Run WinVer and say out loud, "Thank goodness I'm using Windows. For a second, I thought I was lost in OS/2 land."

Secrets You Can Download

The Windows package no longer includes some programs. For example, the MS-DOS Executive—a crude but fast little file shell used before File Manager—was included with Windows versions up to and including 3.0. These and other Windows-based applications that are no longer included, such as the annoying Reversi game (which is now sold with OS/2—kind of like being relegated to operating system hell), are available directly from Microsoft.

If you have a modem, you can access the Microsoft Download Service, a BBS from which you can download software related to Microsoft products. You can dial the service to get the old MS-DOS Executive, Reversi, and several of the interesting programs that come with the Windows Resource Kit. (The Windows Resource Kit is an inexpensive product from Microsoft that includes technical documentation about Windows as well as several utilities for Windows.) You can also get updated device drivers for your hardware.

Additional Help Files

Some of the HLP files on your hard disk are not associated with a particular program. (Not every PC will have these files installed.) APPS.HLP contains up-to-date information on various applications you can run under Windows; GLOSSARY.HLP is an alphabetic listing of Windows terms; NETWARE.HLP and LANMAN.HLP contain useful information about using those networks; and PSCRIPT.HLP, TTY.HLP, and UNIDRV.HLP—all in the WINDOWS\SYSTEM directory—offer useful information about various printers.

Dialing the Microsoft Download Service is a toll call. Configure your communications software for 2400 baud, 8 data bits, 1 stop bit, and no parity. Then dial (206) 637-9009. If you have a faster modem, dial (206) 936-6735, which supports speeds up to 9600 baud. Both numbers are in the Seattle, Washington area.

Call up the system, enter your name and location when prompted to do so, and then follow the menus to the Windows 3.1 Driver Library section. (Choose File Areas from the first menu, Windows from the second, and Windows 3.1 Driver Library from the third.) Check through the list for the software you'd like, and then download away, using your communications program's "binary receive" options. Note that this service is download only; you cannot leave tech support questions or email on the system.

Chapter 5

Taming MS-DOS Programs

Windows works best with Windows-based programs. Of course you can run MS-DOS programs under Windows, but you'll never really get the most from your PC—not like you can with Windows-based applications. Windows just isn't *The Solution* for the tired old MS-DOS software you have laying around.

The problem is that MS-DOS programs can't access all of Windows' powerful features. When you run an MS-DOS program under Windows, you're back in piddly old MS-DOS, having to contend with printer drivers and programs that don't really want to cooperate with each other. But instead of having to leave Windows to run those programs, you can run them from within Windows' environment. There is an art to doing this, which is what this chapter covers in depth.

RUNNING MS-DOS PROGRAMS IN WINDOWS

Perhaps you have a whole cavalcade of MS-DOS software on your PC. Old standbys, such as WordPerfect and Lotus 1-2-3, abound on computers that run Windows. Ideally, you'll want to run the Windows version of your favorite programs. When that version isn't available, or if you're just too attached to the old version, you'll need to run the old version under Windows. This isn't as painless as it sounds.

You can start an MS-DOS program from Windows just like you start a Windows-based program. You can launch it using the Run command in File Manager and Program Manager, double-click its icon in File Manager, or add an icon for it and then double-click the icon in Program Manager. The MS-DOS program will run "full screen," just as it does outside Windows. Or in enhanced mode, you can make the program run in its own cute window—even a graphics program or game (though it can be slow) can run in a window.

The ideal way to run MS-DOS programs under Windows is to create a program information file, or PIF, for the application. Now don't run screaming for the exits. Information about creating a PIF and using the PIF Editor is covered in "Building Program Information Files," later in this chapter. The PIF contains various settings that control how much memory the program can have and dictates how the program looks and behaves as it runs. MS-DOS programs can run with the default PIF that comes with Windows, but they run much better with PIFs made specifically for them.

Using the Run Command

Both File Manager and Program Manager have a Run command on their File menu. Choose that command, and a dialog box appears, allowing you to type an MS-DOS program's command line or the name of a Windows-based program. Essentially, the Run command provides a command prompt from within Windows. You can type an MS-DOS program's command line in the Run dialog box, complete with any options or parameters, and the program runs just as it does under MS-DOS. The Run dialog box you see from Program Manager is shown in Figure 5-1.

The Run Minimized check box allows you to run the program as an icon. This is how you might want to start a program—for example, a network utility—that you don't need to use right away. If you haven't assigned an icon to the program, the minimized program appears at the bottom of the screen as the generic MS-DOS icon.

Figure 5-1. *The Run dialog box accessed from Program Manager.*

The File Manager's Run dialog box looks identical to Program Manager's, except that it lacks the Browse button. That button allows you to cruise around your hard drive, looking for COM, EXE, BAT, or PIF files for Windows to run. When you select one of these files, its full pathname is placed in the Command Line text box, allowing you to add any optional parameters or filenames before you click OK to start the program.

Note: PIFs are considered program files under Windows. Actually, what happens is that Windows loads the PIF, configures an MS-DOS session according to the PIF's settings, and then runs the COM, EXE, or BAT program specified in the PIF.

Using File Manager

File Manager works like many MS-DOS shells: Multiple windows display lists of files and information about your disk hierarchy (see Figure 5-2). At the top of each window are icons for the available disk drives, with a different icon representing each type of drive.

Each File Manager window has two panes. The pane on the left shows all the directories on your hard drive, with each directory represented by a cute little folder. The open folder is the current directory, and its files are listed in the pane on the right. The files appear as icons with adjacent

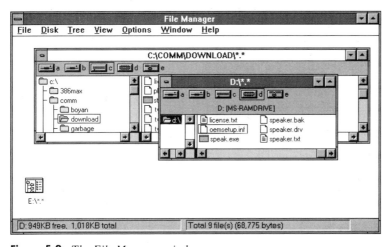

Figure 5-2. *The File Manager window.*

filenames. You can choose the All File Details command from the View menu to see more information about the files.

Four types of icons represent the files in the pane on the right: directory folders, associated files, unassociated files, and program files. These icons are illustrated in Figure 5-3. A directory icon identifies subdirectories. An associated-file icon identifies files that are linked to program files via their extension: BMP to Paintbrush, TXT to Notepad, and so on. (Associated files are discussed in "Associating Files," later in this chapter.) Any file

Windows for Workgroups' File Manager

Windows for Workgroups sports a modified File Manager:

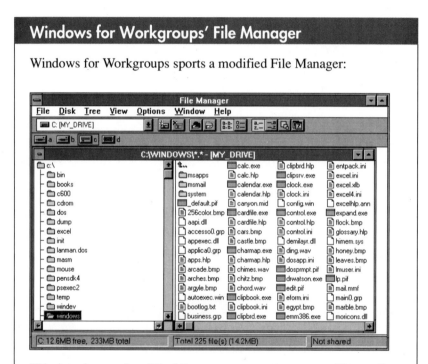

This interface makes File Manager even easier to use: The toolbar, which contains buttons for tasks such as connecting to network drives, sharing directories, and organizing the files in the window, is customizable. So if you use some of File Manager's commands more than others, you can add buttons for those commands to the toolbar.

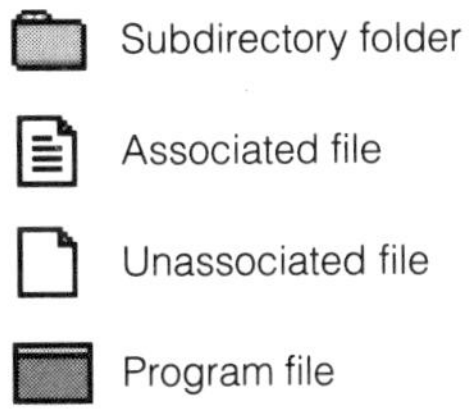

Subdirectory folder

Associated file

Unassociated file

Program file

Figure 5-3. *Icons used in File Manager.*

that doesn't have an associated extension appears with an unassociated-file icon. And all COM, EXE, BAT, and PIF files appear with program-file icons.

All files with associated-file icons and program-file icons are double-clickable in File Manager. For example, Lotus 1-2-3 might appear as 123.EXE beside a program-file icon. To run Lotus 1-2-3, double-click the icon, and the program comes right up. You can also highlight the icon and press Enter, or choose the Open command from the File menu. Whichever way you run an MS-DOS program, you're running the program using a traditional MS-DOS shell method. But these methods are often not the most elegant way of running programs under Windows.

Using Program Manager

You might have had Setup install all of the programs on your hard disk when you installed Windows on your machine. If you did, you have a group called Applications that contains icons for the programs you had when you set up Windows, including both Windows-based programs and MS-DOS programs. You can start an MS-DOS program just as you start a Windows-based application: by double-clicking its icon in Program Manager. If you don't have icons for the MS-DOS programs that you use often, you should add them.

There are three ways you can add an icon in Windows:

■ Dragging the icon from the File Manager window to the Program Manager window

■ Using the New command in Program Manager

■ Using the Windows Setup application

These techniques are covered in the following sections. Of the three, the best is the last one, using Windows Setup. Not only will it install MS-DOS programs, it even gives the programs it recognizes custom icons and custom PIFs. (See "Building Program Information Files," later in this chapter.)

Dragging Files from File Manager to Program Manager

The quickest way to add an icon to Program Manager is to arrange your desktop with both Program Manager and File Manager visible. Open both Program Manager and File Manager, and minimize any other open applications down to icons. Press Ctrl-Esc to bring up the Task List, and click the Tile button to arrange Program Manager on one side of the screen and File Manager on the other.

In Program Manager, open the window of the group to which you want to add the MS-DOS program. For example, click the Main group or open the Applications group window so that it is ready to receive a new item. Or you can create a new group for MS-DOS programs: Choose New from the File menu, select Program Group, click OK, enter a name for the group in the Description box, and then click OK again.

In File Manager, locate the program file for which you want to add an icon in Program Manager. Click the filename, and drag it to the proper group window in Program Manager. Windows hums for a few seconds, and then you see an icon for the file appear in Program Manager. Unless the program is a Windows-based application, it will appear as the generic MS-DOS icon. (You can change the icon later, as you'll read about in a moment.)

Help with Running MS-DOS Programs

Information on running some MS-DOS programs under Windows is included in a file named APPS.HLP. This is a Windows help file. Simply double-click the file's name in File Manager to open the file.

Note: *If the program has an associated PIF—either one that came with the application or a PIF you created—then drag the PIF to Program Manager, not the program file.*

Using the New Command in Program Manager

Instead of using File Manager, you can add a new program icon to Program Manager with the File menu's New command. Start by opening the group window to which you want to add the program or by creating a new group as I described earlier. Then choose New from the File menu, select the Program Item option button if it's not already selected, and click OK to display the Program Item Properties dialog box. Figure 5-4 shows the Program Item Properties dialog box for WordPerfect.

Don't worry about the text boxes for now. Instead, click the Browse button. Use the dialog box that appears to navigate around your hard drives until you locate the program you want to add. For example, you can change to drive D, move to the WP directory, and then double-click WP.EXE to add the MS-DOS version of WordPerfect to Program Manager. (Actually because WordPerfect comes with a PIF, you should select the PIF instead of the EXE file.) Click OK after you've found and selected your program, or double-click the program's filename. Windows then puts the full pathname of the program you've selected in the Command Line text box.

In the Description text box, you type a description of the program using up to 40 characters. (You can include spaces and exotic characters.) The

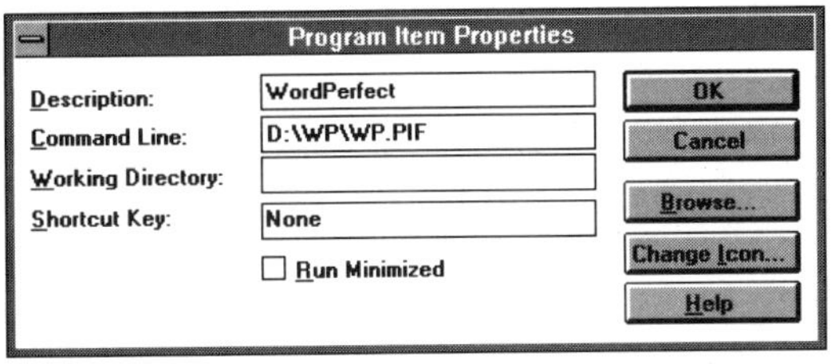

Figure 5-4. *The Program Item Properties dialog box for WordPerfect.*

description appears below the icon in Program Manager. If you don't enter a description, the first part of the filename is used.

Click OK to close the Program Item Properties dialog box, and your program appears in Program Manager, ready to run. You can do more stuff in the Program Item Properties dialog box; I'll cover that in later sections of this chapter.

Using this icon addition technique, as well as File Manager's "drag and drop," you can also add MS-DOS documents, worksheets, and other files to Program Manager. The method is the same, but these types of files won't automatically load themselves unless their extensions have been associated with their programs. See "Associating Files," later in this chapter, for more information.

Massive Installation with Windows Setup

You can use the Windows Setup program to install any or all of the MS-DOS applications stored on your hard drive. Using this tool, you can set up a massive number of programs all at once. However, you can't add files or documents; they can be added only using the methods described in the two previous sections.

In the Windows Setup program, choose the Set Up Applications command from the Options menu. A dialog box appears, allowing you to choose how Windows Setup will find programs. The first option, Search For Applications, directs Windows Setup to scan all the hard drives in your system for programs. The second option, Ask You To Specify An Application, works like the New command in Program Manager.

Select the Search For Applications option when you want to scan for and add a whole gang of files at once. When you select this option, a dialog box appears so that you can select the drives Windows Setup will scan for MS-DOS programs. Click a drive to select it, and click again to deselect it. The Path option limits the search to directories on the MS-DOS search path that you set with the Path command. (Refer to the section titled "Setting the Ideal Windows Path" in Chapter 1 for more information.) After selecting your drives, click the Search Now button.

As Windows Setup scans your hard drive(s), it may stop and ask you about an application. For example, it may see Q.EXE and not know whether it's Quicken or Quattro Pro. A dialog box will list any programs that could match the filename. Select the proper one or the None Of The Above option, and Windows Setup will continue its search. When it's done, you see a dialog box similar to the one shown in Figure 5-5. Listed on the left side of the box are all the applications found and recognized.

To add one or more applications to Program Manager, select them from the list, and then click the Add button. That button merely throws the applications into the list box on the right so that you can take a second look. You can remove any you don't want to add from the list on the right by selecting them and clicking the Remove button. If you want to add them all, click the Add All button.

With the programs you want in the list on the right, click OK. Windows Setup creates the Applications group in Program Manager, and adds icons for the programs to that group. Some of the programs may even be blessed with one of the custom icons Windows keeps handy in the MORICONS.DLL library.

Note: Windows Setup is able to recognize programs mentioned in the APPS.INF file, located in the WINDOWS\SYSTEM directory. It's a text file that contains information about the MS-DOS programs that Windows Setup can locate and install for you.

If you select the second option, Ask You To Specify An Application, in the Setup Applications dialog box, you're presented with a dialog box in

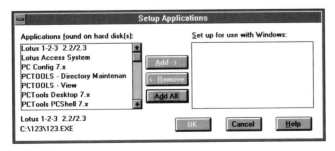

Figure 5-5. *The Setup Applications dialog box.*

which you can either enter the full pathname of your program or use a
Browse button to locate the program's filename. A drop-down list of Program Manager groups allows you to select the group to which you want to
add the program.

If Windows thinks it recognizes the program but isn't certain, you are presented with a Setup Applications dialog box that lists what Windows
thinks the program might be. (For example, the file TM.EXE could either
be the TeleMate program or the Norton Time Mark program.) Select your
program from the group. Windows Setup adds the program to the Program
Manager group you selected—complete with a custom icon, if Windows
has one for the program.

*Note: If Windows doesn't recognize the program, it may refuse to install
it. You'll be told to set up the program using Program Manager instead.*

Changing the Icon of an MS-DOS Program

When you add an MS-DOS program to Program Manager, it's often assigned the dull old MS-DOS icon. This is distressing, especially when all
Windows-based programs—and now, even most MS-DOS programs—
come with their own icons. But don't despair; assigning an icon to a program or file in Program Manager isn't that tough.

To slap a custom icon in place of the lackluster default MS-DOS icon
in Program Manager, select the MS-DOS icon, and choose the Properties command from the File menu. (A shortcut is to select the icon and
then press Alt-Enter.) The Program Item Properties dialog box appears, in

---

Creating Custom Icons

Unfortunately, there is no way in Windows to create icons for your
applications. However, programs for creating icons are available.
The Icon Draw shareware utility allows you to create icons in files
with ICO extensions for use in Program Manager. But in my opin-
ion, the best icon creation program is Icon Editor, which comes with
Norton Desktop for Windows.

which you can see the current icon hovering beneath the words *Shortcut Key* in the lower left corner. To change the icon, click the Change Icon button. The Change Icon dialog box appears, as shown in Figure 5-6.

Windows-based programs store their icons in their EXE files or in an accompanying DLL file. MS-DOS programs don't store icons internally, though some may have an ICO file handy. If no icons are available for the MS-DOS program (which is usually the case), you can select an icon from the Program Manager's internal collection. You pick an icon by scrolling through the list and double-clicking the one you like.

More interesting icons can be found in the file called MORICONS.DLL. To see those, click the Browse button, and select the DDL file from the list. (MORICONS.DLL contains the icons used by the Windows Setup program when it installs MS-DOS programs.)

You can also use the Browse button to open any EXE, DLL, or ICO file and pinch out an icon. A dialog box alerts you if the file contains no icons; simply click the Browse button again and try another file.

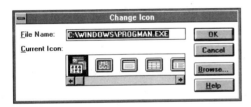

Figure 5-6. *The Change Icon dialog box.*

Associating Files

Associating files is the art of bringing together program and data files based on the data files' extension. Windows recognizes the associated extensions in Program Manager and File Manager and can link the data files with the programs that created them. This works for both Windows-based and MS-DOS programs.

Associated files must have consistent extensions. For example, TXT files are generally text files, and they're automatically associated with Notepad.

You can associate other files with other applications, such as WP files with WordPerfect or WQ1 files with Quattro Pro.

Note: Associating files works only if you can load the files by typing their names after the program filename at the command prompt.

Associating Files in File Manager

The quickest way to associate files is in File Manager. Select the data file you want to associate, such as a worksheet, word processing document, or graphics file. Then choose Associate from the File menu. You see an Associate dialog box like the one shown in Figure 5-7.

The data file's extension appears in the Files With Extension text box, with a list of the programs known to Windows displayed below it. To select an MS-DOS program, you need to click the Browse button and navigate through your drives and directories to locate the program's file. After you select the program, click OK. Files with the given extension will then be associated with that program, and they appear in File Manager with an associated-file icon. You can double-click this icon to launch the application. (You can also add icons for the files to Program Manager.)

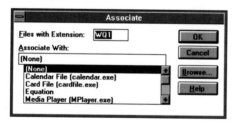

Figure 5-7. *The Associate dialog box.*

Associating Files in WIN.INI

Associations that have been made appear in the [Extensions] section of WIN.INI in the following format:

extension=command_line ^.extension

Here, *extension* is the file's three (or fewer) letter extension—WP for WordPerfect, DOC for Microsoft Word, and so on. *command_line* is the MS-DOS command that starts the program; it's followed by any options or parameters, as required—including the filename in the *^.extension* format.

When Windows runs the program, the caret (^) will be replaced by the name of the file whose icon you clicked. For example, the entry

```
hlp=winhelp.exe ^.hlp
```

associates all files ending in HLP with the Windows Help program, WINHELP.EXE. Because this program is located in the WINDOWS directory, there's no need to specify a full path. When you click the icon of a file with the HLP extension, Windows runs WINHELP.EXE and then loads that help file for viewing.

I don't recommend messing around in WIN.INI as a way of associating files. It's much easier to use File Manager's Associate command. However, you might want to work through the [Extensions] section of WIN.INI to weed out any programs you no longer have installed on your system.

BUILDING PROGRAM INFORMATION FILES

In Windows, a program information file (PIF) acts like a program file that runs an MS-DOS program. Contained in the PIF is a collection of information describing the program and various resources it requires to run under Windows. A typical PIF describes these aspects of an MS-DOS program:

- General information about the program and its startup options, directory, and window title

- How the program runs under Windows: full screen, or in a window (enhanced mode only)

- How much memory—conventional, extended, and expanded—is required by the program

- Which video mode the program runs under

- Multitasking aspects (enhanced mode only)

There is nothing dangerous, mysterious, or even annoying about a PIF. Yet people shun them. One reason is that MS-DOS programs run just fine with the default PIF. Another reason might be that the language used in PIFs is confusing, and some of the options are unclear. The following sections contain information that should shed some light on the topic.

What Needs a PIF?

If an MS-DOS program doesn't have a PIF, Windows runs the program using the settings in the _DEFAULT.PIF file. This file gives the program 640 KB of conventional memory and allows it to run in text mode. Windows itself is more flexible than the default PIF. If you run a program that can pop up a graphics screen, the computer won't die; Windows gracefully shifts your screen into graphics mode even though _DEFAULT.PIF hasn't granted the program access to that mode.

This flexibility may make you wonder whether PIFs are really necessary. The answer is Yes (occasionally) and No (usually). Some programs need a PIF, and other programs run better with a PIF. But for most programs, they aren't totally necessary.

Generally, programs that need PIFs are ones that require you to enter optional parameters when you run them. For example, if you want to run SideKick in nonresident mode (the recommended mode for all TSRs running under Windows), you'll need to create a PIF for it.

For communications programs, having PIFs means they can run "in the background" in enhanced mode. You can download software or upload messages while you're killing aliens or dancing across a minefield—both at the same time. This fancy footwork can only be done by creating a PIF that allows your MS-DOS application to run in the background.

Specifying Optional Parameters

You can specify parameters to a program in the PIF Editor's Optional Parameters text box. For example, you specify /G to direct SideKick to run as a program, not as a pop-up utility. If a program requires optional parameters that vary (such as filenames), you can stick a question mark (?) in the Optional Parameters text box. Then before Windows starts the associated program, you'll be prompted to enter the optional parameters.

Yet another reason may be to run a boring old batch file in a graphical window under Windows. But that's pushing it a bit. Most MS-DOS applications don't need a PIF, so it's nice that they're not required. But keep in mind that Windows-based and MS-DOS applications are more flexible with PIFs than without them.

Using the PIF Editor

The PIF Editor is a utility that you use to create and edit PIFs. Double-clicking the PIF Editor icon in Program Manager displays a window similar to the one shown in Figure 5-8.

The settings available in the PIF Editor vary, depending on the Windows mode. Standard mode has only a limited range of settings. Enhanced mode has more because it supports multitasking of MS-DOS programs. You can display the settings available for either mode by using the PIF Editor's Mode menu. The settings for both modes are saved in the same PIF.

Where you put your PIFs after you create them is up to you. Older versions of Windows had a WINDOWS\PIFS directory. The current trend is to litter the WINDOWS directory with PIFs, or you can put any new PIFs you create in the same directories as their programs. (Some applications come with their own PIFs, which is logical.) I prefer the PIFS directory

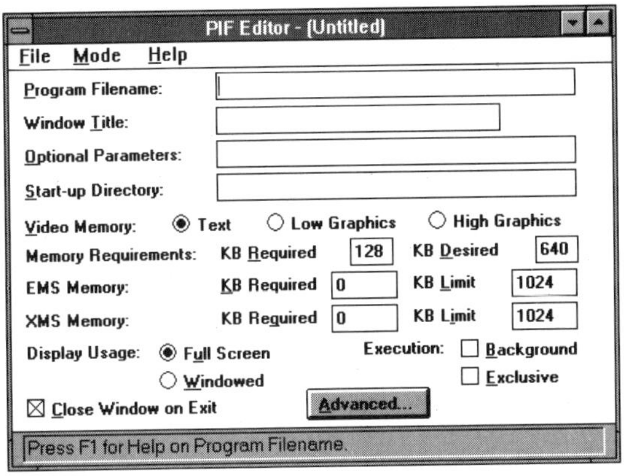

Figure 5-8. *The PIF Editor window for enhanced mode.*

approach, which makes editing a group of PIFs easier because I don't have to hop all over my hard drive.

It would be redundant to repeat information about the PIF Editor that is available in the manual or through online help. Instead, I'll give you a breakdown of the various options in the PIF Editor and what they do, plus some human-readable explanations of the more cryptic settings. Most of this section is specific to the enhanced mode options; descriptions of the standard mode options come at the end of the section.

Enhanced Mode Options

The options available for MS-DOS programs running under Windows in enhanced mode were shown earlier in Figure 5-8.

Video Memory This option doesn't control how the MS-DOS program uses video memory. Instead, it directs Windows to reserve video memory for applications that might need it. For applications that run in text mode, select Text. Most applications that run in CGA and Hercules graphics modes can get by with the Low Graphics setting. If your MS-DOS program ever switches into an EGA or VGA mode, select High Graphics. For example, if you're running WordPerfect and go into print preview, WordPerfect shifts into graphics mode. Providing you have selected High Graphics in WordPerfect's PIF, memory swapping won't be required to enable that mode, and WordPerfect won't give you a "graphics unavailable" error message.

Memory Requirements There can be three types of memory in a PC: conventional, EMS or expanded, and XMS or extended. In the PIF Editor, the Memory Requirements option allocates conventional memory. Set the KB Required value to the minimum amount of memory your application needs to load—typically 256 KB, 384 KB, or 512 KB. Windows won't run the program if the amount you specify isn't available, so never specify the full 640 KB.

The KB Desired setting tells Windows the maximum amount of memory the MS-DOS program can use. Setting this value to 640 KB means that the

MS-DOS program running under Windows will have the full complement of conventional memory, should it need it.

The EMS Memory option doles out expanded memory for MS-DOS applications. This option works only if you've set up Windows to simulate expanded memory, as described in "Giving MS-DOS Programs Expanded Memory," later in this chapter. If you have, set the KB Required value equal to the minimum amount of expanded memory your program would like. Set the KB Limit value equal to all the available expanded memory on your system, or the maximum you want to be available to the program, should it need it.

The XMS Memory option makes extended memory available to your MS-DOS applications. Set the KB Required value equal to the amount of extended memory your application needs, and set the KB Limit value equal to the maximum amount of memory you want the program to have, should it need it.

Display Usage This option controls how your MS-DOS application looks when it runs under Windows. Select Full Screen and your MS-DOS program will run just as it did under MS-DOS: taking up the full screen. This is the best choice for games and graphics programs.

Select Windowed to run the MS-DOS program in a graphical window on the screen with any Windows-based applications. The MS-DOS program then fits in nicely with the Windows motif, and you can access the MS-DOS Window's Control menu. But graphics programs run slowly in these windows, which is a major downer.

Giving Programs What They Need

Set the KB Limit value for both EMS and XMS memory to –1 to allocate as much expanded or extended memory to the program as it needs. If you set the KB Limit values to –1 in the _DEFAULT.PIF file, the value will apply to all MS-DOS programs running under Windows that use the default PIF.

Note: After the MS-DOS program is running, you can switch between full screen and windowed modes by pressing Alt-Enter. The Display Usage option in the PIF Editor describes how the program always starts but doesn't limit you to one display mode or the other.

Execution The Execution option controls the multitasking of MS-DOS programs under Windows in enhanced mode. Selecting the Background check box allows the program to continue running in the background when you're not using the program. This setting is ideal for programs you don't need to sit and watch, but which continue to work without your input—communications programs, databases that are sorting or generating reports, word processors that are printing, and so on.

The Exclusive check box controls how the program runs when it's running in the foreground. When this box is selected, the foreground program has total control of the PC; background programs cease to run. (Windows is still running in the background when the MS-DOS program is running in a window, but it allocates most of the computer's power to the "exclusive" MS-DOS program.) This option is good for CPU hogs, graphics programs that run too slowly when they must "share" the computer, and so on.

Enhanced Mode Advanced Options

Clicking the Advanced button in the enhanced mode PIF Editor window displays the additional options shown in Figure 5-9.

Multitasking The Background Priority and Foreground Priority options control how much time Windows devotes to the MS-DOS program when

---

Game PIFs

Running an MS-DOS "arcade" game under Windows? If so, turn on the Exclusive option in the PIF. Then other programs can't steal the game's resources, and the game runs faster—especially if it's a graphical game. While you're at it, turn off all the reserved shortcut keys so that you can't accidentally switch out of the program during play. (See "Reserve Shortcut Keys," later in the chapter).

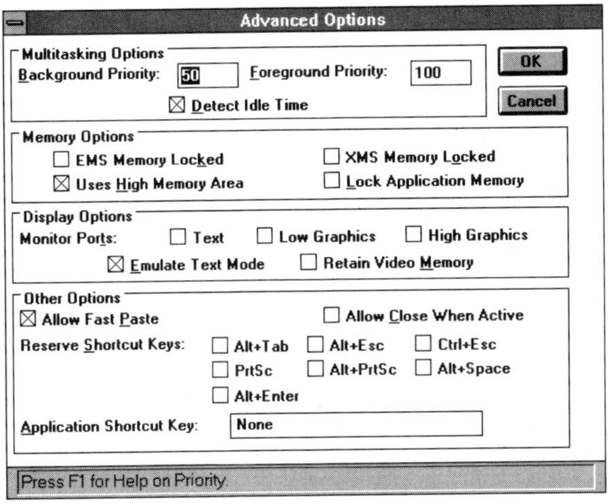

Figure 5-9. *The enhanced mode's Advanced Options dialog box.*

it's in the foreground and background, respectively. The priorities are set by specifying values from 0 for no priority through 10000 for maximum priority. Rarely, however, do you need to go to such extremes. Generally speaking, adjust these values only for programs that really need the PC's horsepower. Most of the time, you can leave them untouched, and Windows will manage everything just fine. If you're curious, here are the rules of thumb:

- The default value for Background Priority is 50. If your program needs twice as much attention when it's running in the background, double the value to 100. If your program doesn't need that much attention, halve the value to 25. Set it to 0 if you don't want the program to run in the background at all.

- The default value for Foreground Priority is 100. If you want to give your program more attention when its running in the foreground, double the value to 200. If you want this program to have exclusive control of your PC, specify a value up to 10000. If you would rather give power to the programs running in the background, halve the value to 50.

A discussion of how these numbers fit into *The Big Picture* is offered in "The Time-Slice Pie: Sharing the Clock" in Chapter 6.

Note: Although boosting the priority values allots more processor time to a program, overall performance depends on how many programs you're running. The more MS-DOS programs you run, the slower the system becomes. This is true for all multitasking environments.

Detect Idle Time When the Detect Idle Time option is turned on, Windows checks the program to see whether it's doing anything. If it isn't—if your application is just sitting around waiting for a keystroke—Windows devotes more memory and processor time to other applications.

This option should be turned on for most of your applications. Leave this item unchecked only if the program somehow fouls up when running in the background. Note that Detect Idle Time is turned on by default, so if your program fouls up without a custom PIF, create one and be sure to turn off this option.

Retain Video Memory This option prevents Windows from stealing back the extra memory used by high resolution graphics modes. For example, after you use WordPerfect's page preview, Windows may free the graphics mode memory and hand it over to some other program. Later, if the other program is using that memory, Windows may be unable to give it back to WordPerfect for graphics mode. Turning on Retain Video Memory prevents Windows from freeing the memory. On the downside, if your program doesn't really need the memory, checking this option may cause other programs to run out of memory. On systems with a lot of RAM, it's best to leave this option unchecked.

Reserve Shortcut Keys If your MS-DOS program relies on some shortcut keys that Windows also uses—for example, Ctrl-Esc or Alt-Tab—you can block Windows' use of these shortcuts with the Reserve Shortcut Keys option. Select the check box of the key combination your program uses. Then when you press that shortcut key, your program acts accordingly, and the Windows function assigned to that key combination is ignored.

Using Reserve Shortcut Keys is a good way to prevent "accidents." For example, pressing Alt-Enter switches your program from full screen mode to windowed mode. If you're running a graphics program and you really do not want that to happen, select the Alt-Enter check box. Table 5-1 describes what each of the shortcut keys does in Windows, in case you want to reserve any for your MS-DOS program.

Shortcut Key	Function
Alt-Tab	Quickly cycles through active Windows and MS-DOS programs; hold down Alt, press Tab to cycle, and release the Alt key to bring the program to the foreground.
Alt-Esc	Switches to the next active program
Ctrl-Esc	Brings up the task manager
PrtSc	Creates a screen image and copies it to the Clipboard
Alt-PrtSc	Creates an image of the active window and copies it to the Clipboard
Alt-Spacebar	Activates the Control menu, or switches a program from full screen mode to windowed mode and displays the Control menu
Alt-Enter	Switches a program from full screen mode to windowed mode and vice-versa

Table 5-1. *Shortcut keys you can reserve for MS-DOS programs by using the PIF Editor.*

Standard Mode Options

The options available in standard mode are shown in Figure 5-10. Notice that some options are the same as the ones for enhanced mode. Refer to the previous section for information about them.

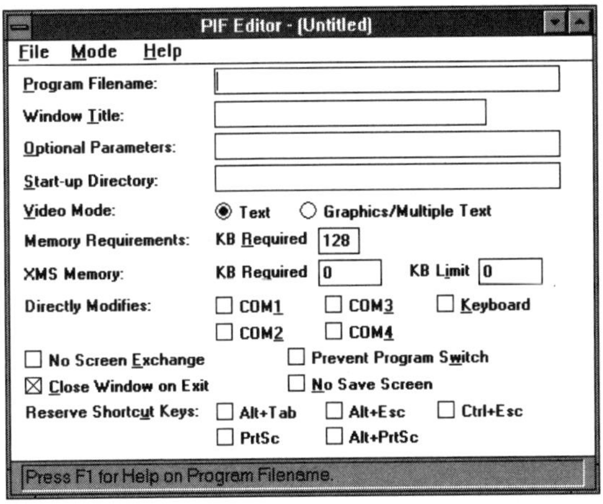

Figure 5-10. *The PIF Editor window for standard mode.*

Video Mode Select Text if your program runs only in text mode. If your program has any graphics displays or screens, select Graphics/Multiple Text instead. Other candidates for Graphics/Multiple Text include any text mode programs that switch text screens. (The old GW-BASIC and its programs would do this.)

This option only reserves memory for graphics and multiple text screen programs. You can still run them without setting the option. But if you don't set the option and Windows runs out of memory, you won't be able to use graphics mode.

Directly Modifies Select a COM port if your program directly controls these ports. For example, for the PIF of a communications program that directly controls a serial port, select the check box corresponding to the proper port to prevent other Windows programs from stealing the port and garbling your data. (This precaution isn't necessary in enhanced mode.)

The same rules apply to the keyboard: Select the Keyboard check box if your MS-DOS program directly modifies the keyboard or its input buffer. If you select any of these check boxes, you can't use any of Windows' shortcut keys, and you have to quit the MS-DOS program to return to Windows.

No Screen Exchange Select the No Screen Exchange option to disable the "print screen" screen capture and save yourself some memory. Normally, pressing PrtSc or Alt-PrtSc copies text from your MS-DOS application to the Clipboard. That requires a bit of memory, and selecting this option releases that memory for Windows to use elsewhere. If memory is tight, select this option.

Prevent Program Switch When selected, the Prevent Program Switch option disables standard mode's program switching. You cannot press Alt-Esc to switch to another program or temporarily exit the MS-DOS program. Instead, you must quit the program and return to Windows to run another program.

Select this option if memory is low or if you're running a program that shouldn't be switched out of memory, such as some communications programs or MS-DOS programs that modify the way your PC works. Use the program, quit when you're done, and then return to Windows.

No Save Screen When you switch out of a program in standard mode, Windows takes a "snapshot" of the screen. That way, when you return to the program, Windows can repaint the screen with the snapshot, making it look like you've never left. This trick takes up memory, so if memory is tight and your program can redraw the screen by itself, then select the No Save Screen check box.

Note: The No Save Screen option has nothing to do with Windows' built-in screen saver, which you turn on or off using the Control Panel's Desktop dialog box.

Giving MS-DOS Programs Expanded Memory

Windows loves extended memory. Some MS-DOS programs love expanded memory. How do you satisfy them both? For an 80286 PC running Windows in standard mode, set up expanded memory by adding an expanded memory adapter and using an expanded memory manager plus a driver for the adapter. For a '386-based PC running Windows in enhanced mode, you must do some fancy footwork, but you don't necessarily need an adapter.

If you create any expanded memory before running Windows, it's available to MS-DOS programs that need it. You can then specify the amount of expanded (EMS) memory in the program's PIF. Or a better approach for enhanced mode is not to create any expanded memory before Windows starts, but to let Windows use some extended memory to simulate the expanded memory. To pull off the simulation, you need to edit your CONFIG.SYS and SYSTEM.INI files.

Windows must use a *page frame* (a 64-KB portion of upper memory) to simulate expanded memory. To create a page frame, you must exclude a 64-KB chunk of upper memory when you run EMM386.EXE. For example, you can add *x=c800-d7ff* to the line that loads EMM386.EXE in CONFIG.SYS. Or a better way is to specify the *ram* option with the EMM386 command instead of *noems*. Although *ram* also creates expanded memory, it makes only 256 KB of it—not enough to quibble over.

Two entries are required in SYSTEM.INI's [386Enh] section to force Windows to fork over expanded memory.

NoEMMDriver=Off This entry is annoying because it's a double negative. Essentially, by setting *NoEMMDriver* to *Off*, you are enabling the EMM (Expanded Memory Manager) driver. The *No* and *Off* cancel. *Off* is the default setting of this option, so you need to change things in SYSTEM.INI only if you see this item set to *On*, *Yes*, *True*, or 1.

EMMSize=*kilobytes* This entry sets the amount of memory Windows will simulate as expanded memory, specified in kilobytes. This memory is then converted on demand by MS-DOS programs according to their PIF settings. For example, to make 1 MB of expanded memory available to programs that want it, specify the following:

```
EMMSize=1024
```

That makes 1024 KB of expanded memory available to MS-DOS programs that need it. For those programs, you need to know how much expanded memory they'd like to have. Say, for example, that WordPerfect (the MS-DOS version) wants 550 KB. In WordPerfect's PIF, enter 550 in the EMS Memory option's KB Required box. In the KB Limit box, enter –1. Other MS-DOS applications that need expanded memory should be set up accordingly.

Using PIFs

Now that you know how to create PIFs, you should use them for all your MS-DOS programs. There are tips and tricks you should know about each type of MS-DOS program that uses a PIF.

Running MS-DOS with a PIF

Windows comes with a file called DOSPRMPT.PIF for running MS-DOS. This PIF basically runs COMMAND.COM, which starts up the MS-DOS command prompt. Ho hum. One of the new things added in Windows 3.1 is a startup banner that is displayed whenever COMMAND.COM runs. This banner offers some information about running the command prompt— that you can press Alt-Enter to switch between full screen and windowed modes, and that you type *exit* to quit the command prompt and return to Windows.

A better plan of attack for running MS-DOS under Windows is to create a custom RUNDOS.BAT batch file and then run the batch file with a PIF instead of using DOSPRMPT.PIF. Start by creating the batch file to run MS-DOS under Windows. I used Notepad to create the file shown in Figure 5-11. Save the file as RUNDOS.BAT in the WINDOWS directory.

```
@echo off
DOSKEY /INSERT
echo +---------------------------------------------+
echo + You're now in an MS-DOS shell under Windows  +
echo + Press Alt-Enter to make this a window        +
echo + Type "exit" to quit this shell               +
echo +---------------------------------------------+
echo
prompt In Windows; type EXIT to return$_($P)
command
echo Back to Windows...
```

Figure 5-11. *The RUNDOS.BAT file.*

Here's a rundown on what RUNDOS.BAT does. First it runs DOSKEY to give you command line editing at the MS-DOS prompt. Next it displays a banner similar to the one displayed when you run COMMAND.COM. It's necessary to create a banner because the default banner isn't displayed when you run a batch file or when you run COMMAND.COM in a batch file, as RUNDOS.BAT does.

No Startup Banner

If you don't want the startup banner to be displayed when you run COMMAND.COM under Windows, edit SYSTEM.INI by adding the following entry to the [386Enh] section:

```
DOSPromptExitInstruc=Off
```

This switches off the startup banner. You'll need to exit and restart Windows for this change to take affect.

The Prompt command then sets up a special prompt for the MS-DOS session in Windows:

```
In Windows; type EXIT to return
(C:\)
```

This prompt will remind you that you're in Windows, not MS-DOS, and will keep handy the command to close the MS-DOS window.

Finally, the batch file runs COMMAND.COM, the program that starts the MS-DOS command prompt. When you type *exit* to quit the command prompt, the batch file displays *Back to Windows...* and you're shuffled back to the Windows environment.

Save the RUNDOS.BAT file to disk, and then start the PIF Editor. Type *RUNDOS.BAT* in the Program Filename text box and *My MS-DOS Prompt* in the Window Title text box. The startup directory should be *C:*, the root directory of drive C.

Set Video Memory to Text. The Memory Requirements settings are 256 for KB Required and 640 for KB Desired. Leave the KB Required entries set to 0 for both EMS and XMS memory, and enter *–1* in the KB Limit boxes. Set Display Usage to Full Screen, unless the idea of running MS-DOS in a window amuses you, in which case select Windowed.

Set the other PIF Editor options as you deem necessary. Then save the PIF information to disk in a file called DOS.PIF, and exit the PIF Editor.

In Program Manager, highlight the MS-DOS icon installed when Windows was set up, and choose Properties from the File menu (or press Alt-Enter).

Other Batch File Candidates

If you want to run memory resident programs in certain MS-DOS windows, consider setting them up using a batch file similiar to RUNDOS.BAT. For example, to load a special TSR before running Prodigy, start the TSR and then start Prodigy from a batch file.

If you've deleted the MS-DOS icon, add a new program item. Either way, you'll end up with the Program Item Properties dialog box.

In the Description text box, enter *MS-DOS Prompt*, and in the Command Line text box, enter *DOS.PIF*, the name of the PIF you just created. If you want an icon other than the default, change the icon by clicking the Change Icon button. The best MS-DOS prompt icon is the big MS-DOS found in PROGMAN.EXE. It's number 10 in the list (if you start counting with 1). Click OK to select that icon. Then click OK in the Program Item Properties dialog box, and, lo, you have your custom MS-DOS prompt.

Batch Files in Windows

You can run a batch file in Windows, just as you can run a COM or EXE file. Windows starts the batch file in its own window, like any MS-DOS program. However, if you want to get fancy, and especially if the batch file needs parameters, you must create a PIF for the batch file to run under Windows.

More Lines on the Screen

Tired of seeing only 25 lines in the MS-DOS window? You can edit SYSTEM.INI to change the number of screen lines—for all MS-DOS applications run under Windows. In SYSTEM.INI's [NonWindows-App] section, add the following line:

ScreenLines=n

The value of n indicates the number of lines on the screen. The default is 25; you can also specify 43 or 50, depending on your video system. (These are the same text resolutions supported by MS-DOS's Mode Con command.)

You will need to save your changes to SYSTEM.INI and then exit and restart Windows for the changes to take effect. Note that some MS-DOS programs assert their own screen mode and may change the number back to 25.

For example, if your batch file requires optional parameters, you need to create a PIF for the batch file and specify a question mark (?) in the Optional Parameters text box. Then when the batch file's PIF runs, a dialog box will be displayed, prompting for input as in Figure 5-12. Of course, the prompt assumes you know what it is you're supposed to type in; no other text is given except for the name that is specified in the PIF's Window Title text box.

The INWIN Program

The following Debug script file creates a utility program named INWIN.COM that can be used in a batch file to determine whether Windows is running. If Windows isn't running, then INWIN returns an Errorlevel value of 0; otherwise, INWIN returns a value greater than 1. (Actually, it returns the Windows major version number; for example, 3 for Windows 3.1.)

Enter the following lines in a text editor, such as the MS-DOS Editor. Double-check your work to make sure you've typed the proper values in the second and third lines. When everything is correct, save the file to disk as INWIN.SCR in your MS-DOS directory.

```
n inwin.com
e100 B8 00 16 CD 2F 24 7F B4
e108 4C CD 21
rcx
b
w
q
```

At the command prompt, type the following command:

```
debug< inwin.scr
```

This creates INWIN.COM. You can now use INWIN in your batch files to determine whether Windows is running.

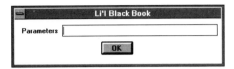

Figure 5-12. *The dialog box that allows you to supply the batch file's optional parameters when its PIF runs.*

TSRs in Windows

There are two types of terminate and stay resident (TSR), or memory resident, programs: pop-up applications, such as Borland's SideKick; and a sort of device driver that sits in memory and modifies the way MS-DOS behaves or adds some new feature to the operating system.

When you run a pop-up TSR in Windows, you should run it only in its nonresident mode. This is usually accomplished by some type of command line option or switch, which you specify in the Optional Parameters text box of the program's PIF. With SideKick, for example, specifying the /G switch allows the program to run in its own Window. If you run Side-Kick as a memory resident program, Windows becomes unstable and crashes, which isn't productive for either Windows or SideKick.

The device driver–type of TSRs are programs such as MIRROR and the MOUSE.COM mouse driver. These programs should be run from within AUTOEXEC.BAT before Windows starts and should be run with Windows only if they serve some purpose. For example, running the mouse driver means all your MS-DOS programs can use the mouse. However, this type of TSR should never be started from within Windows.

To make some types of TSRs more compatible with Windows, there is a *LocalTSRs* entry in SYSTEM.INI's [NonWindowsApp] section. It's followed by a list of memory resident programs that Windows will duplicate each time it runs an MS-DOS program. You should add TSRs to the list only if they are officially approved as working under Windows (so you'll have to dig through your manuals or call the TSR developer's support line to see if they pass muster). Your SYSTEM.INI file may already have the following entry in it:

```
LocalTSRs=dosedit,pced,ced
```

This identifies the Dosedit, PCed, and Ced TSRs as being compatible with Windows and directs Windows to load each of them when it runs an MS-DOS program. MS-DOS's DOSKEY program is automatically loaded into each MS-DOS session if you've included it in your AUTOEXEC.BAT file. Add any other compatible TSRs you feel would be valuable in each MS-DOS session, but remember to load them before you run Windows.

MS-DOS Utility Programs

Some utility programs can wreak total havoc in a multitasking environment such as Windows. It's very dangerous to run utilities such as disk optimizers, defragmentation programs, Undelete, Backup, and even Chkdsk under Windows. Some utility programs, such as Norton's SpeedDisk, are smart and inform you that they cannot be run under Windows. Other

Loading Windows-Only TSRs

If you have a TSR you want to use only while in Windows enhanced mode, put it in a batch file named WINSTART.BAT. That batch file is read by the WIN386.EXE file, and any TSRs it contains are loaded into memory. For example, consider the following batch file:

```
@echo off
REM This is the WINSTART.BAT file that contains
REM TSRs for use in Windows only-
REM not with MS-DOS programs that run under Windows
echo WINSTART.BAT is running...
c:\ndw\smartcan /on /skiphigh
:END
```

This WINSTART.BAT batch file loads the SmartCan program from Norton Desktop for Windows. This TSR, and all others loaded in WINSTART.BAT, is available only to Windows, not to any MS-DOS programs that run under Windows. The advantage here is that only memory for Windows is used by the TSRs—not memory for MS-DOS programs running under Windows. By loading Windows-only TSRs in WINSTART.BAT, you make that much more memory available to your MS-DOS programs.

utilities plow right ahead. Unless the utility was created to run under Windows, don't run it.

Note: If the program has a version that runs under Windows, such as Norton Backup for Windows, then use it instead of the older, text-based MS-DOS application. Programs written for Windows recognize and deal with conflicts that the MS-DOS applications aren't aware of.

Why should you avoid running utilities? Because in Windows it's possible for several programs to be working with different files on disk. If you run a disk optimizer, the utility may pick up the files' pieces and move them without the other programs knowing about it. Chkdsk, for example, may find part of a document you're writing to disk and assume it's a "lost allocation unit."

A further problem with disk optimizers and defragmentation utilities is that you need to reboot your computer after these programs reorganize the files on your hard drive. This is why all hard disk maintenance should be done before or after you run Windows. (Refer to "Routine Housekeeping" in Chapter 4 for more information.)

Another type of utility not worthy of Windows is the diagnostic. These programs compile an inventory of your PC's hardware, test everything, and offer benchmark comparisons between your computer and certain industry standards. Because Windows totally controls your computer, these programs might report inaccurate results. Further, some of these programs may snoop around and modify (or "fix") some of Windows' work, making everything unstable after they quit. As with disk optimizers and defragmentation utilities, run your diagnostic programs before or after you run Windows (preferably from their own self-booting disks).

Virus checking software is handy to have on a Windows system. Most of this software sits in the background and bleeps or pops-up when something suspicious happens. It's best to use the Windows version of any virus checking software. For example, Norton's Anti-Virus, which ships with Norton Desktop for Windows, integrates itself well with the Windows environment. Text-based virus checking programs may be unable to display warning messages in Windows.

Of course, nothing works better for fighting *The Virus* than "safe computing practices": Be wary of strange programs given to you by friends. And
never, under any circumstances, boot your PC from an unfamiliar floppy
disk—especially a pirated game a cohort has urged you to try.

That Bleeping Virus Checker

If your text-based virus checking program bleeps at you in Windows, exit Windows, and run the program's virus "scanning" utility.
Check all the files on your hard drive, as well as the boot sector, for
infection. You should exit Windows first so that the scanning process
doesn't harm a program that is accessing the disk at the same time as
the scan.

MS-DOS PROGRAMS IN A WINDOW

Windows' standard and enhanced modes run MS-DOS programs differently. As you can guess, enhanced mode offers many more interesting and
fun options than you get with standard mode. I'm not in a particularly
cheery mood at the moment, so I'll start by explaining how standard mode
works with MS-DOS programs.

In standard mode, you can start more than one MS-DOS program, but this
mode's DOSX.EXE program allows Windows to run only one MS-DOS
program in extended memory at a time. Unfortunately, the 80286 can't
pull as many tricks as the 80386, so when you duck out of an MS-DOS
program, the DSWAP.EXE program runs, freeing memory by saving much
of the MS-DOS program to disk and then reloading Windows. On disk,
the program no longer runs; it just sits there until you bring it up again,
at which point DSWAP.EXE loads it back into memory. (The MS-DOS
Shell program uses similar tricks to juggle several programs at once.)

Enhanced mode, on the other hand, is where things really cook. When
Windows runs on a '386-based PC, it can create several "virtual 8086

machines," each of which can run an MS-DOS program and all of which can run simultaneously. And you can display each program in a graphical window, instead of being limited to a full screen text window, as in standard mode. There are other exciting things going on as well, which are covered in the following sections.

Multitasking MS-DOS Programs

Windows wasn't designed as a multitasking solution for your MS-DOS software. It works best when running Windows-based applications and only then can you get the most from your PC. However, you may still have MS-DOS programs laying around for which Windows versions aren't available. Until new versions are released, you can use Windows as an MS-DOS multitasker to simultaneously run multiple MS-DOS programs. Here are some hints to make MS-DOS multitasking as productive as possible:

■ Create a PIF for each of your MS-DOS programs.

■ Select the PIF's Background option only if you want the program to continue running when it's placed in the background.

■ Be sure to turn on the PIF's Detect Idle Time option.

■ Edit the PIFs so that all your MS-DOS programs run in full-screen text mode. Run them in graphical windows only if you need to view or share information between MS-DOS and Windows-based applications.

■ If you always run the same group of MS-DOS programs, add icons for them in the Program Manager's StartUp group. Set their properties so that they all run minimized, which avoids Windows having to switch between text and graphics modes as it loads each of them and cuts down the time needed for your start-up sequence.

■ Use Alt-Tab to switch between full-screen MS-DOS programs. Your screen clears and a text banner appears, describing the next running program. Continue to hold down Alt and press Tab until the program you want to switch to is displayed. Then release the Alt key.

Using Alt-Tab to switch between full-screen MS-DOS programs is best because it generally keeps you in text mode. The other methods of switching programs—Alt-Esc and Ctrl-Esc—plop you back into Windows, switching the screen mode,which takes more time.

Note: To enable switching with Alt-Tab, be sure the Fast "Alt+Tab" Switching check box is selected in the Control Panel's Desktop dialog box. The setting of this option is recorded in WIN.INI's [windows] section: Activating Alt-Tab switching sets the value of the CoolSwitch *item to 1.*

Although these tips don't provide the perfect solution for multitasking MS-DOS programs, they will make running those programs less torturous. Again, keep in mind that only Windows-based applications give you the full benefit of running a Windows computer.

The MS-DOS Window's Control Menu

In enhanced mode, all MS-DOS windows have a Control menu (the "hyphen" menu in the upper left corner of the window). When you're running the program full screen, the Control menu isn't visible. You can access the Control menu only when the program is running in windowed mode. There are two ways to switch to windowed mode and display the contents of the Control menu: You can press Alt-Enter to switch to windowed mode and then click the Control menu; or the quick and easy shortcut is to press Alt-Spacebar, which switches to windowed mode and drops down the Control menu all at once.

Figure 5-13 shows an MS-DOS program running in a graphical window with the Control menu dropped down. The first group of commands on the menu—Restore (which is dimmed unless the window is an icon or is maximized), Move, Size, Minimize, and Maximize—are standard for most windows. These all control the window. None of these commands switches the program back into full-screen mode. (You need to press Alt-Enter for that to happen.)

The Close command in the next section of the menu is dimmed. You cannot close an MS-DOS window as you can other windows. If you try—by

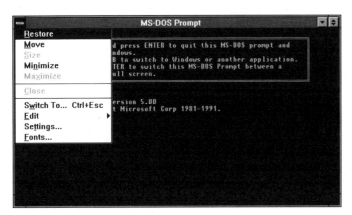

Figure 5-13. *An MS-DOS program with its Control menu displayed.*

double-clicking the Control menu—Windows ignores your request. To close the window, you need to exit the MS-DOS program running in it by using the command to quit the program or by typing *exit* if the window contains an MS-DOS shell.

The bottom section of the Control menu contains the standard Switch To command for popping up the task manager, plus three additional commands that are unique to MS-DOS windows: Edit, Settings, and Fonts. The Edit menu is covered in "Copying and Pasting," later in this chapter. The following two sections describe Settings and Fonts.

Changing Settings

Choosing Settings from an MS-DOS window's Control menu displays a dialog box like the one shown in Figure 5-14 on the next page. The title of the dialog box matches that of the window. Its contents come straight from the PIF Editor's multitasking and display sections. The options let you change the settings of the program on the fly: You can change from windowed to full screen mode; set the foreground or exclusive multitasking options; and reset the foreground and background priorities. These settings apply to the current MS-DOS session only. To make them permanent, you must edit the program's PIF.

Clicking the Terminate button techno-punches your MS-DOS program into oblivion. A warning dialog box is displayed after you click Terminate,

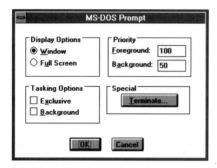

Figure 5-14. *The Settings dialog box available for MS-DOS windows.*

urging you to click Cancel and try to quit the program. Only after all hope
is lost and you're certain that you can't quit the program any other way
should you click OK to annihilate the MS-DOS program. The MS-DOS
session is then removed from the system. In the process, Windows may become unstable, so it's a good idea to restart Windows before continuing.

Changing Fonts

Choosing the Fonts command from the Control menu brings up a nifty dialog box that allows you to set the size of the display font for MS-DOS
programs running in a window. It's shown in Figure 5-15. Font size options are displayed in the Font list box in the upper left part of the dialog
box. The Window Preview area gives you an idea of how big the MS-DOS

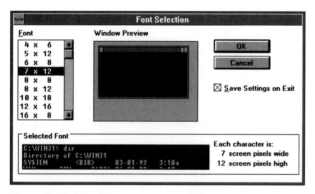

Figure 5-15. *The Font Selection dialog box available for MS-DOS windows.*

window will be with the new font. (The new size is shown relative to the window's current size.)

At the bottom of the dialog box in the Selected Font section, you see a preview of how the font looks. The font's size is specified by the number of horizontal and vertical pixels used per letter. This is how it's described in the Fonts list and how it's drawn in the Selected Font section.

To change the display font's size, select the size from the list. Check the Selected Font preview to see whether the size is right, and then click OK to use that size. If you select the Save Settings On Exit check box, Windows

---

The DOSAPP.INI File

Information about MS-DOS programs that run under Windows is kept in a file called DOSAPP.INI. The format of each entry is un-documented, though many of the settings relate to items in the program's PIF and settings or selections you make from the pro-gram's Control menu—including whether the program is run full screen or windowed, and what font it uses. The format of the entry starts like this:

filename=window horz vert window_size ...

The *window* parameter is 1 if the MS-DOS program is windowed and 0 if it is full screen. The next two values are the number of hori-zontal and vertical pixels that constitute the font size. They are fol-lowed by the size and position of the window on the screen. The other information is probably best left alone. For example, this entry

```
C:\WINDOWS\RUNDOS.PIF=1 4 6 328 178 22 2 3 65535 65535
   124 84 124 84 284 178
```

is typical for an MS-DOS program—in this case, the RUNDOS.PIF program used to run MS-DOS. (DOSAPP.INI puts this entire entry on one line.)

remembers the size and uses it the next time that particular MS-DOS program is running in a window.

Copying and Pasting

The ease with which you use Windows is partly a result of the way information can be copied and pasted among different Windows-based applications. You can do the same among MS-DOS programs, but only with text. You can copy text from an MS-DOS program and paste it into either a Windows-based application or another MS-DOS program, and you can copy text from a Windows-based application and paste it into an MS-DOS program. There are two ways to work this magic.

The first way to copy is to use the print screen key, PrtSc, in a full-screen MS-DOS program. This is not elegant, but it keeps you in text mode. Simply press PrtSc (or Print Scrn, depending on how it's labeled on your keyboard). The screen blinks as Windows reads all the text and saves it *en masse* to the Clipboard.

The second way to copy is to use the MS-DOS program's Control menu, which can be accessed by pressing Alt-Spacebar. Choose the Edit command from the Control menu, and then from the Edit submenu, choose Mark. The title of the window changes, acquiring the prefix *Mark*. You can then use the mouse to select a block of text on the screen. Press Enter when you're done, and the text is copied to the Clipboard.

Text can be pasted from the Clipboard into an MS-DOS program only when the program is in a window. First position the cursor where you want the text to go. Then choose Edit from the Control menu and Paste from the Edit submenu. Windows feeds the text into your MS-DOS program a line at a time.

Using the Mouse in an MS-DOS Window

Many MS-DOS programs support a mouse, and you'll still be able to use your mouse when running those programs under Windows—but only if you load the mouse driver from within either CONFIG.SYS or AUTO-EXEC.BAT. Although Windows itself comes with its own mouse drivers, your MS-DOS programs can use only one installed for MS-DOS.

In full-screen mode, your MS-DOS program's mouse appears as it always has. No problem. In a graphical window, the mouse is available, but there's a trick to using it. Just hover Windows' mouse over the MS-DOS program's window, and your program's mouse appears "beneath" it. As long as you keep Windows' mouse over the window, your program senses it. But if you move Windows' mouse out of the window, you lose control of your MS-DOS program's mouse.

Activating Mouse Support

Mouse support is provided via the "grabber" files installed in your SYSTEM.INI file. If you're using Windows 3.0 grabber files, then you may need to activate mouse support for your MS-DOS windows. This is done by adding the following entry to the [NonWindowsApp] section of SYSTEM.INI:

```
MouseInDosBox=1
```

INI FILE SETTINGS FOR MS-DOS PROGRAMS

Both WIN.INI and SYSTEM.INI have settings that affect MS-DOS programs running under Windows. This information applies to all MS-DOS programs. Specific information about each MS-DOS program that has run under Windows is kept in the DOSAPP.INI file, which is in your WINDOWS directory.

The rest of this chapter is all optional reading. The information I've already given in this chapter is enough to let you run MS-DOS programs in Windows with relatively few hassles. If you care to read this stuff, great! Otherwise, feel free to skim ahead to the next chapter.

MS-DOS Program Settings in WIN.INI

WIN.INI doesn't really control MS-DOS programs. Instead, it provides two sections, [windows] and [programs], where you can manipulate the type of programs run under Windows.

The [windows] Section

The [windows] section contains two items that deal with MS-DOS programs running under Windows. Neither of them is really crucial.

CoolSwitch=*Boolean* Set the aptly named *CoolSwitch* item to 1 to activate fast Alt-Tab switching between running programs. Set it to 0 to disable this feature. (You can also turn this feature on and off in the Control Panel's Desktop dialog box, using the Fast "Alt+Tab" Switching check box.) The default is 1.

Programs=*extension* The *Programs* item is set to the extensions Windows associates with program files. The entry by default looks like this:

```
Programs=com exe bat pif
```

Because of this entry, any file ending in COM, EXE, BAT, or PIF is considered a program by Windows.

The [programs] Section

The [programs] section can come in handy for programs Windows has trouble locating. Windows searches for programs in the WINDOWS directory as well as in all subdirectories on the MS-DOS search path. When it can't locate a program, it displays an error message. To avoid the message, you can specify the program in the [programs] section of WIN.INI in the following format:

> *program=pathname*

program is the name of the program you want to run. *pathname* is the full pathname of the file, including drive letter, directories, and the program's filename and extension. This entry is created by File Manager when it prompts you for a full pathname, or you can edit WIN.INI to enter the pathnames manually.

MS-DOS Program Settings in SYSTEM.INI

Items in SYSTEM.INI's [boot], [NonWindowsApp], [386Enh], and [standard] sections directly control how MS-DOS programs behave under Windows. Obviously, the [386Enh] and [standard] sections contain information particular to those two modes. However, some standard mode–only settings are in [NonWindowsApp], and some enhanced mode–only settings are in places other than [386Enh]. These occurances will be flagged in the following sections.

The [boot] Section

Two items in the [boot] section set up the "grabber" files that allow MS-DOS programs to be displayed under Windows, using this format:

286grabber=*filename*

386grabber=*filename*

filename is the name of the grabber file, which starts with the name of your graphics display type and ends in the extension 2GR or 3GR for the 286 or 386 grabber files. You shouldn't mess with these entries; changing the grabber files does not improve operations.

The [NonWindowsApp] Section

The [NonWindowsApp] section is devoted to entries that support running MS-DOS programs under Windows. Some of these settings apply only if you're using old grabber files. Others are particular to standard mode.

Up-to-Date Grabber Files

Always be sure you have up-to-date grabber files. They keep you current with the fancy things Windows can do, such as changing fonts and using a mouse in an MS-DOS window. If you don't have updated grabber files and you want to change fonts and use a mouse in an MS-DOS window, you'll need to set the values of these two entries in the [NonWindowsApp] section to 1:

FontChangeEnable=*Boolean*

MouseInDosBox=*Boolean*

How can you tell if your grabber files are current? Check their dates and times. For example, all Windows 3.1 files have a date of 3-10-92 and a time of 3:10 A.M. Later versions of Windows have later dates; earlier versions have earlier dates.

None of them is really required, and each must be manually added to SYSTEM.INI and manually set there.

The following entries may be found in SYSTEM.INI's [NonWindowsApp] section.

CommandEnvSize=*bytes* This entry sets the size of MS-DOS's environment to the specified number of bytes. The default value is equal to the size of the environment set by the /E:*nnnn* option for COMMAND.COM when COMMAND.COM was started. You can specify a value of 0 to disable this entry and use the default or a value from 160 through 32768 to set the environment to that size. (The environment size will be equal to the size specified by COMMAND.COM or *CommandEnvSize*, whichever is greater.)

DisablePositionSave=*Boolean* When set to 1, *DisablePositionSave* does not save MS-DOS program information (window position and font) in the DOSAPP.INI file. When set to 0, the information is saved. (You can always save information, and override this option, by selecting the Save Settings On Exit check box in the Fonts dialog box before quitting the MS-DOS program.)

FontChangeEnable=*Boolean* This entry applies only to Windows systems using old grabber files. Set *FontChangeEnable* to 1 to provide font switching in an MS-DOS window. This setting has no effect when you use Windows 3.1 (or later) grabber files.

GlobalHeapSize=*kilobytes* This setting is used to save an area of memory for sharing information between MS-DOS programs run in standard mode. The default value is 0, and should remain that way; do not alter this setting.

LocalTSRs=*list* The list consists of names of TSR programs that will be loaded each time an MS-DOS program runs under Windows. For example, the DOSEDIT command line editor is an acceptable *list* entry. It's specified by default and, if loaded before Windows starts, it's loaded when any MS-DOS program runs. (See the section titled "TSRs in Windows," earlier in this chapter, for more information.)

MouseInDosBox=*Boolean* This entry is grabber-file–dependent. If you are using Windows 3.0 grabber files and you want to use the mouse in an MS-DOS window, set *MouseInDosBox* to 1. If you have updated grabber files, this entry has no effect.

NetAsynchSwitching=0 ¦ 1 This standard mode setting is ignored in enhanced mode. When it is set to 1, Windows prevents you from switching out of any MS-DOS program that has made a network call. This is a good thing. If Windows switches to a different program and another network call is made or received, the system may hang. Setting this item to 0 disables the feature.

ScreenLines=*number* This entry allows you to specify the number of text lines displayed in an MS-DOS program. The default value is 25; 43 and 50 are also accepted on VGA displays. Windows pops up all MS-DOS programs with the number of lines specified, unless the program you are running overrides the setting.

SwapDisk=*drive:directory* This standard mode–only setting directs Windows to a drive and directory on disk to which it can swap an MS-DOS program when it switches away from the program. Normally, the directory specified by the TEMP environment variable is used, but this entry allows you to swap files away to another directory by specifying its drive letter and pathname.

The [standard] Section

The [standard] section can contain three items—*FasterModeSwitch*, *Int28Filter*, and *Stacks*—that control how MS-DOS programs run in standard mode. These settings have no effect when Windows is run in enhanced mode. If you plan on running only in enhanced mode, feel free to skip ahead to "The [386Enh] Section."

FasterModeSwitch=0 ¦ 1 The *FasterModeSwitch* item can be used to make Windows running on an 80286 PC switch from Windows to an MS-DOS program more quickly. It does this by using a faster method of switching between the protected and real modes of the 80286. To speed up the switch, add the following entry to the [standard] section:

```
FasterModeSwitch=1
```

This entry works only for 80286 PCs. It is ignored by all '386-based PCs.

Int28Filter=number The *Int28Filter* item describes how Windows treats the CPU interrupt 28h. That's the "Idle" interrupt, which is generated when the computer is idle. MS-DOS responds to the interrupt by giving processor time to control programs, such as the Print command, that run in the background. Some networks also use the free time indicated by interrupt 28h to schedule their background tasks. In Windows, you use the *Int28Filter* item to control how often interrupt 28h is passed through to MS-DOS programs.

The value of *number* specifies how often interrupt 28h signals are passed through to MS-DOS programs. When *number* is 1, every interrupt 28h signal is passed along to MS-DOS; for 2, every other interrupt is passed along; for 3, every third interrupt is passed along, and so on. Setting *number* to a high value increases Windows' performance but may cause some MS-DOS programs' hearts to skip a beat. The default value is 10. Setting it lower may slow Windows but gives more power to your MS-DOS programs. Setting it higher makes Windows run faster but may cause MS-DOS programs to malfunction.

Stacks=number The *Stacks* item controls how many internal stacks (storage areas) Windows passes along to MS-DOS programs running in standard mode. The default setting is 12. You can specify values from 8 through 64, but the only reason to change this entry is if you see a *Stack Overflow* error message when you run an MS-DOS program. In that case, specify a higher number.

The [386Enh] Section

The settings in this section apply only when you are running MS-DOS programs under Windows in enhanced mode. Most of them are automatically set and shouldn't be messed with.

EGA80WOA.FON=*filename*
EGA40WOA.FON=*filename*
CGA80WOA.FON=*filename*
CGA40WOA.FON=*filename*

These entries set up the Windows OldApp fonts for CGA and EGA 80-column and 40-column modes that might be used by an MS-DOS program. These items are typically set equal to files of the same name.

AllEMSLocked=*Boolean* When set to *On*, this entry locks all expanded (EMS) memory, preventing it from being swapped to disk. This setting overrides the EMS Memory Locked setting in all applications' PIFs. The default value is *Off*.

AllVMsExclusive=*Boolean* This entry puts all MS-DOS programs, or virtual machines (VMs), into the exclusive foreground mode. When set to *On*, *AllVMsExclusive* forces all MS-DOS programs to run in full-screen mode with no interruptions. This setting overrides any PIF settings and can be used to tame some unruly MS-DOS programs.

AllXMSLocked=*Boolean* When set to *On*, the *AllXMSLocked* item locks all extended (XMS) memory, preventing it from being swapped to disk. This setting overrides the XMS Memory Locked setting in all applications' PIFs. The default value is *Off*.

AutoRestoreScreen=*Boolean* This entry specifies whether Windows or the MS-DOS program should update the screen after returning to the program. The entry makes a difference only on VGA systems. If your MS-DOS program can update the screen, set *AutoRestoreScreen* to *Off*. When it is set to *On*, Windows updates the screen, which is often faster. The default is *On*.

BkGndNotifyAtPFault=*Boolean* This entry deals with MS-DOS programs that may access the screen incorrectly, corrupting the display. When it is set to *On*, Windows notifies you at once of the error. When it is set to *Off*, Windows waits until you switch out of the program. Set the value to *On* for VGA displays and to *Off* for special displays, such as the TIGA and 8514 displays.

COMxAutoAssign=*number* This setting controls how Windows reacts to conflicts with the serial ports, where x specifies the COM (serial) port in question. When this entry is set to –1, Windows warns you when more than one program tries to use the same serial port and asks you to choose the program that gets to use the port. All other programs are restricted from using the same port. If the value is 0, all programs can fight over the serial ports fairly. If the value is greater than 0 (up to 1000) that number of seconds must elapse after one application stops using the serial port before another application can start using it. The default value is 2.

Note: The COMxAutoAssign setting can also be controlled using the 386 Enhanced dialog box in the Control Panel. The setting is found in the Device Contention area in the dialog box that appears when you click the Advanced button.

EMMSize=*kilobytes* This entry sets the amount of expanded (EMS) memory Windows makes available to programs that request it. You must add this entry to SYSTEM.INI, in conjunction with *NoEMMDriver=Off*, for your applications to use expanded memory. *kilobytes* indicates the amount of expanded memory to make available.

FileSysChange=*Boolean* Set this item to *On* if you want File Manager to receive updates when you add, modify, or delete files using an MS-DOS program. Set it to *Off* if you don't want File Manager to be notified of any files you change or add. (You'll need to choose Refresh from File Manager's Window menu to actually update the files and directories in the File Manager windows.) The default setting is *On* in enhanced mode. This can slow down your system, so if you're running a lot of MS-DOS programs, change *FileSysChange* to *Off*.

MouseSoftInit=*Boolean* This entry controls how a mouse is used in an MS-DOS window. When it is set to *On*, Windows allows a mouse to be set up and initialized in an MS-DOS program running in a window. However, if this setting causes display problems in the program, change it to *Off*. Note that setting *MouseSoftInit* to *Off* in your SYSTEM.INI file disables the use of a mouse with MS-DOS programs.

NoEMMDriver=*Boolean* This entry turns Windows' expanded memory manager (EMM) driver on or off. The default is *Off*. If you change this entry to *On*, you cannot use expanded memory with your MS-DOS programs running under Windows.

ReservePageFrame=*Boolean* The *ReservePageFrame* item controls an expanded memory (EMS) page frame that Windows might set up in conventional memory for MS-DOS programs. When it is set to *On*, Windows keeps the page frame at the expense of conventional memory. Set this entry to *Off* to give your MS-DOS programs more conventional memory.

ReserveVideoROM=*Boolean* This entry protects video memory and normally need not be set. The default is *Off*. However, you can set this entry to *On* if you notice that text in an MS-DOS program appears corrupted.

UseROMFont=*Boolean* This entry controls the font of the text messages that appear when MS-DOS programs are running in full-screen mode, such as the text that appears when you press Alt-Tab. If the font looks corrupted, set *UseROMFont* to *Off*. The default is *On*.

VideoBackgroundMsg=*Boolean* This entry affects MS-DOS programs running in the background. If the background program is suspended or its video memory runs low, Windows displays a warning when this option is set to *On*. Setting it to *Off* turns off the warning. The default is *On*.

VideoSuspendDisable=*Boolean* When this entry is set to *Off*, Windows suspends a background MS-DOS program if its display becomes corrupted. When the entry is set to *On*, the program keeps on running. *Off* is the default.

WindowUpdateTime=*milliseconds* This entry specifies the number of milliseconds Windows waits before updating a windowed MS-DOS program's display. The default is 50 milliseconds. Setting a higher value gives more time to the MS-DOS program. For example, setting this entry equal to 200 makes some MS-DOS programs run more smoothly in a window.

WinExclusive=*Boolean* When this entry is set to *On*, Windows runs exclusively in the foreground, not giving any processor time to the MS-DOS programs in the background. The default is *Off*. (This entry can be set by using the Control Panel's 386 Enhanced dialog box and selecting the Exclusive In Foreground check box.)

WinTimeSlice=*foreground,background* This entry specifies the number of "time slices" Windows gives itself when it is running MS-DOS programs. The values are identical to the Windows In Foreground and Windows In Background settings in the Control Panel's 386 Enhanced dialog box.

WOAFont=*filename* This entry specifies which font file Windows uses when displaying MS-DOS programs. The default is DOSAPP.FON. To change the font file, run Setup from the command prompt, and specify a new code page or display setting.

Chapter 6

The Multitasking Environment

Multitasking is a big, scary word. It's technical—an advanced subject that most people would rather skirt around. Along with multitasking comes other terms, such as "background" and "foreground," and the concept of "time slicing," which sounds like it could only be done by Albert Einstein with the proper Ginsu knife. Fortunately, the subject isn't that dreadful. Windows deals with multitasking in a sane and painless manner. To put it simply, multitasking works without you having to think about it.

This chapter deals with several topics related to multitasking, or the ability to run several programs at once on a single computer. Additionally, this chapter discusses Dynamic Data Exchange (DDE) and Object Linking and Embedding (OLE), which Windows uses to share information with two or more programs. These mechanisms deal with basic cutting and pasting, though in clever and powerful ways.

ABOUT MULTITASKING

The traditional way to run computer programs is one at a time. You quit one program, start another, work some more, and so on. This is boring. And it's truly a crime to use Windows that way. Windows can run several programs at once. In fact, you might be running more than one program without even realizing it. Program Manager is always running, even when you're using only your favorite Windows-based application.

Perhaps the concept of multitasking is too alien for most MS-DOS users. Typical Windows neophytes will quit a program, start another, quit the second program, and then return to restart the first program. It never occurs to them to *minimize* the first program, run the second, minimize that program, and then *maximize* the first. Because both programs remain in memory, switching between the two is no problem, but it's just not that obvious.

Windows is a graphical environment best suited to running Windows-based applications. It can run multiple MS-DOS programs at one time, but only in enhanced mode. It's not an "MS-DOS multitasker," like Quarterdeck's DESQview.

Multitasking in Windows

Think of multitasking as visiting the library. Each program you run is a book. Say you start with the Program Manager book. You open it and begin using it. Then you open the File Manager book and set it on top of Program Manager, just like two overlapping windows in Windows. Of course, you can read only one book at a time. So when you want to read that meaty Program Manager tome again, you pull it out from under the open File Manager book. This is how Windows multitasks.

Next suppose you open your word processor. You now have another open book sitting on top of the Program Manager and File Manager books. Things start to get crazy, so you mark your place in Program Manager, close it, and set it aside. You do the same with File Manager. This is the same as minimizing a program in Windows: The program's still there, just tightened up into an icon where it won't get in the way.

Windows can open many different applications, and you can switch between them more quickly, easily, and efficiently than shuffling through a stack of books. And you may have noticed that books don't "minimize" well. In fact, in the library you may end up hoarding books and arranging them in a fortress-like wall around your table.

The amazing thing about Windows is that it continues to "read" from all books on the table, even when they are closed or buried beneath other books. Under Windows, any running program can perform such background tasks as printing, sorting, churning, or crunching while it is waiting for you to give it some attention.

Note: *When a PC is multitasking, the program you're currently using is said to be "in the foreground." Other programs—the ones that are running but that you're not using—are "in the background." The foreground/background terms work with Windows because the programs you're not using are literally hidden in the background. However, these terms also apply to MS-DOS programs that you may not be able to see in a window.*

Running Multiple Programs and Using the Task Manager

You can run a program from three different places in Windows: from Program Manager; from File Manager; and from Program Manager or File Manager's File menu (by choosing the Run command and typing the name of the program). You can see a list of all the programs you're running under Windows in the task manager's window, shown in Figure 6-1.

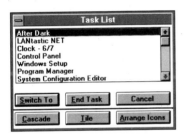

Figure 6-1. *The task manager's window, showing a list of running programs.*

To bring up the task manager, press Ctrl-Esc. If you can see an open area of the desktop uncovered by a window, double-click in the area to display the task manager's Task List window. The name of the program you were just working in appears at the top of the list, with the other programs running under Windows below it.

The top row of buttons in the Task List window control the programs you're running. You click Switch To to change to the selected application; double-clicking the program's name in the list does the same thing. You click End Task to close the selected application; choosing Exit from the application's File menu or double-clicking the Control menu accomplishes the same thing. The End Task button works for all Windows-based applications (the applications let you know if you have unsaved documents), but not for MS-DOS programs running under Windows, which must be shut down from within their own windows. And finally, you click the Cancel button to get rid of the Task List window.

The bottom row of buttons in the Task List window control how icons and windows appear in Windows. The Cascade and Tile buttons arrange all open windows in a cascading or tiled pattern; neither button affects programs minimized to icons. And the Arrange Icons button arranges minimized icons but not open windows.

Program Switching Keys

When several programs are running in Windows, you can switch between them in a number of ways. The most obvious way is to click the mouse in the window of a running program to bring that window to the foreground. Or, if the program is minimized, you can double-click its icon.

When you can't get at a program with the mouse, press Ctrl-Esc to bring up the Task List window. Select the program you want to work in, and then actually move to the program by clicking the Switch To button.

You use the Alt-Esc key combo to "cycle through" all the programs you are currently running. Alt-Esc moves to each program in the order in which they appear in the Task List window. If the program is running in a window, Alt-Esc brings the window to the top of the pile. If the program is minimized, Alt-Esc brings its icon forward and selects it; you can then press Enter to open the icon.

Another program switching key combo is Alt-Tab—the "cool switch." When you press Alt-Tab, a small box appears in the center of your screen. In the center of the box is the program's name (actually, the contents of its window's title bar). To the left of the name is the program's icon. You can cycle through your programs by holding down the Alt key and tapping Tab. Release the Alt key, and Windows brings up the program whose name is in the box, maximizing it from an icon if need be.

Note: You activate the Alt-Tab cool switch in the Control Panel's Desktop dialog box. Select the Fast "Alt+Tab" Switching check box to turn it on.

The quickest and easiest way to switch to a particular program is by assigning it a shortcut key (or hot key) that, when pressed, takes you directly to the program. This method works for both Windows-based and MS-DOS programs. You assign the hot key using the Program Item Properties dialog box in Program Manager.

To see how this works, highlight an icon in Program Manager, and choose Properties from the File menu. Click the Shortcut Key text box so that a cursor appears in the box. (The word *None* in the text box lets you know that no hot key is currently assigned.) To assign a hot key, simply press a letter. That letter appears in the text box preceded by *Ctrl+Alt+*. For example, suppose you're assigning a hot key to File Manager. If you press F, *Ctrl+Alt+F* appears in the Shortcut Key text box. The keys specified in the text box form the hot key. (Yes, I know it would make more sense to call them "hot keys," but that's terminology for you!)

From anywhere in Windows, you can now use the hot key (Ctrl-Alt-F in our example) to switch to the program when it's running. The really neat thing about the hot key is that if you're in Program Manager and you press the hot key when the program isn't running, Windows will start the program for you!

Table 6-1 summarizes the program switching keys.

Key	Function
Ctrl-Esc	Brings up the task manager; select an application from the list
Alt-Esc	Switches to the next application in the task manager's list
Alt-Tab	Displays the names of running programs one at a time in a box; press Tab to change, release the Alt key to switch
Hot key	Switches directly to a program

Table 6-1. *Windows' program switching keys.*

The Time-Slice Pie: Sharing the Clock

Multitasking works by dividing up the processor's resources among several programs. It helps to think of every second of the processor's time as a giant time-slice pie, like the one shown in Figure 6-2. Each program owns a piece of the pie. When the sweep second hand passes over a piece, the program that owns that piece has control over the computer. When the second hand moves on to the next piece, the program that owns that piece is given control, and so on. This system works for all the programs you're multitasking.

For Windows, the sweep second hand is incredibly fast. The processor switches between programs so quickly that everything appears to be running at once.

And now, a secret: When you run several Windows-based applications at the same time, they all share the same piece of the pie. One program takes a bite of time, and if it doesn't need anymore time, it lets another program have the piece so that it can take a bite. Windows-based programs use what's called "nonpreemptive," or cooperative, multitasking. Essentially, all Windows-based applications are run like one huge program. Any MS-DOS programs you pile on are run on a par with Windows and all of its applications. So if you have one MS-DOS program running, the time-slice pie will have only two pieces: one for the MS-DOS program and one for Windows. For the programmers and wizards, that's something to

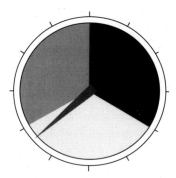

Figure 6-2. *A multitasking time-slice pie.*

stroke the beard over. For you and me, just keep in mind that everything runs at once and it all works, so we're happy.

Enabling Multitasking for MS-DOS Programs

Windows-based applications automatically share the same piece of the time-slice pie. They're designed to work that way. So if you're running only Windows-based applications, there's nothing else to mess with—no switches to throw or settings to make. Like an only child, Windows shares its own toys fairly with itself. By comparison, MS-DOS programs are rude and surly—the typical bratty sibling.

When Windows runs an MS-DOS program in standard mode, it shuts down almost everything else, and switches its attention to that single MS-DOS program. No multitasking takes place between the program and the rest of Windows. Even though Windows-based applications can share the power in standard mode, all sharing stops when you add an MS-DOS program to the picture. If you run another MS-DOS program, the first is saved, or "swapped to disk", and the second one is loaded. Nothing runs in the background. There is no multitasking. End of story.

MS-DOS programs running under Windows in enhanced mode are each given their own "virtual machine"—the special V86 mode of the '386-based processor. This mode allows the processor to simulate multiple 8086 computers. Windows runs your MS-DOS programs on the virtual machines, and each of them assumes that it's running by itself on its own PC. This trick is what makes multitasking MS-DOS programs in enhanced mode possible.

When you use an MS-DOS program in enhanced mode, it runs as it would under MS-DOS. Windows runs in the background, taking care of routine tasks and managing the computer. When you switch away from the MS-DOS program, Windows shuts down the program and proceeds to run in the foreground. To allow the MS-DOS program to continue to run in the background, you must modify its PIF. (Modifying PIFs is covered in Chapter 5, in "Building Program Information Files.")

Five settings in the PIF Editor window control how an MS-DOS program multitasks:

■ The Execution area's Background option

■ The Execution area's Exclusive option

■ The Multitasking Options area's Background Priority setting

■ The Multitasking Options area's Foreground Priority setting

■ The Multitasking Options area's Detect Idle Time option

To bring an MS-DOS program into the multitasking fold, select the Background check box. This is necessary if you want the MS-DOS program to continue running while you do something else. For example, communications programs can continue to receive or send information, database programs can sort and index, and word processors can continue to print without your assistance.

You should reserve the Exclusive option for the programs that require a lot of power to do their job. Graphics and desktop publishing are two categories of application that you might want to run exclusively. If you select the Exclusive check box, no program will be allowed to run in the background when the MS-DOS program is in the foreground. Your typical MS-DOS program doesn't need that kind of power.

The multitasking options for MS-DOS programs running in enhanced mode are kept in the PIF Editor's Advanced Options dialog box. To open it, click the Advanced button in the PIF Editor. The Background Priority, Foreground Priority, and Detect Idle Time settings are grouped in the Multitasking Options area.

The Background Priority and Foreground Priority settings tell Windows how big a piece of the time-slice pie to give the MS-DOS program when it's in the background and foreground. The Foreground Priority should obviously be higher, because when you're actively working on a program you want it to have most of the muscle. How these settings fit into *The Big Multitasking Picture* is covered in the next section.

The Detect Idle Time option is a good time-saver. When it is turned on, Windows spies on an MS-DOS program to see if it's doing anything. Most of the time, the program is just sitting there waiting for you to press a key. If that's the case and Detect Idle Time is turned on, Windows shifts the program to a low priority and allows other programs in the background and foreground to use the time that would otherwise be wasted on the idle program.

Splitting the Pie Between Windows and MS-DOS Programs

Windows-based applications and MS-DOS programs can share the time-slice pie. MS-DOS programs in the background get a piece only when their PIFs have the Background option turned on. Otherwise, Windows gets the whole pie to itself. And, of course, the more multitasking MS-DOS programs you run, the more pieces the pie has to be divided into, and the slower everything runs. But there are ways to create bigger pie slices for certain programs.

All is fair in love, war, and Windows multitasking. The fairness is controlled by setting the foreground and background priority values for both MS-DOS and Windows programs. For MS-DOS programs, you set these values in their PIFs. For Windows, you set them using the Control Panel's 386 Enhanced dialog box, which is shown in Figure 6-3.

The minimum size of each piece of the time-slice pie is set at the very bottom of the 386 Enhanced dialog box. In Figure 6-3, it's set to 20 milliseconds, or 0.02 seconds. That's the amount of time Windows spends on each

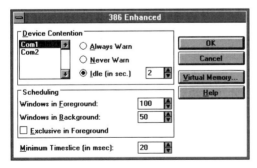

Figure 6-3. *The dialog box displayed when you click the 386 Enhanced icon in the Control Panel.*

task. For example, when you're running Windows and one MS-DOS program, Windows spends 0.02 seconds on itself, then 0.02 seconds on the MS-DOS program, and so on, back and forth.

When you bring more MS-DOS programs into the picture, there's more switching going on and less time devoted to each application, so the system slows down. The same thing happens when you open more Windows-based applications, but they share Windows' one piece of the pie among themselves.

Background priority and foreground priority settings are available for Windows-based applications in the 386 Enhanced dialog box and for MS-DOS programs in the advanced PIF settings. For Windows, the options are called Windows In Foreground and Windows In Background. As we've seen, for MS-DOS, they're called Foreground Priority and Background Priority. No matter where they are and what they're called, these two settings confuse the heck out of everybody because they involve math, which is a subject most of us would rather avoid. Here's the scoop for both the Windows and MS-DOS background priority and foreground priority settings:

- The background priority setting is a value from 1 though 10,000 (don't use a comma in the box, though). It tells Windows how much time to give itself or an MS-DOS program when it's running in the background. The default value is 50.

- The foreground priority setting works the same way: It's a number from 1 through 10,000 (again, no comma) that tells Windows how much time to give itself or an MS-DOS program when it's running in the foreground. The default value here is 100. This value is higher than the background value because programs in the foreground—those you're working on *right now*—deserve more attention.

What the values actually represent is a percentage of a total. The total isn't 10,000. Instead, its the total of all the background priority and foreground priority values of all the programs you're running. Table 6-2 shows how this works when you are running Windows and an MS-DOS program with the standard settings and Windows is in the foreground. Table 6-3 shows the same thing, but this time with the MS-DOS program running in the foreground and Windows running in the background. As you can see, the settings and percentages are reversed.

Application	Setting	Percentage of Pie
Windows in the foreground	100	67
MS-DOS program in the background	50	33
Total	150	100

Table 6-2. *Multitasking priorities with standard settings and Windows in the foreground.*

Application	Setting	Percentage of Pie
MS-DOS program in the foreground	100	67
Windows in the background	50	33
Total	150	100

Table 6-3. *Multitasking priorities with standard settings and an MS-DOS program in the foreground.*

Whether they are in the foreground or background, Windows and the MS-DOS program share resources the same way: The program in the foreground gets two-thirds of the attention, and the one in the background gets one-third. (Obviously, it makes sense to give the foreground task more power because it's the one you're working on.) These relationships are shown graphically in Figure 6-4.

Suppose you needed more time for the MS-DOS program running in the background. To meet the program's needs, you set its Background Priority

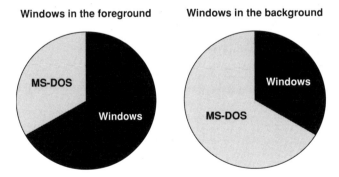

Figure 6-4. *Foreground and background percentages of the time-slice pie.*

value in the PIF Editor to 100. You leave the Foreground Priority value at 100, because the program works just fine in the foreground. This change doesn't affect how the MS-DOS program runs in the foreground; it still gets two-third's of the pie, while one-third goes to Windows in the background. But when the MS-DOS program runs in the background, it eats up half the time. Table 6-4 shows the new settings.

Application	Setting	Percentage of Pie
Windows in the foreground	100	50
MS-DOS program in the background	100	50
Total	200	100

Table 6-4. *Multitasking priorities with custom settings and an MS-DOS program in the background.*

Because the MS-DOS program's background slices are equal to Windows' foreground slices, time is shared equally. If we were to redraw the pie charts in Figure 6-4 for these settings, the pie on the right would look the same, but the pie on the left would be split fifty-fifty.

If you add more MS-DOS programs to the picture, the slices of the pie grow smaller. As long as you don't change the foreground and background priorities for the MS-DOS programs or for Windows, everything is shared fairly: With two MS-DOS programs running under Windows, the program in the foreground uses half the processor's power and the other two each have a quarter. Of course, if you mess with the priority values, the slices of the pie are no longer equal. I will leave it up to you to do the math and draw the cool pie charts for other possible priority combinations.

SHARING INFORMATION BETWEEN PROGRAMS

Multitasking takes care of the bother of starting, stopping, and restarting programs when you use a computer. But you must still hop back and forth as you bring together separate elements into a finished product. Windows' environment helps eliminate those extra steps in a major way: Text and graphics can be cut or copied and pasted between different applications. To make sharing information even easier, Windows offers DDE and OLE power for your cutting and pasting.

Note: Interestingly enough, while DDE is pronounced "Deedee-ee," OLE is pronounced "olé," as in what you say when the bull misses the matador (physically misses, that is). Oh-lay. Interesting.

Don't let the TLAs (Three Letter Acronyms) frazzle you. Think of DDE and OLE as "super cut and paste." DDE is *Dynamic Data Exchange*, the mechanism for sharing information between programs, but a more common term for it is *paste linking*, or just *linking*. With DDE, the information you paste is updated automatically if you change the original. For example, a stock quote retrieved from one spreadsheet would be updated in all the spreadsheets it's been pasted into, thanks to DDE.

More important than DDE is OLE. You can think of DDE as the underlying engine of OLE—the spell Windows incants to make the paste linking possible. The actual process of pasting a picture or chunk of a spreadsheet into your word processor is OLE, which stands for *Object Linking and Embedding*.

Again, don't get lost in TLA-la-land. DDE and OLE are things your software docs. OLE is the feature that gives your programs "super paste" ability. What happens with OLE is that the stuff you paste—called an *object*—contains information about the application that created it. So the little chunk of spreadsheet in your word processor has a long, electronic umbilical cord back to mama spreadsheet. Additionally, you can create a link to the file that originally contained the object, so the DDE engine can make sure the li'l chunk of spreadsheet is updated. If you don't create a link, the object is said to be *embedded*. With the link, the object is *linked*.

The information the OLE object maintains allows you to quickly edit the spreadsheet chunk, picture, sound, or whatever. To do so, you double-click the object, and Windows loads the object into the application that created it. This allows you to quickly edit the object without going through all the motions of starting the original application. When you double-click an object that has a link to the original file, Windows starts the application and loads the entire original file.

Another advantage of OLE is that you can instantly insert an object from another application—without ever actually starting that application in the

File Manager or Program Manager. This is made possible through the Insert Object menu command. Simply select the type of object you want to create from the list, and Windows runs the application used to create the object. You create your object and then exit the application to return to your original application, where the newly created object is pasted.

The best part about all this is that neither application needs to know squat about the other. The only stipulation is that both programs be capable of OLE. In the following sections, I'll tell you how to find out when and where OLE is supported and how it works. You'll also be introduced to the Object Packager application, which allows you to embed full documents or even MS-DOS commands into a document.

Checking for Linking and Embedding Support

To check whether a program works with DDE and OLE—the super paste features—check the Edit menu. Dead giveaways are the following commands and variations of them:

- Paste Special
- Paste Link
- Object
- Insert Object
- Links

These commands may not all be on the Edit menu. For example, the Object command is on the Insert menu in Word for Windows, and the Links command is on the Microsoft Excel File menu. Other applications may have additional OLE commands on other menus. (Although OLE is a standard, its implementation varies from application to application.)

You paste, insert, or link an object from a *source* document to a *destination* document. And the application that created the object is the *object server*. The commands I've listed would be found in the destination document's application. They are what makes all this possible in varying degrees.

The link commands—Paste Link and Links—are used with DDE (and OLE) to "live paste" information. Provided that both the source and destination applications are capable of DDE, you can paste information with an attached link back to the original document. Then any changes made to the original will be reflected in the linked copy. The Links command is used to list a summary of the links in a document—what they are and to what they're linked. The linking process is covered in detail in "Linking Information," later in this chapter.

The object commands deal with objects pasted into a document. The difference between pasting objects and pasting plain text or a graphic is that Windows keeps track of the source application when you paste an object. You can edit the object simply by double-clicking it or choosing the Object command from the Edit menu. Or, if the object is "playable," such as a sound object or bit of animation, you can choose a command that activates it. So the information you paste isn't just another "thing" in your document; it's a "smart thing" that you can change quite easily.

Windows is very flexible about the types of objects it can paste into a document. You can paste text, spreadsheet data, equations, sounds, and so on. A list of possibilities is displayed when you choose the Insert Object command found in most OLE-supporting applications. Some of the objects you might see are listed in Table 6-5 on the next page. The ones you see when you choose Insert Object depend on your installed software. The Package, Paintbrush Picture, and Sound objects are all available with Windows.

The most interesting of all the objects you can insert is the "package"—a collection of information, an MS-DOS command, or a file that you can neatly tuck into a document. Double-click the package object, and whatever is stored "in the box" explodes out on the screen in front of you. Creating an object that performs this feat is covered later in this chapter, in "Using the Object Packager."

Object Name	Object Server	Type
Equation	Equation Editor	Graphic
Microsoft Drawing	Microsoft Draw	Graphic
Microsoft Excel Chart	Microsoft Excel	Graphic
Microsoft Excel Macrosheet	Microsoft Excel	Macro commands
Microsoft Excel Worksheet	Microsoft Excel	Worksheet data
Microsoft Graph	Microsoft Graph	Graphic
MS WordArt	WordArt	Graphic
Package	Object Package	Varies
Paintbrush Picture	Paintbrush	Graphic
Sound	Sound Recorder	Sound
Word Document	Microsoft Word for Windows	Text

Table 6-5. *Some of the types of objects you can paste into OLE-supporting applications.*

The Object List

The list of object types and their creator applications is kept in the WIN.INI file, in the [embedding] section. Each item in the list is stored in this format:

   object=description1, description2, program_file, format

object is the name of the object type. *description1* provides a description of the object, and *description2* is the name that appears in the Insert Object dialog box. *program_file* is the pathname of the program that creates the object. And *format* is the file format, which is usually "picture," the Windows Metafile format.

You shouldn't edit this information directly in WIN.INI. You can use the Registration Editor program, REGEDIT.EXE, to modify object linking information, but most OLE-supporting applications will add their object types themselves during their installation.

Linking Information

Linking the information in two different applications can be done only if both applications are DDE-aware. You can tell when this is the case because the Paste Link command becomes enabled. For some applications, the command may be Paste Special, but then you'll see a Link or Paste Link button in the Paste Special dialog box. Figure 6-5 shows the dialog box displayed when I choose Paste Special from Word for Windows' Edit menu after copying a chunk of an Excel spreadsheet—just a range of cells.

Figure 6-5. *Word for Windows' Paste Special dialog box.*

Listed in Figure 6-5 are several different formats for the information to be pasted. As you can see, the Excel cells can be pasted in five formats, which are listed in Table 6-6.

Paste Special Item	Pasted as Object	Paste Link
Excel Worksheet Object	Yes	No
Formatted Text (RTF)	No	Yes
Unformatted Text	No	Yes
Picture	Yes	Yes
Bitmap	Yes	Yes

Table 6-6. *The different formats available for Excel cells in Word for Windows' Paste Special dialog box.*

The Excel Worksheet Object, Picture, and Bitmap formats are all object types whose content looks the same as it did in the original file. (For more information about objects, see the next section.) If you paste in the cells as text (formats two or three), they will not be objects. However, you can link these two formats back to the original spreadsheet, as you can the final two formats, Picture and Bitmap (which are graphic images of a chunk of Excel spreadsheet, as opposed to being text).

Pasting the cells into Word for Windows using the Paste Link button keeps Word and Excel chatting. When you make a change to the worksheet, the image in the Word document gets updated as well. In fact, you can link a single bit of information to several documents and have all of them updated in real time every time you change the source file. But keep in mind that this updating works only with applications that are DDE-aware.

To confirm that the links have been made, or just to see what's linked in your document, you choose the Links command to display a dialog box that looks something like Figure 6-6. The Links dialog box contains a list of items with links to your document. The items are listed by type and filename, with other information displayed depending on the capabilities of your application.

Using the Links dialog box, you can monitor, make, or break the links. For example, if you want to freeze the data in your document, simply highlight the appropriate link, and click the Cancel Link button. The data remains in your document, but it is no longer updated to reflect changes made to the original file.

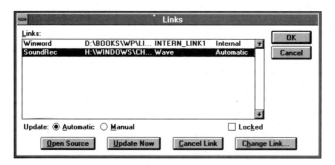

Figure 6-6. *The Links dialog box, showing several links to an Excel spreadsheet.*

Embedding Objects

Your application must be receptive to an object before you can embed one. To find out what kind of reception the object is likely to receive, look for a command named Object or Insert Object. Table 6-7 lists some OLE-aware applications and where to find their "insert object" command.

Application	Menu	Command
Cardfile	Edit	Insert Object
Microsoft Excel	Edit	Insert Object
Microsoft Word for Windows	Insert	Object
Write	Edit	Insert Object

Table 6-7. *Popular Windows-based applications and their "insert object" commands.*

The Insert Object command is designed so that you can create and then insert an object from another document without having to minimize your first application, start the second application, create the object, and so on. With Insert Object, it's all done at once.

For example, to insert an Excel graph in Word for Windows, you pull down the Word for Windows Insert menu, choose Object, and click Microsoft Excel Chart. Instantly, you're transferred to Excel's chart-building environment. Upon choosing Exit in Excel, you're returned to Word for Windows, with the chart object you've created inserted in your document. Like anything else you paste in, you see the object on the screen and can print it; the object is as much a part of your document as the text you've typed. But, covertly, the object is linked to the program that created it.

The old copy-and-paste approach can also be used to embed objects. Suppose you start Excel, create a chart, select it, and copy it. Then you run Word for Windows and choose Paste from the Edit menu to paste the chart into your document. Because both Excel and Word for Windows support OLE, there's nothing else you need to do. Word for Windows has embedded the object.

This old method has its limitations. For example, after selecting and copying a range of cells in Excel, you have several options for pasting them in a Word for Windows document. The traditional Paste command pastes in the cells as a table of text—not as an embedded object. To paste in the cells as an object, you must select the Paste Special command.

Note: *You don't need to save the object in the application in which you created it. For example, if you create a graphic in Paintbrush, there's no need to save the Paintbrush file to disk; the graphic object is saved as part of the document in which you embed it. Of course, you should save the graphic if you want to use it again elsewhere.*

The most amazing aspect of OLE comes into play when you want to update the embedded object. Just double-click it to automatically run the program that created the object and load the object into memory for instant updating. For example, after embedding a Paintbrush graphic, double-click the graphic to run Paintbrush and load the graphic for editing. When you're done editing, choose Exit from the File menu, and you'll be asked if you want to update the object in the destination document. Respond by clicking the Yes button.

With a sound object, you can double-click it to play or edit the object. Some applications may just play the sound. Others may have an Object Edit or Object Play command that comes and goes depending on the capabilities of the object you've embedded.

Using the Object Packager

One of the most interesting objects you can paste into a document is an Object Packager package. Object Packager's icon is an exploding box, which is most appropriate. The stuff you can stick into a package includes files on disk, which must be associated with an application, MS-DOS commands, and anything you copy to the Clipboard from an OLE-supporting application. For example, you could send a document with an embedded MS-DOS command package as mail to everyone on your network. When they double-click the package, the MS-DOS command will run on their systems. This feature has both useful and mischievous applications, as you can guess.

To use the Object Packager, choose the Object or Insert Object command in an OLE-supporting application, and in the list, double-click Package to run the Object Packager application. As Figure 6-7 shows, the Object Packager window has two main panels, Appearance and Content.

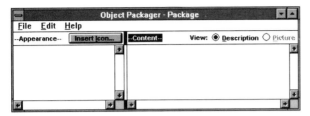

Figure 6-7. *The Object Packager window.*

The Appearance panel on the left shows how the Object Packager will appear in the document. Normally, this panel contains an icon with a label below it, though you can edit the image or create your own using Paintbrush.

The Content panel shows the content of the package—a filename, an MS-DOS command, or a portion of a document pasted from the Clipboard. If the content is a graphic pasted from the Clipboard, it appears in its proper format if you click the Picture button.

To stuff a file in the Object Packager, choose the Import command from the File menu, and select the file you want to include. It must be an associated file—one that's attached to an application that will run and load the file when the package is opened. You can also select a program file, which will then be run when the package is opened.

To put an MS-DOS command line in the Object Packager, choose Command Line from the Edit menu. Type the name of the MS-DOS command to be run, just as you would type it at the command prompt. If the command is not an MS-DOS command and its program isn't on the MS-DOS

Pasting Files into Object Packager

In File Manager, you can choose the Edit menu's Copy command to copy a file to the Clipboard. From there, you can paste the file into the Object Packager's Content panel. If the file changes often, you can paste-link the file so that the embedded object package will be automatically updated.

search path, specify a full pathname to it. Note that this option doesn't package the program that runs the command, only the command line.

On the left side of the dialog box, you control how the object package appears in your document. If the contents are represented by an application, the application's icon appears. Otherwise, you may just see the package icon. To use a new icon, click the Insert Icon button. Select an EXE or DLL file, such as MORICONS.DLL, and select an icon from the list that appears. Or, you can use the Paintbrush program to create your own icon: With the Appearance panel of the Object Packager window active, choose Copy from the Edit menu to copy the icon to the Clipboard. Then start Paintbrush, paste in the image, and edit it. Finally, return to the Object Packager, and paste in your icon.

Note: Creating your own icon works only with the Object Packager; you cannot use Paintbrush to create icons for use by other Windows-based applications.

To stick a descriptive label below the icon, choose the Label command from the Edit menu, and type a description of the package in the text box. Note that you can't add a label to an icon you created.

When everything is properly saved, choose Exit from the Object Packager's File menu, click OK to update the object in the destination document, and voilà: Your object is packaged, inserted, and ready to go.

To test the object, double-click it. Windows loads the file or runs the MS-DOS command in the package. To edit the package, choose an appropriate Edit Object Package command from your application's Edit menu.

Note: You can also open Object Packager by double-clicking its icon in Program Manager. In this case, when you're done creating a package, you choose the Copy Package command from the Edit menu to copy the entire package to the Clipboard. You can then paste the package into any document.

Chapter 7

Managing Windows' Graphical Effects

Calling Windows *graphical* is like saying the Pope is Catholic; both are painfully obvious. What makes Windows graphical is its interface, which displays colors, images, and text elegantly in windows. The contrast with the monotonous world of MS-DOS—boring text characters and stick graphics—is dramatic. This chapter looks at only part of Windows' graphical interface by exploring how Windows deals with fonts, icons, and the desktop.

WORKING WITH FONTS

Almost any Windows-based application that lets you type text also lets you select a font. The exceptions are the primitive "text-editor" applications, such as Notepad or Cardfile. Everything else, from Write on up to Microsoft Word for Windows, Aldus PageMaker, Microsoft Excel, and the rest, allows you to select different fonts for your documents. This flexibility can really liven things up and make your work expressive.

Applications typically allow you to select several attributes for the text you type:

- The font
- The style
- The size
- Effects

A *font* is what typesetters refer to as a *typeface*. It's the name of a family of characters that all sport a similar design. For example, Avant Garde,

Souvenir, and Times Roman are all typefaces. In Windows, everyone calls them *fonts*.

The *style* of a font describes its characteristics. Popular styles are bold, italic, and bold italic. (Underlining isn't a style; it's an effect.) The basic font is called *roman*, or sometimes *normal*, *regular*, or *plain*. Just as vanilla is really a flavor of ice cream (not the absence of flavor), roman is a true font style (not the absence of style).

The *size* describes the size of the font, measured in points, with 72 points to an inch. A 12-point font has capital letters that are ⅙ inch in height. In some contexts, you'll see *points* used instead of *size* in Windows; both describe the same thing.

Effects describe some interesting modifications Windows-based applications can make to the font. The most popular effect is underlining. Other effects include strikeout or strike through, double underlining, small caps, and assigning colortext;colors to the text.

Different Windows-based applications provide different mechanisms for manipulating fonts. Some use menus; others offer a dialog box, and so on. With some applications, you have even more control over the text and can manipulate some of the interesting elements listed in the tip titled "Typesetting Terminology." With other applications, you're limited to a few basic options.

How Windows Uses Fonts

The variety of fonts you can choose from in the menus, dialog boxes, and lists of your Windows-based applications depends on the fonts installed by Windows, the fonts available on your printer, and any extra fonts or font utilities you may have added to your computer. All systems running Windows have a basic assortment of fonts, called *screen fonts*, that Windows uses to display information on the screen. These fonts fall into three categories:

- Raster fonts
- Vector fonts
- TrueType fonts

Note: *Another set of fonts is used by Windows to display MS-DOS programs. These fonts are the files with WOA extensions that you may have seen in SYSTEM.INI. They can't be selected from any font menu.*

Typesetting Terminology

Here are the definitions for the typesetting terms you'll see in this chapter. These terms are only the tip of the iceberg of the language used by typesetters.

Fixed	A font in which all the characters take up the same amount of horizontal space, regardless of the actual width of the character. Examples are the Courier font in Windows and the text font used by MS-DOS. Compare with *Proportional*.
Monospaced	Another term for *fixed* (see above).
Point size	The height of the capital letters in a font, measured in points. There are 72 points in an inch, so a 36-point character is half an inch tall.
Proportional	A font in which the horizontal space occupied by each character varies according to the character's width: An *I* takes up less space than an *M*. Nearly all of Windows' fonts are proportional and are displayed that way on the screen.
Sans serif	Literally, "without stroke." A font with no ornamental projections or short lines hanging from its ends. These fonts are usually used in headlines because they stand out.
Serif	A font with ornamental projections that extend from the ends of the letters. For example, the letter *T* has serifs hanging from its ends like the eaves on a roof. Serif fonts are generally used for blocks of text because they're easier to read.
Typeface	In traditional typesetting, each style of each font is a unique typeface; Times Roman and Times Roman Bold are two typefaces. In Windows, these two typefaces are the same font with different styles.

Raster fonts are available in a given assortment of point sizes. For example, the MS Sans Serif raster font comes in 8, 10, 12, 14, 18, and 24 points on VGA systems. These sizes are fixed, set according to the SSERIF*x*.FON font file, which is directly related to your video display. (The *x* is a letter representing the display adapter you have installed.) The available point sizes may be different on your system, depending on your display adapter.

Windows can double or halve the point sizes for a raster font, but you can't select in-between values. Sometimes, when you reduce or enlarge a raster font, the font develops a sick case of "the jaggies." The other font formats don't have this problem. Unlike raster fonts, which are essentially bitmaps, vector and TrueType fonts are *scalable*.

The characters in vector fonts are created line by line using Windows GDI (graphics device interface) functions. You can enlarge or reduce them to any size, and they still look good. The problem is that creating vector-font characters takes time, which is why the TrueType fonts were developed.

You may see vector fonts referred to as *plotter fonts*, because they print well on a plotter where bitmapped fonts can't be used. Because vector fonts can be scaled, Windows may use a vector font to display a raster font that you have enlarged to the extreme. Windows makes this substitution internally to keep the display from looking like a low-res arcade game.

TrueType fonts were introduced with Windows version 3.1. They were designed to look good on both the screen and your printer. Like vector fonts, TrueType fonts can be scaled to any size, from 1 to 999 points. Windows comes with five TrueType fonts: Arial, Courier New, Times New Roman, Symbol, and Wingdings. The first three fonts come with four styles: book, bold, italic, and bold italic. (The book style isn't labeled as such in dialog boxes; only the font name appears.) The last two are fonts that contain symbols or pictures instead of letters and numbers.

The fonts that Windows installs are listed in Table 7-1. Your system may have more or fewer fonts, depending on how they are set up in the Control Panel's Fonts dialog box.

Font Name	Font Type
Arial	TrueType
Arial Bold	TrueType
Arial Bold Italic	TrueType
Arial Italic	TrueType
Courier	Raster
Courier New	TrueType
Courier New Bold	TrueType
Courier New Bold Italic	TrueType
Courier New Italic	TrueType
Modern	Vector
MS Sans Serif	Raster
MS Serif	Raster
Roman	Vector
Script	Vector
Small Fonts	Raster
Symbol	Raster
Symbol	TrueType
System	Raster
Terminal	Raster
Times New Roman	TrueType
Times New Roman Bold	TrueType
Times New Roman Bold Italic	TrueType
Times New Roman Italic	TrueType
Wingdings	TrueType

Table 7-1. *Windows' installed fonts and font types.*

Courier and Terminal are fixed, or monospaced, fonts; the rest are proportional. Only the raster fonts have fixed sizes, which are determined by your display adapter. The vector and TrueType fonts can be scaled to any size.

This selection of fonts is truly rich and suitable for almost any application. You can add more fonts by buying any of the many TrueType font packages available, or you can add third party font packages to suit your designing needs.

Old Windows Fonts

Old versions of Windows were shipped with four basic fonts: Helv, Tms Rmn, Times, and Helvetica. These raster fonts have been replaced in newer versions of Windows. To stay compatible with older software, Windows assigns *font substitutes* for the old fonts. Table 7-2 lists these substitutes.

Old Font	New Font
Helv	MS Sans Serif
Tms Rmn	MS Serif
Times	Times New Roman
Helvetica	Arial

Table 7-2. *Windows' old fonts and their new substitutes.*

Font Information in WIN.INI

Windows keeps information about its screen fonts in three sections of your WIN.INI file: [fonts], [FontSubstitutes], and [TrueType].

The [fonts] section lists the names of your fonts, their type, and the name of the font resource file located in your WINDOWS\SYSTEM directory. The following format is used:

font_name (type)=filename

font_name is the name of the font. Some raster fonts may be followed by their point sizes, like this:

```
MS Sans Serif 8,10,12,14,18,24 (VGA res)=SSERIFE.FON
```

type indicates whether the font is a raster, vector, or TrueType font. Raster fonts are designated by the display adapter's name, as shown above; vector fonts are designated by (*Plotter*); and TrueType fonts are designated by (*TrueType*).

filename is the name of the font resource file in the WINDOWS\SYSTEM directory. The file is copied from the Windows distribution disks when you set up Windows, or it may have been installed in the WINDOWS\ SYSTEM directory by a TrueType font setup program. Raster font files are specific to your display adapter, which explains why you need to reinstall font files if you ever change display adapters.

The [FontSubstitutes] section lists the names of old fonts, each followed by an equal sign and the name of the new substitute. The contents of this section reflect the entries in Table 7-2.

Finally, four entries in the [TrueType] section control how Windows deals with TrueType fonts, as follows:

OutlineThreshold=*number* This entry tells Windows when to render a TrueType font as an outline and when to use a bitmap. Bitmaps are faster to display but take up more memory. *number* equals the number of "pels per em"—the number of pixels used across the width of the letter *M*. This value determines when Windows will start rendering the font using outlines instead of a bitmap. The default value is 256; specify a lower value if memory is tight. Do not specify a value over 300.

TTEnable=0¦**1** If set to 1, this entry makes TrueType fonts available to your Windows-based application. The default is 1. To change the setting, use the Control Panel's Fonts dialog box.

TTIfCollisions=0¦**1** This entry controls how Windows deals with two fonts of the same name, one of which is a TrueType font. If set to 0 (the default), the TrueType font is always used. Set this entry to 1 if you want to use the non-TrueType font.

TTOnly=0¦**1** If set to 1, this entry makes *only* TrueType fonts available to your Windows applications. The default is 0, which means that all font types are available. To change the setting, use the Control Panel's Fonts dialog box.

Adding and Removing Fonts

Windows' screen fonts are controlled using the Control Panel's Fonts dialog box. Double-click the Fonts icon to display a dialog box similar to the one shown in Figure 7-1 on the next page. The Installed Fonts list shows all the raster, vector, and TrueType fonts installed on your system, including any TrueType fonts you may have purchased and installed. Three buttons control the fonts: Remove disables the selected font and optionally removes the font file from disk; Add allows you to add a new font; and TrueType controls the settings for TrueType fonts.

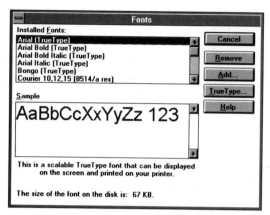

Figure 7-1. *The Control Panel's Fonts dialog box.*

Note: Windows uses the System font as its screen font and uses the MS Sans Serif font in many dialog boxes. Do not delete these fonts!

To preview a font, select it in the list. A text sample is displayed in the Sample box. The font's description appears below the box, letting you know whether it is a TrueType font or a screen or plotter font. If it is a raster font with multiple resolutions, a sampling of the available sizes appears in the box.

You remove a font by clicking the Remove button. Unless you select the Delete Font File From Disk check box in the dialog box that appears, the font is removed only from WIN.INI. It remains on your hard disk and can be reinstalled using the Add button, but it isn't available in any applications.

You add a new font by selecting it and clicking the Add button. Most fonts are stored in the WINDOWS\SYSTEM directory. If you have moved the font files to another directory on another drive, select this drive and directory and then select the font. (Moving fonts is covered in "Dealing with Font Files" in Chapter 4.)

The TrueType button controls two aspects of TrueType. Turning on the Enable TrueType Fonts option tells Windows to make TrueType fonts available to your applications and to render those fonts on the screen without jaggies. Turning on the Show Only TrueType Fonts In Applications option selfishly tells Windows to make only TrueType fonts available in your applications.

My advice is to turn on only the Enable TrueType Fonts option. Turning on Show Only TrueType Fonts In Applications frees up the memory used by non-TrueType fonts, but leaving the option off allows you access to printer fonts and other non-TrueType fonts installed in the system.

Printer and Third Party Fonts

Raster, vector, and TrueType fonts are all used by Windows to display characters on the screen. Your system may have additional fonts associated with your printer or special third party fonts you may have added, such as Adobe PostScript fonts. These fonts are not controlled using the Control Panel's Fonts dialog box because they're not supplied with Windows, nor are they controlled via WIN.INI. But they are available in your applications, as you'll see if you display a Font menu or dialog box. For example, Figure 7-2 shows the Fonts dialog box from the Write application on my machine. In addition to Windows' screen fonts, the dialog box lists various fonts associated with my printer. (Printer fonts appear with a small printer icon next to them, TrueType fonts have the TT icon, and other screen fonts have no icon.)

The best type of fonts to use are printer fonts. They print the fastest. Windows displays these fonts using a similar screen font but, for the best results, prints them using the font that is resident in your printer. For

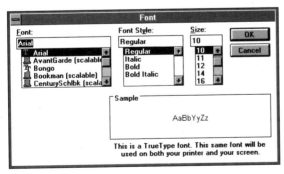

Figure 7-2. *The Write application's Font dialog box.*

example, if you have a PostScript printer and you select the Palatino font, Windows may show the Times New Roman font on the screen. In the Write application's Font dialog box, Palatino is described like this: *This is a printer font. The closest matching Windows font will be used on your screen.* When you print, the printer uses its Palatino font.

The second best type of fonts to use are TrueType fonts. Windows attempts to print these fonts properly on most printers. First, it tries to use a similar printer font; for example, a printer might use Times in place of Times New Roman. If that doesn't work, Windows creates and downloads a bitmapped version of the TrueType font in the proper point size and for the resolution of your printer.

Note: It's best to select a font with a printer icon by it. Because those fonts are resident in your printer, they print faster than TrueType fonts. TrueType fonts print on all printers supported by Windows, but because Windows must often render the fonts as bitmaps, printing takes longer.

Controlling Printer Fonts

Printer fonts are set up using the Control Panel's Printers dialog box, which is displayed when you double-click the Printers icon. Each printer installed under Windows has its own dialog box, which contains some items for controlling printer fonts. The box might contain a Fonts button, an area where you can select optional fonts, font cartridges, emulation modes, or an area for downloading "soft" fonts to the printer.

Note: Printer fonts do not appear in the Control Panel's Fonts dialog box, nor are they editable in WIN.INI. Information about those fonts is stored only in your printer driver. Keep in mind that Windows substitutes screen fonts when displaying printer fonts on the screen. Check with your printer manufacturer to see whether screen font versions of your printer fonts are available; for example, Hewlett-Packard supplies the Intellifont-for-Windows utility to render HP printer fonts on the screen.

For a Hewlett-Packard LaserJet IIIP printer, you would select an optional font cartridge from the Cartridges list shown in Figure 7-3. To add additional fonts, you would then click the Fonts button. The fonts associated with the selected cartridge would appear in the Fonts list along with the

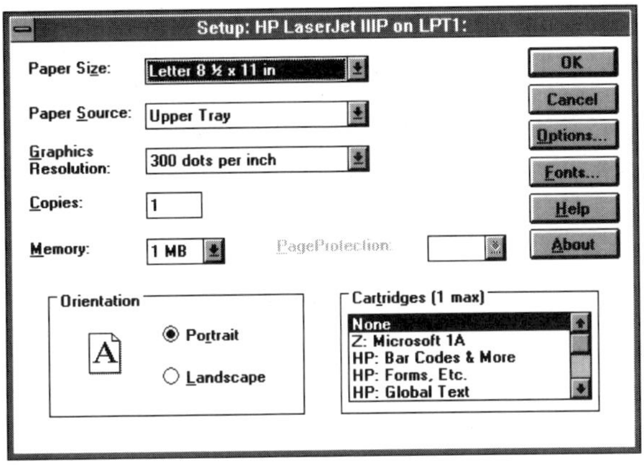

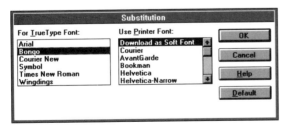

Figure 7-3. *The Setup dialog box for an HP LaserJet IIIP.*

standard printer fonts. You would then install the fonts from disk and download them to the printer.

PostScript printers come with a base of fonts, usually 35 typefaces. During printing, the PostScript printer driver uses its own resident printer fonts in place of Windows' screen fonts. To control this substitution, display the Printers dialog box, click the Setup, Options, and Advanced buttons, and in the Advanced Options dialog box, click the Edit Substitution Table button. The Substitution dialog box is shown in Figure 7-4.

TrueType fonts are listed on the left, and PostScript fonts—both resident printer fonts and fonts you may have installed using a font package such as Adobe Type Manager—are shown on the right. This dialog box doesn't control how the fonts appear on the screen, only which TrueType fonts will be replaced by printer fonts in the printer. (If you want to send the

Figure 7-4. *The Substitution dialog box for a PostScript printer.*

TrueType fonts as bitmaps, go back to the Advanced Options dialog box, open the Send To Printer As drop-down list box, and select Bitmap.)

Other types of printers have different options in their Setup dialog box for dealing with fonts and font cartridges. Mechanisms for downloading fonts to the printer are also included in the dialog box. If you have any trouble, the online Help should get you through.

Using Nonprinter Fonts

You can buy font packages from third party developers, among them the popular Adobe Type Manager (ATM), which includes a PostScript screen rendering utility as well as several PostScript printer fonts. ATM and similar packages from other developers use their own control panels to manipulate their fonts. ATM's control panel, which is shown in Figure 7-5, lists several PostScript font files installed for Windows.

Because these ATM font files aren't Windows screen fonts, you won't see them in Windows' Control Panel or in WIN.INI. Like printer fonts, they appear in your application's Font menu or dialog boxes with a little printer icon by them. Unlike printer fonts, however, they can be accurately rendered on your screen. For example, when you select the 13-point Tekton font, ATM displays it as best as it can on your screen. It even converts the

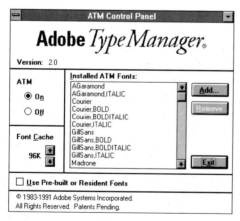

Figure 7-5. *The ATM Control Panel.*

font into bitmaps for use on non-PostScript printers. As with TrueType, what you see on the screen is what you get on the printer.

Windows allows you to easily mix and match a variety of fonts in a document (keeping within the realm of good taste and design, of course). For example, you can print a document using TrueType, ATM fonts, and fonts native to your printer. The only problem is dealing with "font overload," which results in diminishing hard disk space and slow printing.

Font overload occurs when your list of fonts is about four times longer than your screen. (Macintosh users have suffered from font overload for years.) The cure for this malady is to use the Control Panel's Fonts and Printers dialog boxes, as well as any third party font control panels, to reduce the total number of installed fonts to those you use often. You can keep the rest of the hoard on disk, adding them only when you need them.

Using the Character Map Application

What's in the name of a font? Who knows. Garamond is Garamond is Garamond, yet by any other name would look just as pretty. It's the shape of its characters that counts. You can peer at a font's character set using the Character Map program, which was described in Chapter 4. (See Figure 4-5 on page 142.)

The Character Map displays the full character set for a given font. Its Font drop-down list box lists all the fonts installed on your system, but not the ones resident on your printer. (Remember, printer fonts are tied into your printer, and Windows uses a substitute screen font to display them "under the glass.") However, ATM fonts do show up in the Character Map.

Inserting Special Characters in Word for Windows

Microsoft Word for Windows allows you to insert special characters using the Symbol command on the Insert menu. The character is inserted without your having to change the current font. Simply double-click the symbol you want to add.

In addition to seeing all the characters and their styles in the Character Map, you can select characters and copy and paste them into your applications. Simply double-click the character you want to plop into the Characters To Copy text box. When you click the Copy button, the characters in the Characters To Copy text box are copied to the Clipboard. From there you can paste them into another application. For example, you might select the Symbol or Wingdings font to scope out the interesting characters available. You can then copy odd characters, like ♥ or ✌, and paste them into your document.

Creating Your Own Fonts

Windows doesn't come with any font creation or modification software, but TrueType fonts can be created using utilities such as these:

- Fontographer from Altsys Corp.
- FontStudio from Letraset Graphic Design Software
- Ingredient and SplineLab from Projective Solutions
- TypeMan from Type Solutions, Inc.

For converting other fonts to TrueType fonts, check out Ares Software's Fontmonger software. These and other programs are available through mail order houses as well as local software vendors.

CONTROLLING ICONS AND THE DESKTOP

You control some aspects of the icons in Program Manager, as well as various aspects of Windows' desktop, through the Control Panel's Desktop dialog box, shown in Figure 7-6. This dialog box contains an assortment of controls and settings for both the desktop and the icons on it.

Messing About with Icons

Icons are used throughout Windows. Program Manager is the first place you see them; each icon represents an application stored on your hard disk. The applications themselves also use icons to represent your printer, disk drives, documents, and so on.

Figure 7-6. *The Control Panel's Desktop dialog box, with which you control icons and the desktop.*

The Icons area of the Desktop dialog box has two settings: Spacing, which determines how close together icons appear on the desktop; and Wrap Title, which directs Windows to wrap long icon titles and increase the vertical space between icons to accommodate the longest title. (Icon titles can be up to 40 characters long.)

The Spacing box tells Windows how far apart you want to position icons on the screen, in pixels. The default value is 75; a value of 53 still looks good as long as you wrap the titles. This setting controls only the horizontal distance between icons, not the vertical distance. To control the vertical distance, you need to edit WIN.INI, as I'll explain in a minute.

The Wrap Title option is usually turned on to permit longer titles to wrap and look good on the screen. If you're using short titles, you can turn off this option. Then remember to use short titles, or your screen will look junky.

WIN.INI's [Desktop] section contains entries that reflect the settings you made in the Desktop dialog box, as well as several additional settings that control the way icons look on the screen.

IconSpacing=*pixels* This entry sets the horizontal distance between icons in pixels. The default value is 75, with smaller values decreasing the distance between icons and larger values increasing the distance.

IconSpacing can be edited in WIN.INI or changed using the Control Panel's Desktop dialog box.

IconTitleFaceName=*fontname* This entry selects the font used to display the icon's title. The default is MS Sans Serif, the font Windows uses to display information in dialog boxes. However, you can use any raster font. Symbol is a good font for playing practical jokes.

IconTitleSize=*points* This entry sets the point size used to display the icon's title. The default value is 8; smaller values may be hard to read. Experiment to find the best size for the font you're using.

IconTitleWrap=0¦1 This entry reflects the status of the Wrap Title check box in the Control Panel's Desktop dialog box. If this entry is set to 1 (the default), Windows wraps long icon titles. If it is set to 0, Windows does not wrap the title.

IconVerticalSpacing=*pixels* This entry sets the vertical distance between icons, in pixels. The default value varies, depending on the resolution of your display adapter and the font you use for your icon titles. Larger values push the icons apart; smaller values bring them closer together. Setting this entry requires experimentation. A value of 50 is snug but not too close on VGA systems. Delete the entry to return to the default spacing.

Messing About with the Desktop

Four areas in the Control Panel's Desktop dialog box deal with the desktop's appearance: Pattern, Screen Saver, Wallpaper, and Sizing Grid. You will probably want to use either a background pattern or wallpaper— not both. Mixing the two rarely looks good. If you select a background pattern and then select a tiled wallpaper design, the wallpaper covers the entire desktop and the background pattern with one exception. Your background pattern will show up in the background of icon titles. It'll look bad. Trust me. So which should you use? Wallpaper consumes more memory, and on some systems Windows takes a long time to draw the wallpaper. If memory and speed is an issue, use a background pattern. See "Changing the Background" later in this chapter for more information about wallpaper and background patterns.

You use the Screen Saver box in the Control Panel's Desktop dialog box to set up Windows' built-in screen saver. Select None to disable the screen saver entirely, or select a screen saver from the list. The Delay value sets the length of idle time before the screen saver is activated.

The Sizing Grid area controls the appearance and position of windows and icons on the desktop. The Granularity option describes how windows and icons can be positioned on the screen. A value of 0 means Windows can stick a window or icon anywhere. A value of 1 tells Windows to create a grid of 8-by-8 pixels and to snap the windows and icons on the screen to that grid. Each succeeding value increases the size of the grid by 8. The maximum value of 49 gives a grid of 392-by-392 pixels, which significantly constrains the positioning of windows on the screen. The Border Width option in the Sizing Grid area sets the width of a window's border in pixels. The default value is 3; you can set a width from 1 through 49 pixels.

As with the icon settings, the desktop settings have counterparts in WIN.INI. In the [windows] section, you'll find the following settings:

BorderWidth=*pixels* This entry sets every window's border width in pixels. Values range from 1 through 49, with 49 being very thick. The default value is 3.

ScreenSaveActive=0¦1 When set to 1, this entry directs Windows to turn on its automatic screen saver. A setting of 0—the default—disables the screen saver.

ScreenSaveTimeOut=*seconds* This entry sets the length of idle time before the screen saver is activated, in seconds. The default is 120 seconds, or 2 minutes. When you set this value in the Control Panel's Desktop dialog box, you set it in minutes. You'll need to remember which place takes which type of setting.

The following settings appear in WIN.INI's [desktop] section:

GridGranularity=*number* This setting is equal to the Granularity value in the Control Panel's Desktop dialog box. It sets the size of the grid used to position windows on the screen. Values range from 0 through 49, and each step represents 8 pixels. The default value is 0.

Pattern=*pattern* This entry specifies the pattern used for the desktop's background, represented as eight values, each specifying a row of pixels in an 8-by-8 grid. The names of the available patterns and their values are stored in the CONTROL.INI file. The default is *(None)* for no pattern.

TileWallpaper=0: 1 This setting describes how Windows arranges wallpaper (if you have selected it). A setting of 1 tiles the wallpaper; 0 directs Windows to center the wallpaper pattern on the screen. The default is 0. Set this value in the Control Panel's Desktop dialog box.

Wallpaper=*filename* *filename* is the name of a bitmap (BMP) file that Windows should use as the desktop's wallpaper. The bitmap file is usually selected in the Control Panel's Desktop dialog box. Be sure to include the full pathname if the file isn't in the WINDOWS directory. The default is *(None)* for no wallpaper.

Creating Your Own Icons

Windows applications come with icons that appear in Program Manager or when the application is minimized. MS-DOS programs, on the other hand, don't come with icons. They're usually assigned a generic MS-DOS icon, which is boring—the hallmark of a stubborn MS-DOS program being run under Windows. You can assign a new icon to an MS-DOS program by using Program Manager's Properties dialog box. The new icon can be plucked from Program Manager's file (PROGMAN.EXE) or the icons library file (MORICONS.DLL).

But can you create your own icon in Windows? No. Unless you have your own icon editor, you'll have to steal an icon from a Windows application's file, a dynamic link library (DLL) file, or an icon (ICO) file (which is created by an icon editor).

Windows doesn't come with an icon editor. I really wish it did, but alas, it just ain't so. It comes with the Paintbrush paint program, but Paintbrush does not save its images to disk in the icon file format. So you're left yearning for a public domain, shareware, or third party icon editor to help you design your own icons.

The most popular shareware icon editor is Icondraw for Windows. The author is Philip B. Eskelin, Jr. As a shareware programmer, he does not market this utility through the usual outlets. You can download this file from a national online network or local BBS, or you can get it from a software warehouse or user group.

If you have Visual Basic, you can make your own icons with the Icon-Works application that comes with it. And don't forget that Visual Basic comes with a wealth of icons. Even if you can't use any of them, they provide the basis for creating new icons.

My favorite icon editor comes with the Norton Desktop for Windows. Not only does it let you create and edit icon files, but you can also build your own icon libraries and cut and paste icons between EXE and DLL files. I used this utility to give Dr. Watson a dye job; he's now a brunette on my system.

CHANGING THE BACKGROUND

For Windows' background, you have three choices: You can select a plain color using the Control Panel's Color dialog box; you can select a background pattern using the Control Panel's Desktop dialog box; or you can opt for wallpaper, which is a centered or tiled bitmapped image selected from the Control Panel's Desktop dialog box. What you select is up to you. However, note that tiled wallpaper consumes more memory, and Windows takes longer to paint over it (just like I took ages to paint over the gaudy silver wallpaper in our old house).

Selecting Wallpaper

A wallpaper file is nothing more than a bitmap picture. You can create or edit a wallpaper bitmap using the Paintbrush program. You assign it as wallpaper using the Control Panel's Desktop dialog box. Larger images look best centered on the screen; intricate patterns can be tiled.

Table 7-3 on the next page lists the wallpaper files that come with Windows 3.1. All except WINLOGO.BMP should be tiled. The WINLOGO wallpaper can be tiled, but I think it looks better centered. You may find other wallpaper patterns on your system—files from older versions of

Windows or files you have collected from friends. (Thanks to Jim Fuchs for the cool Macintosh and NeXT bitmaps he's sent me.) If the file isn't in your WINDOWS directory, it won't show up in the Desktop dialog box. Don't despair. Simply specify the file's full pathname in the text box to select it.

Wallpaper File	Description
256COLOR.BMP	256-color wallpaper (balls)
ARCADE.BMP	Little squares, turned 45 degrees
ARCHES.BMP	Roman-like aqueduct arches
ARGYLE.BMP	Blue argyle pattern
CARS.BMP	Little blue Volvos driving up steep hills
CASTLE.BMP	Cinderblock/brick pattern
CHITZ.BMP	Zigzag pattern with square freckles
EGYPT.BMP	Interlocking curves
FLOCK.BMP	M.C. Escher bird pattern
HONEY.BMP	Honeycomb
LEAVES.BMP	Brown, green, and gold leaf pattern (excellent for fall)
MARBLE.BMP	Blue marble pattern
REDBRICK.BMP	Red bricks (red CASTLE.BMP)
RIVETS.BMP	Steely blue with uniform bumps
SQUARES.BMP	Grape flavored squares
TARTAN.BMP	Scotch tape dispenser pattern
THATCH.BMP	Silver gray thatched pattern
WINLOGO.BMP	Windows' flag, carved in marble
ZIGZAG.BMP	Cool zigzag pattern (reminds me of San Francisco)

Table 7-3. *Wallpaper bitmaps that come with Windows.*

Wallpaper files are available everywhere, even as part of professional third party programs. To create unique images, you can use a scanner.

Browsing Through BMP Files

The handiest wallpaper selection tool is the Graphics File Viewer, which comes with the Windows Resource Kit. You can use it to browse through the BMP files on your disk and then select one as wallpaper with the touch of a button.

Scanning in your photograph, a comic book, Captain Kirk, or Miss May is simple, provided you have a scanner and the software to run it. You must convert the image to the bitmap (BMP) format for use as wallpaper.

Selecting a Pattern

Using the Control Panel's Desktop dialog box, you can select an interesting background pattern for the desktop, instead of wallpaper. This choice is better when memory gets low. First disable the wallpaper by selecting (None) from the drop-down list in the Wallpaper area. Then select the pattern you want from the drop-down list in the Pattern area. To preview the pattern, click the Edit Pattern button to display the Edit Pattern dialog box shown in Figure 7-7.

You select a pattern using the drop-down list at the top of the screen. The Sample area on the left displays a preview of the selected pattern. In the middle is the *editing cell*, where you can edit the pattern by clicking to change each pixel from the foreground to the background. Click again to switch the pixel back to its initial color.

To create your own pattern, type its name in the Name text box, and then build the pattern pixel by pixel in the editing cell. Save the pattern by clicking the Add button, and then clicking OK. Your pattern is created and is added to the drop-down list in the Pattern area of the Desktop dialog box. Select it and click OK, and the pattern appears on the desktop.

Note: You select the foreground and background colors for the pattern using the Control Panel's Color dialog box. You select the Desktop item from the Screen Element drop-down list, and then select the background

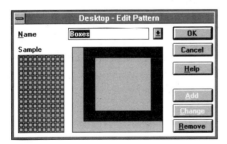

Figure 7-7. *The Edit Pattern dialog box.*

color. Select the Window Text item for the foreground color. These two set-
tings appear in the WIN.INI file's [colors] section. The background color
is set by the Background *entry, and the foreground color is set by the*
WindowText *entry.*

Working with the Control Panel

As you have seen, the Control Panel allows you to customize and control
Windows' interface, options, and hardware. Actually, the Control Panel is
nothing more than an interface. It makes it easy to adjust various settings
in your WIN.INI and SYSTEM.INI files without having to use the System
Editor or Notepad to make adjustments yourself.

To display the icons you see in its window, the Control Panel loads special
control panel (CPL) files, which are stored in the WINDOWS\SYSTEM directory. For example, the MAIN.CPL file contains the primary Control
Panel icons: Color, Fonts, Ports, Mouse, Desktop, Keyboard, Printers, International, Date/Time, and Network (providing you have a network installed). If you're running in enhanced mode, you see the 386 Enhanced
icon because the Control Panel automatically loads the CPWIN386.CPL
file. The same holds true for the Sound and Drivers icons. Sound is displayed by the SND.CPL file, and Drivers is displayed by DRIVERS.CPL.

Icons for third party drivers could also be added to the Control Panel, but
most of the ones I've seen use their own control panel icon. For example,
LANtastic has its own separate icon, the Adobe Type Manager's control
panel is a unique application, and so on. In the future though, many of
these types of programs will probably appear in Windows' Control Panel.

The Control Panel has its own INI file, CONTROL.INI. There is absolutely
no reason to edit the CONTROL.INI file, but there's nothing wrong with
peeking at it. So use Notepad to open CONTROL.INI. Following is a list
of the sections you may find there and their contents. Remember, you are
only satisfying your curiosity; I don't recommend editing this file.

[current] This section contains one keyword, *color schemes*, which is set
to the color scheme you've selected for the desktop. For example:

```
color schemes=Ocean
```

[color schemes] This section lists all the predefined color schemes available in the Color dialog box. Each scheme is defined by 21 color values, which are specified as hexadecimal numbers.

[Custom Colors] This section stores the custom colors you may have created using the Control Panel's Color dialog box. Windows lets you create 16 colors, so this section contains 16 entries. (If a six pack of *F*'s follows an entry, then the color is white, so you know a custom color for the entry hasn't been created.)

[Patterns] This section contains the background patterns available for the desktop. The following format is used:

> *pattern_name=row1 row2 row3 row4 row5 row6 row7 row8*

pattern_name is what appears in the Desktop dialog box. It's followed by eight numbers (all in decimal—thank you) that represent the bit values for the eight rows in the editing cell. You could create your own pattern here, but it's much easier to do it in the Desktop dialog box.

[MMCPL] This section's header stands for Multimedia Control Panel. The values here relate to the various multimedia items that appear in the Control Panel.

[Screen Saver.*] Several sections may record information related to your screen saver settings. One section may list an encrypted password, another may have settings for a specific screen saver, and so on. For example, the section [Screen Saver.Mystify] would contain the settings for that screen saver.

[Userinstallable.drivers] This section describes various multimedia drivers installed using the Control Panel.

[Drivers.Desc] This section draws a connection between various multimedia driver files and the names that appear when you click the Drivers icon.

[Installed] This section contains entries that describe your installed printers. You may see an entry that specifies the CAN_ADF.EXE file, which is used to install soft fonts, and you may see the Windows version in the following format:

```
3.1=yes
```

Chapter 8

Networks, Telecommunications, and Faxes

Our PCs are still *personal* computers. They're each used by one person (or one person at a time), and one person working alone can get a lot done. But there may be times when you need to access information in another computer. Or perhaps you want several computers to share a single printer. Or maybe your computer is a *workstation* that runs Windows and other applications from another computer called a *file server*. In these situations, your PC is probably part of a network. Believe it or not, this can be done painlessly under Windows.

This chapter covers networking with Windows. Rather than focusing on one particular network, I take a general approach. The idea here is to talk about working with Windows on a network, not about buying or installing network hardware and software. In addition, I briefly discuss the subjects of telecommunications and faxes, which also involve using more than one computer. The telecommunications discussion touches on using a modem and serial ports under Windows, and the fax discussion covers the interesting ways Windows can send and receive facsimile images.

Note: You don't have to have a network to use Windows. If you don't have a network, please skip ahead to the section titled "Communications from Within Windows."

A NETWORKING PRIMER

Networks let individual PCs share information and resources. Information consists of files located on a PC. Resources consist of PC hardware—the disk drives, printers, tape backup systems, and modems available to the computers connected to the network. When the network is properly set up, sharing information and resources is simple.

A computer network has both software and hardware components. Both are set up outside of Windows. (If you've just installed a network, you'll also need to run the Windows Setup program to tell Windows about your network.)

The network hardware connects each computer using what I generically call the "network hose." The hose attaches to a nozzle on the back of each PC, chaining them all together. Information is squirted out of your PC's nozzle, through the network hose to another computer. Likewise, other computers can spew information through the hose to your PC.

The network software is what you use to talk with other computers connected to the network hose. It consists of various elements: a driver for the network hardware; a NetBIOS that serves as intermediary between the hardware and the driver; a redirector that sends and receives system information across the network; and control programs that let you hook up to other computers and share resources.

I won't bore you with tedious network details. It's usually best if someone else sets up your network, though anyone who's ever upgraded a hard drive or installed extra memory in a PC can set up a simple network in a small office. Some of the simpler networks, such as LANtastic and Windows for Workgroups, are quite easy to set up.

You should test your network before running Windows. Make sure that all aspects work: that you can log onto the file server, access files and programs,

Designating Accessible Drives

If you're going to access drive letters higher than E, then you'll need to use the Lastdrive configuration command in your CONFIG.SYS file. You should also check out the Fcbs configuration command. These commands are discussed in Chapter 1.

use remote printers, or whatever it is you want the network to be able to do. Only then should you set up the network for use with Windows. (This process is covered in "Configuring Windows for Networking," later in this chapter.)

Two Types of Networks

All networks have the same basic components: network hardware in your PC and the network hose that connects your system with other systems. Then there's the network software that controls everything. Beyond that, networks come in two different flavors: server-based and peer-to-peer.

A server-based network resembles an old minicomputer in computing days of yore. One or more large, powerful central computers called *servers* run the networking software and can store thousands of programs and files on their huge disk drives. The other computers on the network are called *workstations*. Each workstation can access the servers and use their files and programs, and any printers attached to them. Several users can work on a single database, update files, and use special network programs, all at the same time. You'll find this type of network in large organizations or companies that do a lot of data processing. Examples of server-based networks include Novell NetWare, Banyan VINES, 3Com networks, DEC Pathworks, IBM's OS/2 LAN Server, and Microsoft's LAN Manager.

A peer-to-peer network is more friendly and more in keeping with the spirit of personal computing. Each computer on the network can act as a workstation, as a server, or as a combination of both. You can access another computer, save files there, run programs from there, or use the other computer's printer. Each computer can be configured to share or not to share its resources, and sharing is controlled by the networking software. Examples of peer-to-peer networks include Artisoft LANtastic and Novell NetWare Lite.

For small offices, I recommend a peer-to-peer network. I run one in my home office so that my two computers can share files back and forth and run programs from one another's hard drive. It sure beats swapping files with a floppy disk. The peer-to-peer network also lets my two computers share a single laser printer. And when it comes time to backup, a single tape backup system handles both computers' hard drives.

Windows works with both types of networks, and you use the same commands in similar ways with both. Subtle differences occur beneath the surface, and different networks have different interfaces, as I discuss in "The Control Panel's Network Dialog Box," later in this chapter.

The Advantages of Networking

Networks for PCs came about because several people working on several computers often have to share a lot of information. Walking disks back and forth wasn't the answer. To make file transfer easy, networks were designed so that computers could beam files back and forth. They also allow several computers to share one or two powerful printers. And they enable a single file server to become a home for everyone's software and file storage (not to mention multiplayer games, network mail, and so on).

Networks offer many advantages. Sharing files, printers, and disk drives is just one of them. Other advantages you might not be aware of, especially with regard to Windows, include

■ Faster printing. Printing on the network involves "spooling" a file to the network printer server. For example, when you select a network printer under Windows, all your files print directly to the network. With the file squirted down the network hose, your computer is available for you to do other work. This is much more efficient than using Print Manager, which sits in the background and snatches processor power from other applications.

■ Larger file storage. Server-based networks have the advantage of a large, central disk drive, sometimes *gigabytes* in size. You may have your own special area on that drive where you can store files. Just think of it. You could have files megabytes in size and not impact your disk space!

■ Automated backup. By putting your files on a network drive, you're ensured of regular backup because the network administrator backs up the network drive as part of his or her job. You can back up your files each day simply by copying them to your area on the server's hard drive.

Network users of Windows may not benefit from all of these advantages. For example, my two-node network hard drive doesn't get backed up unless I sit here and do it. And if I'm printing a lot, the computer connected to the printer—my "printer server"—slows down just as it always does when printing. But for sharing information and resources, nothing beats a network—even in the smallest office.

CONFIGURING WINDOWS FOR NETWORKING

Windows is well-geared for networked PCs. You can use the Control Panel's Network dialog box to log onto your network or change your password. File Manager allows you to make or break network connections, as well as manage files on remote hard disks. You use Print Manager to connect to and print on network printers. You can also connect to those printers using the Control Panel's Printers dialog box. Program Manager can even have network group windows, shared by dozens of users. Provided your network is compatible with Windows (and only a few aren't), networking under Windows is a cinch.

Note: Windows for Workgroups was made for networked PCs. The information in this section pertains only to Windows 3.1. For more information about Windows for Workgroups, see "Networks and Windows for Workgroups," later in this chapter.

Generally speaking, it's best to install your network hardware and software, make sure it all works, and then configure your network as much as possible before starting Windows. The configuration work can be done in your AUTOEXEC.BAT file, or you can use the Call command to run a STARTNET.BAT or similar batch file to run the network. In that batch file, do the following:

■ Set up and configure the network hardware and software. (You can do some of this setup work in CONFIG.SYS as well.)

■ Log onto the server(s).

■ Set up your networked disk drives.

■ Connect to any network printers.

■ Make your PC's resources available to a peer-to-peer network.

Your networking software may have a configuration program that performs these tasks for you. For example, on installation, some networks create a batch file that configures the network hardware, logs you onto a server, and makes the network connections. If your networking software doesn't create such a file, you can create one using your network's Net or Use commands, or you can include the commands in AUTOEXEC.BAT.

As an example, Figure 8-1 shows the STARTNET.BAT batch file I use to start my LANtastic network. The name of the computer on which I run this program is Behemoth, and the program is called by my AUTO-EXEC.BAT file before Windows starts.

```
@echo off
cd \lantasti
set net=yes

aex irq=15 iobase=300 verbose
ailanbio
redir behemoth logins=3
server

net login/wait \\behemoth behemoth
net login/wait \\pickle behemoth
net use h: \\pickle\h-drive
net use l: \\pickle\i-drive
net use lpt1: \\pickle\@printer
net lpt timeout 10
:end
```

Figure 8-1. *STARTNET.BAT, used to start LANtastic before Windows runs.*

The second set of commands in Figure 8-1, starting with *AEX*, loads the LANtastic hardware drivers, NetBIOS, redirector, and the server software. Some networks may install these commands in CONFIG.SYS, along with the MS-DOS Share command.

The final set of commands configures the Behemoth server and my second server, which is called Pickle, and makes disk drive and printer connections. This set of commands totally configures Behemoth to use the network. When Windows starts, the network will be ready.

Network devices are designated by their *network path*, which takes the following format:

\\server\device

server is the name of the network server. It's usually an MS-DOS filename that identifies one of the servers on your network. *device* is the name of a device on the server—a disk drive, printer, or some other device.

Setting up your disk drives and printers in MS-DOS has two advantages. The first is that it's done automatically. The second is that you don't need to memorize weird server names and complex device names; just put the command in a batch file and you're instantly connected—before starting Windows.

Note: Some networks enable Windows to have persistent connections. That is, when you quit Windows, Windows remembers the drive and printer connections you had and reconnects you the next time you start. If your network supports persistent connections, don't worry about making your connections at startup.

Figure 8-2 shows the portion of an AUTOEXEC.BAT file that sets up a Windows workstation under Microsoft's LAN Manager network. The first command, *net start workstation*, sets up the workstation under LAN Manager. The other commands log you on and then connect a network printer and disk drive.

```
REM Start this LAN Manager workstation
net start workstation
net logon dang
use lpt1: \\msprint04\L141037a
use r: \\products\data
```

Figure 8-2. *AUTOEXEC.BAT commands that connect a LAN Manager workstation.*

Your system should be similarly set up before Windows runs. Although it's possible to log onto some networks while Windows is running—as well as make or break disk and printer connections—you should try to start Windows with the same network configuration every time. Even if your server changes its configuration, you should maintain the same local drive letters and printer reassignments. This consistency helps keep you sane.

For Windows to be able to use your network, you must tell it that your network exists. If you installed your network before you installed Windows, Windows' Setup program recognizes that the network exists and makes the necessary changes to its configuration to make the network available in Windows. If Windows was already installed when you set up the network, let Windows know about it by using the Windows Setup program within Windows.

Start Windows Setup, and choose the Change System Settings command from the Options menu. Next select your network's name from the Network drop-down list box, and then click OK. (If your network isn't listed, select the Other Network option. You'll need a disk from your network vendor with the files Windows needs.) Windows will probably prompt you to insert one of Windows' distribution disks. When it's done, you'll be prompted to restart Windows so that the changes you made can take effect.

Before using any networking commands, load the NETWORKS.WRI file into the Write application. Read through it for additional information regarding your network.

Pop-Up Messages

If possible, tell your network not to display "pop-up" messages. These messages work fine when you're running MS-DOS programs, but they totally foul up Windows. Instead of pop-up messages, configure your network to beep at you when it has something to tell you. In response, you can run the network software from within Windows to check things out. Of course, if you have a Windows version of the pop-up software, you can always use it instead.

General Windows Network Tips

Here's a few general tips about using Windows on a network:

- As I've said, configure your network completely before starting Windows. The more you do in AUTOEXEC.BAT or in a START-NET.BAT file, the better.

- Consider creating batch files for quickly logging on or off your network and connecting to or disconnecting from network drives and printers. You can put these batch files in a networking group in Program Manager for quick access to network functions. (Although most networks—and Windows—let you perform these operations from within Windows, the batch files are custom made for your system and make everything double-click simple.)

- You cannot put a swap file on a network drive. If you're using a peer-to-peer network, you must disable the network software before setting up a permanent swap file.

- If you run a network program in an MS-DOS shell in Windows and the program crashes, press Ctrl-Alt-Delete to reset that MS-DOS shell. Windows displays a warning message, describing the consequences of rebooting. From the options listed, select the one that closes the network program and allows you to continue running Windows. In most cases, selecting this option shuts down the network program and lets you continue using your PC without losing anything.

The Control Panel's Network Dialog Box

After reading through NETWORKS.WRI, your next stop is the Control Panel. A new Network icon appears in the Control Panel window when you're running a network with Windows. Double-click the icon to bring up the Network dialog box for your network.

Figure 8-3 shows the Network dialog box for Microsoft's LAN Manager version 2.1 Enhanced network, which displays a user name, computer name, and domain. This information may have been provided before you started Windows—for example, in AUTOEXEC.BAT. If it wasn't, you can use the Network dialog box to log on or off the network, change your password, select a name, and perform other network maintenance. You can use menus to control the various network options and settings.

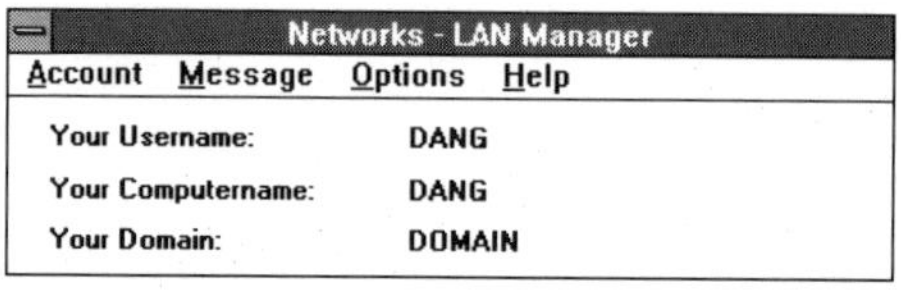

```
┌──────────────────────────────────────────────┐
│ ▭          Networks - LAN Manager             │
│ Account   Message   Options   Help            │
│                                               │
│   Your Username:          DANG                │
│   Your Computername:      DANG                │
│   Your Domain:            DOMAIN              │
│                                               │
└──────────────────────────────────────────────┘
```

Figure 8-3. *The Network dialog box for LAN Manager.*

What you see in the Network dialog box depends on your network. Not every network supports the Control Panel's Network icon. Your network may just pop up with a message saying *Hello, I'm your network. OK.* In that case, you have to control your network from somewhere else. You probably have to run the network software under MS-DOS.

Note: If you don't see a Network dialog box when you double-click the Network icon, then your software may have its own control panel. Skip ahead to the next section, "Custom Network Control Panels."

Don't worry if your Control Panel's Network dialog box isn't very useful. Most of the standard networking chores—connecting disk drives, using network printers, and so on—are handled elsewhere in Windows.

Custom Network Control Panels

If your network cannot be controlled from the Control Panel's Network dialog box, then you can use an MS-DOS window to access the network's shell program, or you can create a PIF for the network shell and run the shell as a program under Windows. Pick one of these methods and then experiment to make sure it works, by running your network shell in Windows and testing your drive and printer connections. If these methods are incompatible with Windows, you can still use File Manager and the

Control Panel's Printers dialog box to make or break network connections. (These procedures are covered in "Using Windows with Your Network," later in this chapter.)

Note: Do not log on or off your network from within an MS-DOS window. Some networks work without a hitch when you do this; others may become unstable.

Some network software comes with special Windows programs that become the "control panel" and more for the network. (In a similar way, the Adobe Type Manager program is a custom control panel for PostScript fonts in Windows.) For example, the LANtastic for Windows network has a custom control panel that gives you network control from within Windows.

LANtastic for Windows' program displays buttons that let you control network connections, printers, disk drives, and servers and perform general network management. It also has buttons for network mail and chat. This program fits very well with the Windows way of doing things. Figure 8-4 shows the Drive Connections control panel, in which you make network disk drive connections by dragging hard drive icons to drive letter slots—a simple, logical, and graphical way to make network drive connections. You use a similar panel for printer connections.

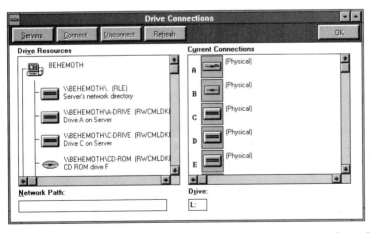

Figure 8-4. *The LANtastic for Windows Drive Connections control panel.*

Note: LANtastic for Windows is a networking product separate from LANtastic versions 3.x and 4.x, which you can also run with Windows.

SYSTEM.INI Network Settings

In this section, I describe the network settings in three SYSTEM.INI sections: [boot], [standard], and [386Enh]. The [Network] section in WIN.INI contains additional information; I cover that in the next section of this chapter.

I provide this information for reference only. Generally speaking, there's no need to change the settings made by Windows Setup. You should edit SYSTEM.INI only if you're directed to make additional tweaks by the NETWORKS.WRI file.

In SYSTEM.INI's [boot] section, you'll find a single entry that deals with networks:

network.drv=*filename* This entry specifies the name of your network driver.

The [standard] section can contain two entries related to networks:

NetHeapSize=*number* This entry specifies the size of the buffer that Windows creates in conventional memory for transferring information over the network. *number*, which indicates the number of kilobytes, must be a multiple of 4. The default is 8.

Int28Filter=*number* This entry describes how Windows treats interrupt 28h (hexadecimal)—the "idle" interrupt—which is used by some networks to schedule background tasks. In the *Int28Filter* entry, *number* specifies how often Windows passes interrupt 28h through to MS-DOS programs that are running in standard mode. The default value is 10, which means every tenth signal is passed. You can set this number lower if you notice inconsistent network performance. For additional information, refer to Chapter 5.

The [386Enh] section contains a wealth of settings that affect network performance. Two settings, *AllVMsExclusive* and *FileSysChange*, are discussed in Chapter 5. The *EMMExclude* setting is described in Chapter 4. (This setting is required for network adapter hardware that sits in upper memory. You need to exclude the adapter's address using *EMMExclude*—as well as the *x* option of EMM386.EXE—so that the memory it occupies is not stomped on by a TSR or device driver that is loaded high. Excluding areas of memory is also explained in Chapter 1.)

Here are the rest of the network-related entries in [386Enh]:

InDOSPolling=*Boolean* This entry directs Windows to be kinder to TSRs—including network drivers. These programs set the "in DOS" or "MS-DOS is busy" flag when they use MS-DOS functions. If *InDOSPolling* is set to *On*, Windows waits while the program accesses MS-DOS. The wait slows down Windows but makes it more compatible with some networks (and TSRs). The default value is *Off*.

Int28Critical=*Boolean* When set to *On*, this entry prevents networks from hanging up during critical operations made while handling interrupt 28h. Setting this entry to *Off* may improve performance on non-networked machines.

NetAsynchFallback=*Boolean* This entry enables Windows to allocate extra memory to networks that make "asynchronous NetBIOS requests." When *NetAsynchFallback* is set to *On*, Windows attempts to save a network call that would otherwise fail because of lack of space in the network buffer. Windows allocates another buffer, suspends other applications, and waits for a specified time for the network function to succeed. How long it waits is specified by the *NetAsynchTimeout* entry.

NetAsynchTimeout=*seconds* This entry specifies the number of seconds Windows waits for a successful asynchronous NetBIOS request. The default value is 5.0 seconds; a single decimal value is accepted. This entry is used only when *NetAsynchFallback* is set to *On*.

NetDMASize=*kilobytes* This entry specifies the size of the network DMA (direct memory access) buffer. The default size is 32 on machines, such as the IBM PS/2, that use the Micro Channel Architecture. The default is 0 for all other machines.

NetHeapSize=*number* This entry sets the size of a buffer that Windows creates in conventional memory for transferring information over the network. *number*, which indicates the number of kilobytes, must be a multiple of 4. The default is 12.

Network=*devicename ¦ filename* This entry specifies the name of your network driver. *devicename is an internal driver name; *filename* is the name of a network driver with the extension 386 that came with your network. You might see both options, and sometimes more than one *devicename is used. You change this entry by changing networks in the Windows Setup program.

PSPIncrement=*number* This entry, which is used in conjunction with the *UniqueDOSPSP* entry, specifies the amount of memory Windows reserves to prevent two MS-DOS programs from conflicting over a network. (PSP stands for *program segment prefix*, which is a block of information that MS-DOS creates and places in memory right before the rest of the program.) *number* sets the number of 16-byte blocks Windows reserves between each MS-DOS program or virtual machine.

ReflectDOSInt2A=*Boolean* This entry tells Windows how to deal with interrupt 2Ah (hexadecimal). If your network requires that interrupt, then setting this entry to *On* directs Windows to pass the interrupt to other applications. Setting this entry to *Off* makes Windows run more efficiently.

TimerCriticalSection=*milliseconds* This entry tells Windows to go into a "critical section" when it receives a timer interrupt and specifies a timeout period for the interrupt. Setting a timeout period causes Windows' performance to suffer, but the timeout period is necessary for some networks that need to use the timer interrupt without being interrupted by anything else. The default value is 0.

TokenRingSearch=*Boolean* This entry needs to be set to *On* if you're using a token ring type of network. Windows then searches for the token ring network hardware.

UniqueDOSPSP=*Boolean* This entry prevents certain networks from crashing by directing Windows to start every MS-DOS program at a different address. Some networks use the addresses in the program's PSP (program segment prefix) to determine which program is running. Because Windows is a multitasking environment, it is possible to have multiple programs sitting at the same address. If you quit one, the network may assume you've quit them all, which probably isn't what you want. Setting this keyword to *On* prevents such an assumption. The related entry, *PSPIncrement*, specifies the amount of memory Windows uses to separate various programs.

WIN.INI's [Network] Section

WIN.INI has a [Network] section that describes a few attributes of your network, including any network connections made in Windows. These settings are controlled either from File Manager's Network Connection dialog box or from the Control Panel's Network dialog box. (Using File Manager with your network is covered in "Using File Manager on a Network," later in this chapter.)

drive=\\server\device Entries using this format show which disk drive connections you've set up using File Manager. *drive* is a local drive letter, which is set to the network path of the drive. The network path, in turn, consists of the names of the server and device. Several entries may specify various drives to which your computer is connected. An equal sign followed by nothing designates a drive that was formerly used.

port=\\server\printer Entries using this format indicate printer port reassignments or the connection of a network printer. *port* is the name of the local printer port—say LPT1. The port is set to the network path, which consists of the server and printer names. As with disk drive entries, more than one printer port entry may appear in the [Network] section.

InRestoreNetConnect=0 ¦ 1 If this entry is set to 1, Windows automatically reestablishes the network disk drive and printer connections made the last time you ran Windows. If the entry is set to 0, Windows does not reestablish the same connections. The default is 1. You can set the value using the Control Panel's Network dialog box, or you can edit WIN.INI directly. The *InRestoreNetConnect* keyword might be abbreviated to *Restore* for some networks.

Note: The location of the information about disk drive and printer connections varies depending on the type of network you have. For example, if you're running Microsoft LAN Manager 2.1, the drive and port entries are stored in the file LMUSER.INI instead of WIN.INI, and the In-RestoreNetConnect *information is stored in LANMAN.INI in the* autorestore *entry. If you're running Artisoft LANtastic, the information is stored in WINFILE.INI in a special section called [Previous].*

USING WINDOWS WITH YOUR NETWORK

When your network is up and running and your network connections have been made, Windows works just like it did before, except for differences in four areas: The Network icon appears in the Control Panel; the Network Connections command is enabled on File Manager's Disk menu; the network commands are enabled on Print Manager's menus; and you'll be able to use the Network button when selecting a printer connection in the Control Panel's Printers dialog box.

The network configurations you can make in these four areas affect only how you use the network under Windows. If you've already made your network connections at the command prompt, then you have nothing else to do. Windows works the same with or without a network installed. But with a network installed, you can use the network's resources to do all sorts of things: access files on other systems, use network printers, send mail, play multi-player games, and more.

Using File Manager on a Network

All disk drive connections (both the ones you make before you start Windows and the ones you make in Windows) are reflected in File Manager. Icons for the network drives appear at the top of the File Manager window, along with ones for the floppy and hard drives (plus RAM drives, CD-ROM drives, and so on) installed on your system. The icon for network drives is shown in Figure 8-5, along with File Manager's other drive icons.

For example, suppose you issued a command at the command prompt to connect your PC to a hard drive on a server, which you assigned the drive letter *W*. When you click the network drive's icon to access drive W in File Manager, you're accessing the hard drive on the server. The files and

Floppy drive

Hard drive

Network drive

CD-ROM drive

RAM drive

Figure 8-5. *The drive icons used in File Manager.*

directories you see in the drive window are actually on the server, though you can access and use them as if they were on a local drive called W.

Note: You don't have to go through File Manager to access drive W. You can also type w: *at the command prompt to access the network drive.*

You can connect to several network drives on several servers, and they'll each be represented as a network drive icon and be as accessible as if they were local drives on your system. The only time you'll need to change anything is if you want to make or break a network drive connection.

You can easily make or break a network drive connection from File Manager. Simply choose the Network Connections command from the Disk menu to display a dialog box like the one shown in Figure 8-6. (For some networks, Windows offers two commands on the Disk menu: Connect Network Drive and Disconnect Network Drive. If you're using such a network, choose the command that suits your needs.)

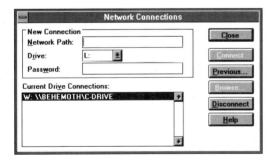

Figure 8-6. *The Network Connections dialog box in File Manager.*

Note: You might find it easier to work with network connections outside File Manager. Some networks supply their own control panel that offers easy ways to make or break connections. You can also modify network connections from an MS-DOS window. Choose whichever method you want. The results are the same.

Current drive connections are listed in the box with that name. The drive letter is shown first, followed by the network path (the server name and drive device name). To break a connection, highlight it in the list, and then click the Disconnect button.

To make a new connection, enter the network path in the Network Path text box. This is the tricky part because network paths can be hard to remember. After entering the network path, assign it an available drive letter from the drop-down list. If you need to enter a password to access that drive, type the password in the Password text box. (This box does not assign passwords; it lets you enter them when they're required by your network.) Click Connect to connect to the network drive.

Note: Clicking the Previous button displays a list of the network drives you've previously connected to. If you've entered the pathname before, you can fetch it from this list quicker than retyping it.

On networks that allow you to look around for the server you want, the Browse button in the Network Connections dialog box is enabled. Figure 8-7 shows the Network Disk Resources dialog box that appears on LAN Manager networks when you click the Browse button. You can select a domain and view that domain's available servers, as well as its resources. Browsing is particularly handy if you are not very familiar with your network's drive nomenclature.

Network Printing

Printing on a network printer in Windows works as seamlessly as accessing a network drive. The best way to ensure that printing is hassle free is to configure your network printer before you start Windows. Then, using the Control Panel's Printers dialog box, select your network printer's type from the list, click the Connect button, and then click Network. Windows

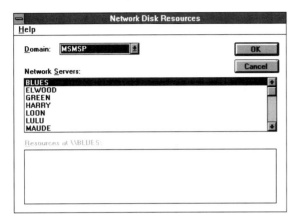

Figure 8-7. *The Network Disk Resources dialog box.*

displays a Printers-Network Connections dialog box that is similar to File Manager's Network Connections dialog box (see Figure 8-6).

Current network printer connections are listed in the Current Printer Connections box. Each network printer's path is assigned to a printer port device, typically LPT1 or LPT2. The path specifies the name of the printer's

When You Lose a Connection

Some networks log you off a network drive after a period of inactivity. You'll need to reconnect to the drive before you can use it again. If you don't reestablish the connection File Manager reports that the drive is unavailable. You may want to manually disconnect from drives you are not using, rather than have the network do it. Networks that log you off inactive drives might do so for a couple of reasons. The first is security. Leaving an unattended PC connected to a sensitive network drive might enable someone else to log on—using your name—and you'll be held accountable for what they do. The second reason is server availability. Some networks allow only a certain number of people to be connected to a server at one time. The network logs you off to make room for others who might be trying to connect. To be safe and courteous, log off the drive yourself.

server and the printer itself. To make a connection to a network printer, specify the printer's path in the Network Path text box, and click the Connect button. To break a connection to a network printer, select the printer's path from the Current Printer Connections list, and click Disconnect. As in File Manager's Network Connections dialog box, the Printers-Network Connections dialog box might offer Browse and Previous buttons that make it easier to figure out the path of the printer you want.

Note: Windows for Workgroups' Print Manager makes it easy to manage network printer connections. See "Networks and Windows for Workgroups" later in this chapter for more information.

When you tell Windows to print to a network printer, it sends the file to Print Manager, which flushes the file right on out the network hose. To see the status of the file, you can use Print Manager, but you'd better be quick. Network files flow so fast that you have to be pretty swift to see them in Print Manager.

Note: Some networks don't use Print Manager; for example, LANtastic for Windows has you disable Print Manager in favor of its own spooler.

Using Multiple Network Printers

You may have a choice between several printers on your network. The best way to switch between printers is to configure Windows for each of them. First set up and install each network printer according to the type of printer and its network connection. For example, suppose you have a LaserJet III attached to a server called Gzunda. Using the Control Panel's Printers dialog box, install the LaserJet III as you would any printer. To make the printer connection, click the Connect button and then the Network button. Select a port for the printer, and then type in the network path—something like *gzunda\ljetiii* (or whatever the proper network printer name is). Repeat this process for the other printers on your network. You can use either the same port for each network connection or different ports—it doesn't make any difference.

After you install and connect to the network printers you want to use, their names appear in the list of installed printers in the Control Panel's Printers dialog box. You can switch among them by choosing the Print Setup command from any application's File menu.

Some networks have specific quirks when it comes to connecting multiple printers. This description is generic, though it should work with most networks. If the procedure I've described doesn't seem to work with your network, check your network's documentation for the specifics.

Note: *With Artisoft LANtastic, you can use only LPT2 and LPT3 for remote printer connections. LPT1 is reserved for a printer that is connected directly to your own PC.*

Your network may log you off a printer after a period of inactivity, and you may have to reconnect your network printers when you want to use them. A possible solution to this problem is to write a short batch file that reestablishes printer links using network commands. You can then run the batch file before you print. Figure 8-8 shows an example of such a batch file.

```
@echo off
REM Re-link LaserJet III down the hall
use lpt1: /d
use lpt1: \\gzunda\ljetIII
```

Figure 8-8. *A batch file that re-establishes printer connections.*

In this example, the first Use command disables the connection. This command may cause an error if the connection is already disabled, but it avoids a worse error if you attempt to reconnect to a printer to which you're already connected. The second Use command reconnects you to the printer.

Network Groups for Program Manager

If you work in an office where several people access the same set of programs and files on a server—for example, client or product information files—you can create icons for those files, put them in a single Program Manager group, and put that group on a network server. Then anyone can add the group to his or her Program Manager window. Giving everyone point-and-click access requires a lot of setup.

Start by creating the group in Program Manager on your own PC. Choose New from Program Manager's File menu, select the Program Group option button, and then click OK. Give the group a description—something like *Network Group*—and then give it a filename (one that is not already used on the server). For example, you might name the group SHARED. Click OK to create the group.

Next add the server's files and programs to the group. To do so, choose New from Program Manager's File menu, select the Program Item option button, click OK, and fill in the resulting dialog box. The files and programs that you add are all stored on the server, so you must be sure to specify their full pathnames, network drive letter and all. Each time you add an item, Windows warns you that because the item is on a network drive, you might not always have access to the file or program. Click OK in response to the warning. When you're done adding items, use File Manager to copy the group's file (in our example, the file is named SHARED.GRP) from your PC to the server, and use the Properties command on File Manager's File menu to set the group's read-only status.

With the network group file copied and protected on the server, go back to Program Manager, and delete the original network group from your PC. Then use the File menu's New command to add the network group (now found on the server) to your Program Manager. Specify the server's network drive letter and the group's filename to add the group. Add the group in this way to each workstation that needs to access the group.

Note: Setting up a network group is much easier if each workstation accessing the network group uses the same drive letter for the server on which the group is stored. If the workstations use different drive letters, you'll need to reset the item properties for each icon in the network group on each workstation.

Setting up network groups is complicated stuff, but it works. If you want to slap further protection on Program Manager network groups, consider adding the [restrictions] section to the PROGMAN.INI file on each workstation. Table 8-1 lists some of the settings you may want to include. (More information on the restriction settings in PROGMAN.INI is given in Chapter 2.)

Restriction	Setting
Disable Run command	*NoRun=1*
Disable File menu entirely	*NoFileMenu=1*
Disable Exit Windows command	*NoClose=1*
Don't save settings on exit	*NoSaveSettings=1*
Cannot create, move, copy or delete item	*EditLevel=1*
Cannot create, move, copy, or delete anything	*EditLevel=2*
Disable Command Line text box in Properties dialog box	*EditLevel=3*
Disable Properties dialog box	*EditLevel=4*

Table 8-1. *Restrictions you can impose by editing PROGMAN.INI.*

Using Windows on a File Server

You may be running some applications from a file server and others directly from your own hard drive. Or you may be running Windows and any applications entirely from a file server, perhaps because you are working on a *diskless workstation*—essentially a *smart terminal.* An example of a server/diskless workstation setup might be a Windows system in a library, where security reasons prohibit local hard drives.

Setting up a diskless workstation to run Windows on a file server requires that the workstation be booted remotely. In some cases, the boot program on the server sets up a PROM (programmable read-only memory) chip on the diskless workstation's network adapter. The PROM is programmed to boot MS-DOS and then load Windows from the server. In other cases, the workstation is booted from a floppy drive. Either way, only the programs required to start both MS-DOS and Windows are loaded on the workstation.

Each network system does things differently, and a diskless workstation running Windows will be customized by the network administrator to work best with that network. However, note that you need a local swap file when you run Windows in enhanced mode and that this swap file must be on a hard drive or a floppy drive, not a RAM drive.

Under most circumstances, I recommend using a peer-to-peer network rather than a file server for running Windows in enhanced mode. This setup may make your system susceptible to some security risks, but by fully implementing passwords, locking directories, and attaching timeouts to network drives and printers, you can create and maintain a secure system.

NETWORKS AND WINDOWS FOR WORKGROUPS

In most small offices, the ideal solution for networking your computers running Windows is to buy Windows for Workgroups. Essentially, it's a custom version of Microsoft Windows 3.1 that includes peer-to-peer networking abilities, mail and chat programs, workgroup scheduling software, plus special enhancements to the File Manager and Print Manager. All you need is the networking hardware (adapter cards and hoses); Windows for Workgroups supplies the brains (the peer-to-peer networking capabilities).

Note: Windows for Workgroups allows you to create a peer-to-peer network in your workgroup. You can share files, disk drives, subdirectories, and printers with other PCs in your workgroup that also run Windows for Workgroups. If you need a powerful, central file server system, however, you should look into Windows NT or some other solution.

To set everything up, you'll need to install Windows for Workgroups on each of your networked PCs. That's about the toughest part. Everything else—all the network hassle, the configuring and setup, almost all of the rough edges smoothed over in this chapter—is gone. Windows for Workgroups makes working with a small group of networked PCs a snap, because you control your network from within Windows' environment.

New Goodies with Windows for Workgroups

A version of Windows specific to networking is bound to include a lot of interesting networking goodies. These aren't things that you'd miss if you're running standard Windows on a lone PC, but some of these tools are missing from third-party, peer-to-peer solutions for Windows. Specifically, Windows for Workgroups gives you the following bonus features and applets:

An enhanced File Manager The most obvious change to File Manager is the addition of a handy toolbar—similar to the ones you get with Microsoft Excel or Word for Windows. The buttons give you quick access to common File Manager functions, including some new network-specific items. (The toolbar is elaborated on in the next section.)

An enhanced Print Manager Print Manager displays information in readable columns and includes information on documents sent by other PCs to various printers. As with File Manager, a handy toolbar helps you control printing, connect to network printers, share your printer with other people in your workgroup, and so on.

Chat The Chat program enables you to "type" back and forth with other members of the workgroup—similar to the way you would talk on the phone but much more slowly because people can type at a fraction of the speed they can talk. (Using Chat is a great way to contribute to the office gossip without going to the water cooler—and you look like you're working while you do it.)

Custom Network dialog box in the Control Panel The Control Panel's Network dialog box, which is shown in Figure 8-9, serves as the Windows for Workgroups network control center. You can set up the network, configure your hardware, change your password, select your computer's name, and describe how your PC shares its resources.

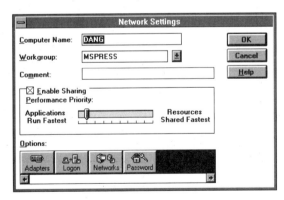

Figure 8-9. *The Control Panel's Network dialog box in Windows for Workgroups.*

Electronic mail Windows for Workgroups comes with its own electronic mail, or "e-mail," application called Mail. You can compose and send messages to one or more members of your workgroup, read replies, send responses, and so on. After you receive a message, you have many options for what to do with it: You can store the message for later retrieval, print it, edit it, send it along to someone else, and more. Mail will likely become a vital communications resource in your workgroup.

Net Watcher The Net Watcher utility provides a summary of who's doing what on the network—which computers have been using which resources and for how long. You can use this utility to see whether someone's been loitering around your system for too long and, if the loiterer is below you on the corporate ladder, you can log them off if you suspect foul play.

Schedule+ Schedule+ is a personal organizer, but on a workgroup scale. It allows you to schedule appointments and projects, record memos, and cross-reference information with other members of your workgroup. With Schedule+, you no longer have to spend hours trying to figure out a time for a meeting. You just specify all the people you want to attend the meeting and ask Schedule+ to let you know when everyone is free. Schedule+ uses the network to check everyone else's schedule and come back with a quick response to your query.

The ClipBook Viewer The ClipBook Viewer is a "super Clipboard" application that allows you to cut and paste—and save—bits of text, charts, graphics, and so on, which can then be shared among members of the workgroup. The ClipBook Viewer lets you copy and paste objects (using OLE) across the network. You can even maintain a link to the original file—and its application—so that if the contents of the original file change, your pasted object's contents are updated.

WinMeter WinMeter is a silly, but occasionally useful, program that monitors your PC's performance. It shows you a graph that describes how much of your processor time is being spent. You can see what percentage of the time is being taken up by computers connected to your machine and the percentage being taken up by the programs you have running on your machine. If you notice your system unexpectedly slowing down, you can use WinMeter to determine the cause and possibly remedy the situation by shutting down a power-consuming task (or by telling Bob in Finance to stop playing Solitaire on your computer).

Windows for Workgroups' File Manager

The first thing standard Windows users get jealous about is Windows for Workgroups' File Manager. The standard version of File Manager has a few scattered menu items for connecting to directories and such, but doesn't have the customized tools that Windows for Workgroups' File Manager packs. (And, face it, some of those tools could be put to good use in standard Windows; the rest of us will just have to sit on the sidelines and be jealous for a while.) The obvious enhancements to File Manager—and those items best-suited to networking—are the toolbar, the ability to share directories with others in your workgroup, and the ease of connecting to other PCs in your workgroup.

Note: You can share directories on your system only if you're running Windows for Workgroups in enhanced mode. In standard mode, you're allowed only to use directories on other systems, not share your own.

The toolbar allows you to perform several network-specific tasks with ease in File Manager. Using various buttons you can connect to or disconnect from a network drive (which could be a directory on a PC) or share or unshare one of your own directories. Other buttons allow you to perform more traditional File Manager duties; for example, view all details or sort by name, type, size, and so on. The toolbar can be customized—or even hidden from view—using commands on the Options menu. When you customize the toolbar, you can add buttons for the File Manager commands you use most frequently or remove buttons you never use.

To share a directory with other people in your workgroup, all you have to do is select the directory in File Manager and click the Share Directory button on the toolbar. File Manager then displays the dialog box shown in Figure 8-10 on the next page. In the dialog box, you can specify the name of the directory, whether it will always be shared, and the type of access people will have to it. To connect to a directory on another computer, click the Connect Network Drive button on the toolbar, select the computer's name and the name of the directory, and click OK. You can then access the directory just as you would a local drive on your machine.

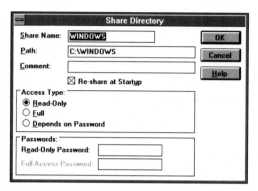

Figure 8-10. *The Share Directory dialog box.*

Other than the networking enhancements, toolbar, and status line, the File Manager in Windows for Workgroups works identically to the File Manager in standard Windows. Just remember that some of the drives you are using or directories you are connected to may be on another user's computer and not your own. (The icon by the drive or directory in the bar below the toolbar is your clue as to what's yours and what's someone else's.)

COMMUNICATIONS FROM WITHIN WINDOWS

A network can be defined as two or more computers communicating. That communication doesn't have to involve a network adapter card and a file server. You can use a modem to connect one PC to another PC or to an online service such as CompuServe, GEnie, or Prodigy. This type of communication isn't like a file server connection, and it doesn't offer a practical way of using a remote printer. But it's still a network.

To access an online network with a PC, you need a modem and the software to control it. You install the modem either internally or externally and connect it to one of your PC's serial ports. You then use telecommunications software to control the modem. Before we go any further, let me warn you: Of all the software in the universe, telecommunications software is the most primitive and ugly.

Setting Up for Communications

Modems come in two flavors: external and internal. Both models connect to a serial port: The external model plugs into a real serial port at the back of your computer, whereas the internal model is usually assigned a serial port through software or some hardware doohickey. The telecommunications software then communicates with the modem through this serial, or COM, port. Four serial ports are standard for MS-DOS, though most PCs have only one or two serial ports: COM1 and COM2. (Your PC may have more than four serial ports, in which case they are handled by the special driver software supplied for the task that requires so many serial ports.)

You may have already plugged a mouse into one of your serial ports. This type of mouse is known as a serial mouse, as opposed to a bus mouse, which plugs into its own port or a custom adapter card. A serial mouse uses a COM port, typically COM1 or COM2, just like a modem. As long as either COM1 or COM2 is still vacant for your modem, you'll have no trouble. Problems may arise, however, if COM3 and COM4 are brought into the picture.

Although MS-DOS supports up to four serial ports, it can really handle only two because of a limitation in the PC's design with respect to interrupt request lines (IRQs), which the computer uses to communicate with its serial ports. Other conflicts may arise with the COM port's *base address*, the location in memory where the port's "control registers" are placed. Things can get quite messy when two ports start duking it out for the same IRQ.

Table 8-2 on the next page lists the serial ports available in a PC, along with their common base addresses and IRQ values. What determines these numbers? Typically, they're chosen by the serial port hardware or a sctup program that configures the hardware. The object here is to configure everything so that no two serial ports conflict.

Note: Always reboot your PC after changing a serial port's base address or IRQ.

Serial Port	Base Address	IRQ
COM1	3F8	4
COM2	2F8	3
COM3	3E8	4
COM4	2E8	3

Table 8-2. *MS-DOS's serial ports and their common base addresses and IRQs.*

Dealing with Conflicting Ports

You know that two ports are in conflict when something—your mouse, your modem, or whatever else you have plugged into a serial port—doesn't work. Or perhaps the modem works, but characters appear slowly. Another telltale sign is this Windows error message: *The COMx port is assigned to an MS-DOS application. Do you want to reassign the port to Windows?* When you see this, you have a conflict.

If you don't have a serial port conflict right now, you can skip ahead to "Setting Up Serial Ports in the Control Panel," later in this chapter. If you do have a conflict, here's how you can resolve it.

Fixing Your Hardware's COM Port Base Addresses

First you should make sure that your serial port hardware is properly configured. Check your computer's documentation to see whether the serial

---

Mouse-Modem Conflicts

Here's an easy solution for the serial mouse vs. modem problem: If your mouse is on an even-numbered serial port, put your modem on an odd-numbered port, or vice-versa. The goal is to avoid putting the mouse on COM1 and the modem on COM3, or the mouse on COM2 and the modem on COM4. Because the even ports share one IRQ and the odd ports share another, this arrangement avoids any conflict.

Here's another tip: Try to avoid installing a serial mouse on COM3 or COM4.

ports have the addresses and IRQ values shown in Table 8-2. If they don't, make a note of the values used. Then exit Windows.

Next run the Debug program that comes with MS-DOS by typing *debug* at the command prompt. At Debug's hyphen prompt, type the following command:

```
-d40:0 L10
```

That's the D (Dump) command, 40-colon-0, a space, then an *L*, and 10. (All the numbers are in hexadecimal, but that's no big deal here.) Debug displays a row of text on your screen that looks similar to this one:

```
0040:0000 F8 03 F8 02 00 00 00 00-78 03 00 00 00 00 00 00
```

Debug is showing you the base address values for the serial ports and printer ports in your PC. The eight values to the left of the hyphen between 00 and 78 are serial port base addresses; the values to the right are printer port addresses. Each address is stored as two digits *in reverse order*. In the example, that translates into the following port values:

COM1 = 03F8
COM2 = 02F8
COM3 = 0000 (no COM3 on this computer)
COM4 = 0000 (no COM4 either)

The values you see on your screen may be different. I've listed the output for my PC, which uses the default values (and has no conflicts). Type *q* to quit Debug. If the values on your screen match the base addresses assigned for your hardware or the defaults shown in Table 8-2, you're okay at the hardware end. Now all you have to worry about is the Windows end. Skip ahead to "Fixing Windows' COM Port Base Addresses."

If the base addresses don't match your hardware specifications or the defaults, you can patch them using a Debug script. The idea is to "poke in" the proper base addresses, correcting the inaccurate addresses your computer is using. Here is how the script should look for COM1:

```
e40:0
f8 03
q
```

The first line shows the memory location of the COM port. The second line lists the base address (03F8), but in reverse order; the last two digits are specified first, followed by the first part of the base address. Type this script into a text file, making sure you press Enter at the end of each line. Save the file to disk as COM1FIX.SCR.

Figure 8-11 shows the script files you would create to patch the COM ports to the default values MS-DOS uses. You must create a separate file for each COM port that needs fixing. Remember to specify the proper values for your ports—in reverse order.

```
e 40:0            e 40:2
f8 03             f8 02
q                 q
COM1FIX.SCR       COM2FIX.SCR


e 40:4            e 40:6
e8 03             e8 02
q                 q
COM3FIX.SCR       COM4FIX.SCR
```

Figure 8-11. *The Debug scripts for changing incorrect COM port base addresses.*

To apply the patch to the COM1 port, add the following command to AUTO-EXEC.BAT:

```
debug < com1fix.scr > nul
```

Be sure to specify the proper pathname for the COM*x*FIX.SCR file and for Debug. Insert the command toward the beginning of your AUTO-EXEC.BAT file, and use as many commands as you need to correct the serial port conflicts in memory.

Note: Many computers have setup programs that enable you to configure your hardware. If you can use the setup program to correct the COM port base addresses, use the program instead of Debug.

Fixing Windows' COM Port Base Addresses

Once you're certain that your hardware is configured properly, you should check the settings that Windows uses for base addresses, and fix them if necessary. Go back into Windows and open the Control Panel's Ports dialog box. Double-click the port whose base address you want to check, and then click the Advanced button in the dialog box that appears. The dialog box that appears next allows you to specify the base address and IRQ number for the port. If the base address value is different from the one your hardware uses, change it. The change is reflected in the *COMxBase* entry that can be found in the [386Enh] section of your SYSTEM.INI file. Be sure to check the base address for each COM port you are using.

Setting Up Serial Ports in the Control Panel

In addition to setting the proper base address, you can use the Control Panel's Ports dialog box to enter other information about your PC's serial ports. The Ports dialog box lists all four ports, whether they're installed on your PC or not. To check the values of a port, double-click it to display a Settings dialog box like the one in Figure 8-12, which allows you to set the baud rate, data bits, parity, stop bits, and flow control for the port.

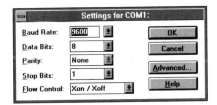

Figure 8-12. *The Settings dialog box, which allows you to make serial port settings.*

The settings you see mirror the values for that serial port specified in WIN.INI's [ports] section. (These settings are covered in the next section.) Clicking the Advanced button allows you to specify the base address and IRQ number for the port. If you change these values, you'll be prompted to restart Windows so that the new base address or IRQ values in your updated SYSTEM.INI can take effect.

Most of the time, you won't need to alter any of these settings. Telecommunications programs under Windows can control the serial port attached to your modem. And serial printers are controlled using the Printers dialog box in the Control Panel. However, you use the Settings dialog box to control the serial port settings for other devices not specifically controlled by Windows—devices you may have configured under MS-DOS using the Mode command.

COM Settings in WIN.INI

Windows' initialization files contain oodles of interesting tidbits regarding your serial ports. Most of these settings are controlled using the Control Panel's Ports dialog box; others are technical in nature. Everything is described here.

There are descriptions in WIN.INI's [ports] section of the various ports attached to your PC and how they're set up. You may have previously set this information using the Mode command at the command prompt. For all COM ports, the following format is used in WIN.INI:

> *port-name:=speed,parity,word-length,stop-bits[,flow-control]*

port-name is the name of an output device—or a filename. Windows accepts COM*x* for serial ports, LPT*x* for printer ports, EPT for an IBM hardware port, FILE for a filename, or LPT*x*.DOS for the MS-DOS printer port (which circumvents Windows).

The *speed*, *parity*, *word-length*, *stop-bits*, and *flow-control* values are all based on the settings in the Settings dialog box (see Figure 8-12), accessed from the Control Panel's Ports dialog box. For *flow-control*, the values used are *x* for Xon/Xoff and *p* for Hardware. If you select None in the Settings dialog box, a value for flow control is not included in WIN.INI.

In addition to being set by the Control Panel's Ports dialog box, these entries can also be controlled by Window's telecommunications programs and any serial printer configurations you may have made. There is no reason to edit these values directly.

COM Settings in SYSTEM.INI

In SYSTEM.INI's [boot] section, you'll find the serial communications driver specified by the *comm.drv* keyword. Under most circumstances, the COMM.DRV file is specified.

comm.drv=*filename* The COMM.DRV driver controls all the serial ports in your PC.

In the [386Enh] section, a whole clot of COM settings can appear. Not all of these are required to configure and use the serial ports on your PC. Note that for each COM*x* entry, four items can appear, each specifying a value for one COM port.

COMxAutoAssign=*number* These entries describe how Windows deals with two programs that are trying to use the same serial port. A value of −1 specifies first-come, first-served. Windows warns you that two programs are trying to use the same port and asks you to select one or the other. A value of 0 specifies a free-for-all. Otherwise, a positive value indicates the number of seconds (less than 1000) Windows waits after one application stops using the port before it allows the second application access. The default is 2.

COMxBase=*address* These entries set the base addresses for the COM ports. Windows assumes the values specified in low memory unless these entries appear in SYSTEM.INI, so you should always specify all four values. You can change these entries by using the Control Panel's Ports dialog box and clicking the Advanced button in the Settings dialog box.

COMBoostTime=*milliseconds* This entry indicates how much time a program has to process a serial port interrupt. The default value is 2. If you notice your MS-DOS telecommunications programs are losing characters, specify a higher value.

COMxBuffer=*characters* These entries set the size of the communications buffer. The default is 128 characters. Set these entries to a higher value if you notice your telecommunications program is dropping characters during transmission. Check the *COMxProtocol* entry (discussed later in this section), which may also help solve the problem of lost characters.

COMdrv30=*Boolean* This entry specifies whether the virtual device driver for serial communications should use its own copy of the serial ports driver. Set this entry to *On* if you're using a Windows 3.0 communications driver. Under Windows 3.1, set this entry to *Off*.

COM*x*FIFO=*Boolean* These entries are set to *On* by default, which directs Windows to use the FIFO (first in, first out) buffer of the serial port's 16550 UART chip. This is technical stuff, so you should set this value to *Off* only if you know what a UART chip is and why FIFO should be disabled.

COM*x*Irq=*number* These entries set the IRQ number for the various serial ports. To disable a port, specify a value of –1. Set these entries by using the Control Panel's Ports dialog box and clicking the Advanced button in the Settings dialog box.

COMIrqSharing=*Boolean* This entry specifies that your serial port interrupts can be shared between COM1 and COM3 and between COM2 and COM4. The default is *On* for most machines.

COM*x*Protocol=XOFF¦*blank* These entries control how Windows deals with lost characters during text transmission through a serial port. If an entry is set to XOFF, Windows pauses when an XOFF character (Ctrl-S) is sent and waits for the next character to be received before resuming transmission. If you don't have a problem with lost characters, you can leave these entries blank. If you still lose characters with XOFF specified, try increasing the value of the *COMxBuffer* keyword.

MaxCOMPort=*number* This entry specifies the maximum number of serial ports you can use in enhanced mode. The default value is 4. If you're using more than four serial ports, you can specify a higher value.

The Terminal Program

Windows comes with a practical, though primitive, telecommunications program called Terminal, which allows you to use Windows with a modem to connect to various online services. This book isn't going to provide a tutorial on the Terminal program, but here are some tips and suggestions for using it:

■ Like any other Windows-based application, it's best to maximize the Terminal window to fill the entire screen.

■ Enter all the settings for an online session with a particular online service, and save them to disk in a TRM file. Enter the service's phone number, terminal emulation, terminal preferences, and communications settings. (The settings can all be modified using the commands in the Settings menu.) Then when you want to connect with the service, all you have to do is load the TRM file and call.

- If you're calling a typical PC bulletin board service (BBS), you may want to set terminal emulation to DEC VT-100 (ANSI) and select the Terminal font from the Terminal Preferences dialog box. The Terminal font contains all the IBM line drawing characters used by many bulletin boards. Display the dialog box by choosing the Terminal Preferences command from the Settings menu.

- Always remember to properly log off an online service before you hang up. Usually, the other computer drops the line when you log off. If it doesn't, choose Hangup from the Phone menu.

Terminal allows you to send or receive files from a remote system or "host" computer. Sending files is called *uploading*; receiving files is called *downloading*. Terminal lets you send and receive both raw text (ASCII) and binary (programs and non-text) files.

To send a text file, choose Send Text File from the Transfers menu, specify the filename in the dialog box, and click OK. To receive a text file, choose Receive Text File, and specify the filename.

When you send or receive a binary file, you must specify the *protocol* that both computers will use in the transfer. The protocol helps to assure that the file isn't corrupted during transmission. Terminal supports the XModem and Kermit protocols.

To select between XModem and Kermit, use the Binary Transfers command on the Settings menu. XModem is a general purpose, file transfer protocol, supported by nearly all PC online services. Kermit is a 7-bit protocol used on some mainframes (and, yes, it's named after the frog).

If you're sending a binary file, direct the host computer to receive using either XModem or Kermit. Follow the instructions on your screen. When the host is ready, begin sending the file by choosing Send Binary File from the Transfers menu. If you're receiving a file, direct the host to send using either XModem or Kermit. When the host is ready, choose Receive Binary File from the Transfers menu.

As you're uploading or downloading files, you can do other work on your PC. My advice is to work (okay, play Solitaire) on top of the Terminal window instead of minimizing Terminal to an icon. That way, you can check the progress of the file transfer and dodge right back into Terminal when the transfer's complete.

Setting Up a Null Modem Connection

It's possible to "network" two single PCs using nothing more than a phone cable or a special serial cable. This type of networking is known as a *direct connection*. It's impractical for true networking, but it is a convenient way to send files between two PCs, especially two PCs with different disk formats.

To directly connect two PCs, both must have serial ports or modems. If they haveserial ports, you need to connect them using a special null modem cable or a standard serial cable with a null modem adapter. In either case, the null modem switches the send-receive lines between the two PCs, allowing them to both talk and listen to each other. If the PCs have modems, you need to string a phone line between them, plugging the line into the Line Out jack on the backs of both modems.

With the computers umbilically connected, fire up Terminal on each of them. Set the serial port using the Settings menu's Communications command, like this: Set the baud rate to 9600 data bits to 8, parity to None, and stop bit(s) to 1. Click OK. Then type something on one of the PCs. Whatever you type should appear on the second PC. If it doesn't, they're either not connected properly or they're talking at different speeds. Make sure both systems are hooked up and check that the speed settings used by Terminal are the same.

When everything is working, you can use the Send Binary File and Receive Binary File commands on the Transfers menu to send files back and forth between the two PCs. On the computer that's sending the file, choose Send Binary File, and on the other computer, choose Receive Binary File. The XModem protocol works best.

Note: Run a few experiments to see how the file transfer goes. Then if everything works okay, try a higher speed. Windows Terminal can handle up to 19,200 baud.

This way of sending files back and forth is rather primitive, but it works fine for quick PC-to-PC transfers. If you often make this kind of transfer, I recommend getting a third party program—something like Traveling Software's Lap-Link. Lap-Link and similar programs come with software that performs high speed file transfer between two computers, even between a PC and a Mac. Some programs also come packaged with the required cables, so there's nothing more to buy.

SENDING A FAX IN WINDOWS

One of the niftiest communications crazes is the combined fax/modem. This device can be used like a modem for traditional online cruising and can also send and receive type-3 facsimiles. Unlike a traditional fax machine, which uses paper to send and receive images, a fax/modem uses digital information. (Obviously, you can't stuff a sheet of paper into your disk drive or plaster a paper image against the monitor and trace it using Paintbrush.)

The fax/modem does have some disadvantages. Fax/modem software is sluggish, and the fax/modem draws on the PC's processing power when receiving a fax; everything slows down. The image is received as a digital bitmap, often a PC Paintbrush file that takes up an incredible amount of storage space on your hard disk. Typically, you'll want to print out faxes rather than store them because disk space disappears quickly if you often receive faxes.

On the other hand, the fax/modem offers terrific advantages. First it uses only one device and a single phone line to accomplish what two devices and usually two phone lines were required for in the past.

There's no paper to shuffle and no requirement that you stand and feed in one sheet at a time. You can also fax information to several people by issuing a single command.

Under Windows, fax/modem software offers another advantage. In the past, most fax/modems were limited to sending boring old text—no graphics—and you couldn't send scanned images unless you had an expensive desktop scanner. Now you can use Windows' graphical power to create custom faxes and send them directly from Windows, totally eliminating the problem of ugly or boring faxes on a fax/modem.

In Windows, fax/modem software works like a printer driver. You create your fax in Word for Windows, PageMaker, Excel, Corel Draw, or any other application you use to produce hard copy. When the document is ready for faxing, you choose Print Setup from the File menu and select the fax/modem driver from the list of printers. When you choose the Print command, your file is "printed" to the fax/modem. It retains all the graphics, fonts, and layout, just as if a true hard copy were being made.

Receiving faxes also works better under Windows. The fax/modem software can run in the background, receiving a fax while you're doing something else. When the fax is ready, a pop-up message may appear, or the fax/modem software's icon may start blinking at the bottom of the screen.

Various applications are available that give you control over your fax/modem under Windows. Two of the most popular ones are Faxit for Windows from SofNet and WinFax Pro 2.0 from Delrina Technology Inc. Both install as print drivers and come with various utilities for sending, receiving, and working with faxes under Windows.

Chapter 9

Windows and Multimedia

Microsoft's latest, greatest step toward making Windows the PC operating system of the '90s is building in multimedia extensions, a group of drivers that allow your computer to use sound, graphics, and animation to display information and entertain. That's the software part. For hardware, you need a sound card, speakers, a CD-ROM drive, and other optional equipment that will make your PC do incredible things. This chapter gives you a peek at the strange and wondrous stuff multimedia is made of. Consider it dessert.

GETTING SET UP FOR MULTIMEDIA

Multimedia is truly what Windows is made for. Nothing astonishes a friend like having Ethel Merman belt out *There's No Business Like Show Business* through your PC's speaker when you start Windows. Or seeing a four-year-old "reading" a story from a CD-ROM disk that's complete with narration, sound, and animation. Even without all the fancy stuff, you can slide your favorite music CD into a multimedia PC and listen while you work. (I'm listening to Mozart as I'm typing.)

To fully exploit the potential of your PC and to use every part of Windows you paid for, you need multimedia. For hardware, here's the shopping list:

- '386-based PC
- VGA monitor
- Sound card and speakers
- CD-ROM drive

For software, you have Windows 3.1. You'll also need drivers to control your sound card and CD-ROM drive. These drivers should be shipped with the hardware, though some sound drivers do come with Windows.

The official hardware specs for a multimedia PC, or MPC, are as follows:

■ You need a PC with an 80386SX or higher-number processor; 2 MB of RAM minimum (though I recommend 4 MB); a 30-MB hard drive (though, seriously, 80 MB or more is a good size); serial, parallel, MIDI I/O, and joystick ports; and a keyboard and mouse. Basically, any system capable of running Windows in enhanced mode can be used as an MPC. Note that the MIDI I/O and joystick ports aren't required, but they are listed as part of the MPC specs.

■ You need at least a VGA monitor to display multimedia stuff. I highly recommend a 256-color display, with 1 MB of video memory.

■ You need a CD-ROM drive that has an average seek time of 1 second or less and—this is the technical stuff—a "sustained 150 KB-per-second transfer rate without consuming more than 40 percent of CPU bandwidth in the process." In English: Any CD-ROM drive that can output digital audio. Installing and using a CD-ROM drive is covered in "CD-ROM Drives," later in this chapter.

Multimedia and 80286 Machines

The fact that an 80286 PC does not meet multimedia specifications doesn't mean you can't use it as a multimedia machine. An 80286 can be equipped with a sound card and can play music and other sounds just like a '386-based PC can. In fact, Windows' ability to make sound isn't tied to the multimedia extensions at all. You can even add a CD-ROM drive to your 80286 and use Windows with multimedia. The problem is that what you see and hear on an 80286 won't be as clear as it is on a faster PC; sound tends to stutter, and everything works slowly. Adding more memory helps, but the best solution is to get a faster machine.

■ The most exciting part of the MPC specification is the sound card, which gives your PC more oomph than its quaint speaker. Using the sound card, you can play and record sounds and store them in the computer. The sound card also contains a music synthesizer, which can generate and play back music. Some sound cards also have MIDI hookups, bringing musical instruments into the picture.

■ To hear all these lovely sounds, you need speakers, which are usually purchased separately and must have an external power source or batteries. You can also use headphones, which just plug into the back of the sound card.

■ For software, you need Windows 3.1, which comes with the multimedia extensions.

There are three ways to get all this stuff off your shopping list and into your PC:

■ You can buy everything one piece at a time.

■ You can buy a multimedia upgrade kit.

■ You can buy a multimedia PC.

If you already have a PC, consider a multimedia upgrade kit, which comes with a sound card, CD-ROM drive, speakers (sometimes), the drivers, special software, and a few CDs tossed in for effect. Buying the kit is generally cheaper than buying all the pieces separately. However, if you already

Microsoft CD-ROM Extensions

You need the latest version of the Microsoft CD-ROM Extensions (MSCDEX.EXE) to drive your CD-ROM drive. Older versions of the Extensions don't work with MS-DOS version 5 unless the Setver program is loaded. The latest version of the driver doesn't have this limitation. If you don't have the latest version of the MSCDEX driver, you can download it from the Microsoft Download service. Refer to "Secrets You Can Download" in Chapter 4.

have a sound card and speakers, it's cheaper to buy a CD-ROM drive and the software separately.

Several manufacturers market PCs that are specially equipped as MPCs. The only difference between these systems and nonmultimedia PCs is the addition of the sound card and CD-ROM drive.

WINDOWS' SOUND

You don't really need a full multimedia PC to get Windows to talk and squawk. Any computer with a sound card can use Windows' Media Player application to play sound files, Sound Recorder to play and edit the files, and Control Panel to attach sounds to system events. Whether you have a full MPC or an 80286 with a sound card installed, sound works the same way under Windows.

Note: There are lots of sound cards available, many of which work with Windows and play sounds. However, only sound cards that are MPC-compatible can be used with multimedia. If you're buying a separate sound card—not one that is part of a multimedia upgrade kit—make sure it's MPC-compatible. Be buyer-savvy here: Not all sound cards that are compatible with Windows are MPC-compatible.

Selecting a Sound Card

There are many sound cards on the market today, some very cheap and some outrageously expensive. Windows is compatible with just about any of them. If Windows doesn't come with the proper drivers, they're often included with the sound card.

Two of the most popular sound cards are the Sound Blaster and the AdLib. The Roland music cards are also popular, though they command premium prices. In addition to drivers for those brands, Windows also ships with a driver for the Media Vision Thunder Board.

Preferably, your sound card should be able to use one of the sound drivers that comes with Windows. If it can't, the card needs to supply its own driver. For example, the Pro AudioSpectrum sound card comes with its own sound driver, though it can also use the Sound Blaster driver.

My advice for selecting a sound card is to listen to it in the store because some of the cheaper sound cards have an annoying buzz or hum. The stereo cards have interesting demos, but the MPC standard doesn't require stereo; buy a stereo card only if your software (okay, a game) supports it and uses the stereo well. (Stereo sounds take up lots more disk space.) While shopping around, bear in mind that the 16-bit sound cards are much more flexible in their configuration than the 8-bit cards.

The technical specifications of the MPC sound card standard are as follows:

- 8-bit DAC, linear PCM sampling, 22.05 and 11.025 kHz rate, DMA/FIFO with interrupt
- 8-bit ADC, linear PCM sampling, 11.025 kHz rate, microphone level input
- Music synthesizer
- On-board analog audio mixing capabilities

Knowing what all that means will probably land you a job as a stereo salesperson. The best way to tell if the sound card meets these specifications is to look for these specs on the side of the box.

Installing the Sound Card

You install a sound card just like any other expansion card: Turn off your PC, and open the case. Locate an available expansion slot, and plug in the sound card according to the instructions. Then attach the external speakers to the proper connection on the back of the sound card, and close up your PC. Finally install the sound card software under MS-DOS. If the software includes a test program, run it to make sure the sound card performs properly.

Some sound cards have a connection for the internal speaker cable. Hooking up this connection enables your PC to beep through the sound card and over the external speakers instead of over the internal speaker. If your sound card has the proper software, this connection opens the door to interesting system beeps under MS-DOS. If you're setting up a multimedia PC, you may have to connect the CD-ROM drive to the sound card so that sound and music from a CD can play over the external speakers.

Your sound card may have several connections on the back:

- An external microphone or sound input jack
- An external speaker or headphone jack(s)
- A joystick connection
- A SCSI port connection
- A MIDI port connection

Attach whatever devices you plan on using to the various jacks. For starters, you will probably connect external speakers or headphones to the speaker jacks, plus any other devices you own—joysticks and external SCSI devices, for example. (Some CD-ROM drives connect through the external SCSI port.)

Updating the Sound Driver

To use your sound card with Windows, you must install and configure its drivers. If the sound card's installation software doesn't perform these tasks for you, you can use the Control Panel's Drivers dialog box to install and configure your sound card.

When you double-click the Drivers icon in the Control Panel, a list of installed drivers is displayed in the Drivers dialog box. To add a new driver, click the Add button to display a list of the drivers that come with Windows. Double-click your sound card's driver to install it. If your sound card isn't in the list, select Unlisted Or Updated Driver, and follow the directions on the screen.

After your sound driver is installed, you can highlight it, and click the Setup button in the Drivers dialog box to make adjustments. The Setup dialog box you see will be custom designed for your sound card. Figure 9-1 shows the Sound Blaster Setup dialog box for the Sound Blaster sound driver.

After installing a new sound driver, or adjusting an existing one, you may have to restart Windows. If a message box appears, click the Restart Windows button, and soon your PC will be making sweet music.

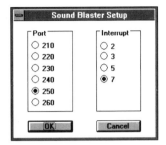

Figure 9-1. *The Sound Blaster Setup dialog box.*

Playing Waveform Files

Windows comes with an assortment of sounds you can play over your sound card's speakers. These sounds are stored in *waveform files* that generally have WAV extensions. The waveform files are played by the Sound Recorder, an application that you use not only for playing but also for creating and editing sounds. (You can also use the Media Player application to play the sounds.)

Because the Sound Recorder is associated with the WAV files on your hard disk, double-clicking a WAV file in File Manager brings up the Sound Recorder window shown in Figure 9-2 on the next page. Click the Play button (the one in the middle at the bottom), and you'll hear the sound played over your speakers. A graphical image of the sound wave appears in the center of the Sound Recorder window.

The PC Speaker Sound Driver

If your system lacks a sound card, you can hear sounds over your computer's internal speaker by using the PC Speaker sound driver. Download this driver from the Microsoft Download Service, and install it by using the Control Panel. Over your computer's speaker, sounds are fuzzy and tinny, but you can at least hear them. Refer to "Secrets You Can Download" in Chapter 4 for more information on the Microsoft Download Service.

Figure 9-2. *The Sound Recorder window.*

The scroll bar allows you to position the Sound Recorder at any spot in the sound recording. You can then use the Delete Before Cursor Position or Delete After Cursor Position commands on the Edit menu to pare down the sound file, but you cannot select, copy, or paste parts of the sound.

The five buttons at the bottom of the Sound Recorder window have the following functions, from left to right: Move to the start of the sound; move to the end of the sound; play the sound; stop playing/recording the sound; and start recording a new sound. The Record button (the tiny microphone) is enabled only if you have a microphone or other sound input device connected to your sound card. (See "Creating Your Own Sounds," later in this chapter.)

If you want to play back a number of sounds in sequence, I recommend opening multiple copies of the Sound Recorder and loading a different sound into each one. The Sound Recorder is really a simple playback and record program, and it lacks the sophistication of advanced sound editing tools. But for most applications, it's fine—and it's fun to play with. (Don't tell the boss!)

Assigning Sounds

Given the proper configuration, you can have your computer constantly making noise.

Assigning Sounds to System Events

One practical thing you can do with sounds in Windows is assign them to various "system events" using the Control Panel's Sound dialog box. Double-click the Sound icon to display the dialog box shown in Figure 9-3.

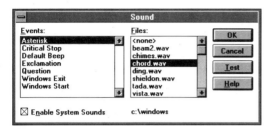

Figure 9-3. *The Sound dialog box.*

On the left side of the box are the various Windows system events to which you can assign sounds. The system events and what they represent are listed in Table 9-1.

Event	Event Description
Asterisk	A warning dialog box with an asterisk (*) icon in it
Critical Stop	A warning dialog box or error box
Default Beep	Windows' typical beep (you've heard it a million times)
Exclamation	A warning dialog box with an exclamation point (!) icon in it
Question	A warning dialog box with a question mark (?) icon in it
Windows Exit	Windows shutdown—the final Alt-F4
Windows Start	Windows startup, after the desktop (background) is drawn

Table 9-1. *Windows' system events.*

On the right is a list of the WAV files stored in your WINDOWS directory. (You can also hunt down files in other directories.) To assign a sound to a system event, highlight the event, and then double-click a waveform file. Experiment a bit, and select the sounds you like best. My advice is to use the shortest possible sound for the Default Beep event. Longer sounds can be selected for Windows Exit and Windows Start. Everything

Short and Sweet

The PC Speaker sound driver halts all system activity during sound playback. This interruption can be really annoying if your PC beeps a lot. That's why I recommend assigning a short, sweet sound, or <none> to the Default Beep event.

else is a matter of choice, though in my travels I've rarely experienced the other events.

If you don't want to associate a sound with an event, select <none> as the waveform file. For example, selecting <none> for Windows Start decreases the amount of time it takes Windows to start because Windows doesn't have to read the sound file. (Windows plays the sound file while doing other things; it's reading the sound file from disk that takes the time.)

Note: The Enable System Sounds check box at the bottom of the Sound dialog box has nothing to do with the sound card and the WAV files. Turning on this option tells Windows to beep as a warning or when an error occurs. This option controls the Beep entry in WIN.INI's [windows] section.

Assigning Sounds to Other Events

With Windows, you can assign sounds only to the seven system events listed in Table 9-1 (and in the Sound dialog box). To slap sounds on other events, such as opening specific programs, selecting menus, and so on, you'll need a third party utility.

One such utility is the Whoop it up! shareware program, which is available from Advance Support Group. They're asking $29.95 for it, a portion of which is donated to the World Wildlife Fund. Whoop it up! allows you to assign sounds to the usual seven system events, to seven "generic" events, and to specific applications. The generic events include maximizing and minimizing a window, changing its size and appearance, and so on.

Another set of utilities is the Microsoft SoundBits sound clip collections. Three collections are available: Classic Cartoons from Hanna-Barbera, Classic Hollywood Movies, and Musical Sounds from Around the World. SoundBits lets you assign sounds to 32 events. Practically anything you do can elicit a sound if you want it to.

Sound Stuff in WIN.INI

Records of your meddling in the Sound dialog box are kept in the [Sounds] section of WIN.INI. Seven entries, one for each system event, appear in the following format:

system_event=filename, description

system_event is the event that causes the sound file to play. *filename* is the name of the waveform file, and *description* is the description that appears in the Sound dialog box. The default Windows sound setup has the following entries in WIN.INI's [Sounds] section:

```
SystemDefault=ding.wav, Default Beep
SystemExclamation=chord.wav, Exclamation
SystemStart=tada.wav, Windows Start
SystemExit=chimes.wav, Windows Exit
SystemHand=chord.wav, Critical Stop
SystemQuestion=chord.wav, Question
SystemAsterisk=chord.wav, Asterisk
```

There is no reason to edit this information because it's so easily changed in the Control Panel's Sound dialog box. And you can't stick any additional "secret" system events in here.

Inserting Sounds into Files

The Sound Recorder application fully supports OLE (Object Linking and Embedding). If you copy the file's sound to the Clipboard, choose the Object or Insert Object command in an OLE-friendly application, and select the Sound option, the Sound Recorder icon is dropped into your document. You can then double-click the icon to play the associated waveform file, or choose Object Edit or a similar command to edit the sound object.

In the Sound Recorder, you can choose the Copy command from the Edit menu to copy a sound to the Clipboard. From there, you can use any Edit menu's Paste command to insert the sound into a file. The application must support OLE for this to work. Additional information about OLE is provided in Chapter 6.

Creating Your Own Sounds

Megabytes of sound files—most of which were created by people like you and me who have a sound card and a microphone—are available for downloading from online services such as CompuServe. These files come from a variety of sources and include interesting sound effects, quips from

TV and movie characters, tidbits of songs and music, and the ever-popular body noises. You are not limited to these prerecorded selections, however. It's quite simple to create your own sounds, often using "things you can find around the house."

I went down to Radio Shack recently and bought $15 worth of stuff that allows me to use my sound card and Windows as a home-brew recording studio. My first purchase was a mini-microphone, the second was a small jack plug and cable for my sound card's input, and the third was a larger converter for the back of my stereo. Together, they constitute a complete hardware setup for recording a variety of sounds.

To record your voice, plug the microphone into the "audio in" jack on the back of your sound card. In the Sound Recorder, click the Record (microphone) button, and jabber away. Click the Stop button or press Enter when you're done. Click the Play button to listen to the sound. You can choose the Delete Before/After Cursor Position commands from the Edit menu to eliminate any extra sounds before and after your recording. Then save your sound to disk as a WAV file.

Recording from your TV, VCR, or a CD is possible, but only if you connect the "audio out" on your stereo to the "audio in" on your sound card. What I do is record the sound using a cassette recorder, just as I would create a tape for my car. Then I connect a portable cassette recorder to my PC, press Play (or whatever) to play the sound on the cassette recorder, and click the Record button in the Sound Recorder to digitize the sound in the computer. Click Stop when you're done.

The Sound Recorder's Effects menu allows you to add a few special effects to the sound. You can increase and decrease the volume, double or halve the speed of the sound, add an echo (but not remove it), and reverse the sound. You don't really need much more than that unless you're into studio-quality sound production. Eventually, Windows products that allow you to incorporate more effects and offer better control over waveform files will be available. Until then, you can have lots of fun using your sound card and a microphone.

CD-ROM DRIVES

CD-ROM drives were once magical things that would never really catch on. For years, the gurus predicted that every PC would soon have a CD-ROM drive, even though at the time there was really no purpose for the drive, nor was there any software to control it. Multimedia now provides the purpose and the software.

Essentially a CD-ROM drive is like a large, write-protected floppy drive. A CD-ROM can store hundreds of megabytes of information, but the CD-ROM drive accesses that information about four times slower than the typical hard drive. Also, the information is read-only. You can only access the information on a CD-ROM; you can't change the information, and you can't use a CD-ROM to store your own information. You can, however, copy files from a CD-ROM to a hard disk and edit them there.

As part of the MPC standard, CD-ROM drives provide ready access to an incredibly large volume of information. Huge graphic images, dozens of fonts, sound files, and animation can all be conveniently stored on a single CD-ROM. For example, Microsoft Bookshelf, which includes a dictionary, thesaurus, almanac, atlas, and other reference texts, contains almost 650 MB of information on a single CD-ROM. That's impressive. All this information can be at your fingertips if you have MPC hardware and Windows on your PC.

Setting Up a CD-ROM Drive

CD-ROM drives come in both internal and external models. Internal models fit inside your PC like a hard drive (though the CD-ROM is removable like a floppy disk). They either have their own special controller or attach internally to a SCSI card. External models typically attach to a SCSI port, so you must have a SCSI card inside your PC to use them. Some sound cards come with SCSI ports built in, which means many MPC upgrades entail adding only one expansion card (for sound) to your PC.

If your CD-ROM drive comes as part of a multimedia upgrade kit, you'll probably plug its digital sound output into your sound card. That way, you can play sound samples from a CD-ROM on external speakers. Other internal connections may be necessary as well, depending on the type of CD-ROM drive. External drives connect via a cable and may have their own speakers.

To use the CD-ROM drive as part of your disk system, you must load a series of drivers—usually two sets. The first is loaded from within CONFIG.SYS to configure the CD-ROM hardware. The second, MSCDEX, is loaded from within AUTOEXEC.BAT. (MSCDEX is the Microsoft CD-ROM Extensions, which makes the CD-ROM drive a recognizable part of your disk system.)

Using Your Home Stereo CD Player

It's at this point in the lecture that an astute student usually asks the following question: "Can I use my compact disc player with my computer?" Don't laugh, class. It's a serious question.

The truth is, you can—provided your CD player is capable of top-flight performance. Some of the inexpensive players can't keep up with a computer. You will also need a way of interfacing your CD player with the computer, which is something most of these devices lack. My advice is not to cut corners. Buy a CD-ROM drive for your PC. If you love to tinker, consider converting the CD player for use with your computer—but only

Loading MSCDEX

Load the MSCDEX driver after loading your network software. If you load it before, your network may assume that the CD-ROM drive is another "network" on your system, and may refuse to load. While running AUTOEXEC.BAT, keep an eye on the screen after loading the drivers to make sure this problem doesn't occur.

Some network software may refuse to recognize the CD-ROM drive or may assume the CD-ROM drive is another network "server"— one it cannot connect to. If this happens, you'll need to use your network software to configure the CD-ROM drive as a network resource. Better still, have a network guru do that for you.

after convincing your family that you won't break it, and only after negotiating usage terms.

CD-ROM Buyer's Guide

Here are some suggestions for buying a CD-ROM drive:

- Make sure the drive is MPC-compatible. It must have a transfer rate of 150 KB-per-second *or better* and a maximum seek time of 1 second while using no more than 40 percent of the processor's power. If the drive is any slower than that, the sound and animation don't play smoothly.

- Avoid drives with an access time that is slower than 500 milliseconds—400 or less is great.

- Internal drives are harder to install than external drives, but my advice is to buy an internal drive if you have room for it in your PC. An external drive just adds to the clutter on your desk.

- Make sure the drive comes with the following: the SCSI controller and cable, driver software (you need MSCDEX version 2.2 or later for multimedia), and the ability to play compact discs—including the necessary software. (Some drives even come with headphones.)

- Shop around. You need to shop for price, but also for service and support. At this point in time, the folks selling these devices are not always aware of how they work. If you find a multimedia guru, buy the drive (or upgrade kit) from him or her, even if it's more expensive than buying from a place where the salespeople know nothing more than how to take your money.

Using a CD-ROM Drive

A CD-ROM drive works just like a hard drive. You can click its icon in File Manager to display the directories and files contained on the currently inserted CD-ROM. You can access the drive from File Manager or from the command prompt. For example, my CD-ROM drive is drive F, so I simply type *f:* at the command prompt and I'm there.

CD-ROMs contain megabytes of files and information. How you access that information depends on the purpose of the disc. If it contains utilities, sound files, clip art, and so on, you'll probably work with them just as you would the files on a hard drive. When the CD-ROM contains a particular multimedia program and its data files, you must install the program before you can use it.

For example, Microsoft Bookshelf has an installation program, named SETUP.EXE, in the root directory of its CD-ROM. When you run the setup program, it installs the multimedia Viewer program in a directory called WINDOWS\VIEWER (which it creates), as well as sets up a program group for Bookshelf in Program Manager. After installation is complete, you're ready to use the Bookshelf CD-ROM. Other multimedia applications install themselves similarly.

When a disc contains one program and that program gets its data from the disc, you can use the program only when its disc is in the CD-ROM drive. So before you start a multimedia application, remove its disk from the jewel case, insert the disc in your CD-ROM drive's disc caddy, and slide the disc into the drive. (You can buy drives with more than one caddy so that you don't have to keep handling your disks.)

Playing CDs

Your PC's CD-ROM drive can also be used by the Media Player program to play music from CDs. Start the Media Player, and choose CD Audio from the Device menu. The Media Player reads the tracks from the CD and displays them above the scroll bar, as shown in Figure 9-4. Click the Play button (the right-pointing triangle) to hear the music.

Some MPC computers have their own applications for listening to CDs. For example, the Media Vision MPC upgrade kit comes with two pro-

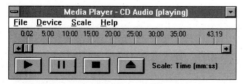

Figure 9-4. *The Media Player, which can be used to play music from compact discs.*

grams: Music Box and Mix. Music Box is a stereo CD interface for playing musical CDs on your computer. It reads the CD and displays the tracks and their times. A special Program button is used to record a database of the songs on each track, which you can reload for each of your CDs.

Mix is basically a volume control program that provides a slider switch for turning the speaker volume up or down. (This control is important because many sound cards and speakers don't have volume knobs.) The Mix program also monitors sound inputs from various devices and can be used when creating multimedia packages and recording sounds.

PUTTING IT ALL TOGETHER

Multimedia is still in its infancy. It's like hard drives were in the early days of the PC. People had them but didn't quite know how to use them. They would copy floppy disk after floppy disk to the hard drive without regard for directories. We're at a similar point with multimedia; we have the hardware and the software, but we still don't quite know what to make of it all.

The most immediate impact of the multimedia revolution is in the area of sound. Having a sound card and Windows makes using the PC fun. This was one area of personal computing in which the Macintosh always outshone the IBM computers and their clones: The Mac could sing, giggle, and burp. The PC went "Bleep." With Windows, PCs finally have a way to use sound like Macintoshes always have. And eventually applications will take advantage of this new capability, producing different sounds for different program modes, much in the same way color is now used in programs to display different types of information.

But multimedia is more than just sound. It is a learning tool that brings a third and fourth dimension to education and entertainment. For example, a multimedia encyclopedia (which is a mouthful) contains much more than the traditional encyclopedic text. Not only can you bring up pictures on the screen while you're reading (see Figure 9-5 on the next page), but you can also click a button to make the pictures move—for example, to demonstrate how a CD player works or how an internal combustion engine goes through its four cycles. And you could also listen to an announcer explaining the process.

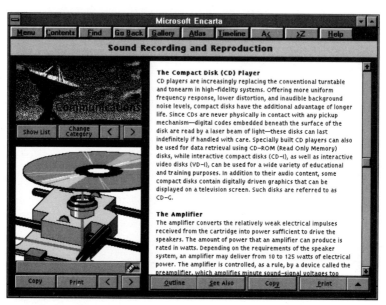

Figure 9-5. *Microsoft Encarta, a multimedia encyclopedia, in action.*

Animation and sound are fun, and they are good tools for an encyclopedia. But because you're on a computer, if you see a reference to *Rudolf C. K. Diesel* in the text, you can simply double-click it with a mouse and read about what he did in a pop-up window. This is truly how an encyclopedia should be used: As a tool for quickly gathering knowledge. Only with a computer can you explore information in this fashion.

As multimedia evolves, more and more uses will be developed for it. Presently, as a learning and information tool, nothing can beat it. Eventually more applications will incorporate multimedia, and as they do, hopefully more Windows users will upgrade to a multimedia PC and take advantage of what it offers.

Appendix A

Command Reference

SMARTDrive

The SMARTDrive utility creates a disk cache on your system using either extended or expanded memory. Starting with Windows version 3.1, SMARTDrive is supplied as SMARTDRV.EXE, a program that you run from AUTOEXEC.BAT. Previous versions of Windows used SMARTDRV.SYS, a device driver that you ran from CONFIG.SYS. Here is the format for SMARTDRV.EXE:

> smartdrv.exe *drive±* /e:*elementsize init win* /b:*buffsize* /c /r /l /q /s /?
> /double_buffer

where *drive* indicates the letter of a drive you want SMARTDrive to cache. If you don't indicate a drive, SMARTDrive caches all your drives. A plus sign (+) following the drive letter activates both read and write caching. A minus sign (−) disables caching. You should disable caching on network, Stacker, and RAM drives. If you specify a drive letter but give no plus or minus sign, SMARTDrive enables read caching and disables write caching.

The /e:*elementsize* switch sets the number of bytes in the chunks of data that SMARTDrive moves around. The *elementsize* can be 1024, 2048, 4096, or 8192 bytes. The default is 8192.

init specifies the initial and maximum size for the cache in kilobytes.

win specifies the minimum size for the cache in kilobytes. This is the size to which Windows can reduce the cache should it need more memory.

The /b:*buffsize* switch sets the size of SMARTDrive's read-ahead buffer. *buffsize* is given in bytes. The default value is 16, though any value that is a multiple of the *elementsize* value can be used.

The /c switch clears the write cache. Use this switch after SMARTDrive is loaded to direct SMARTDrive to write all information in any buffers to disk. Ideally, a *smartdrv /c* command is used before you shut off your PC.

The /r switch is the restart switch. It clears SMARTDrive's cache and restarts the program anew. Use this switch only after you have loaded SMARTDrive.

The /l switch directs SMARTDrive to load in conventional memory, not upper memory.

The /q switch runs SMARTDrive in the "quiet" mode. When /q is specified, no information is displayed on the screen when you load SMARTDrive.

The /s switch is used at the MS-DOS prompt to display SMARTDrive's status. Use this switch only after you've loaded SMARTDrive.

The /? switch displays help information.

You need the /double_buffer option only if you have a hard drive with a SCSI or ESDI controller that uses physical memory addresses. To find out whether you need this option, open an MS-DOS window in Windows, and type *smartdrv*. If every item has *no* in the Buffering column, you don't need the /double_buffer option. If you do need the option, add the following entry for SMARTDrive in CONFIG.SYS. (You'll also have a SMART-Drive entry in AUTOEXEC.BAT.)

```
device = c:\windows\smartdrv.exe /double_buffer
```

In general, you don't need to specify any options with SMARTDrive; it configures itself properly for your system based on available extended memory. (Note that this version of SMARTDrive works only with extended memory.) All the parameters are optional.

Note: There is no need to load SMARTDrive high. If UMBs are available, SMARTDrive finds them and loads itself high.

RAMDrive

The RAMDrive device driver is used to create a RAM drive in either conventional, extended, or expanded memory. For Windows, you'll want your

RAM drive in extended memory, and only if you have memory to spare. RAMDrive is loaded in CONFIG.SYS using this format:

device[high]=*pathname*\ramdrive.sys *size sector entries* [/e ¦ /a]

pathname indicates the location of the RAMDRIVE.SYS device driver, complete with drive letter and directory.

size is the size of the RAM drive in kilobytes. Values for *size* range from 4 through 32767 for a 4-KB through 32-MB RAM drive. (Of course, you can't specify more memory than you have.) When *size* isn't specified, a 64-KB RAM drive is created.

sector is the size of the RAM drive's sectors in bytes. Values for *sector* can be 128, 256, or 512. The default value for *sector* is 512, just as it is on most hard and floppy disks.

entries indicates the number of directories and files RAMDRIVE.SYS allows in the RAM drive's root directory. Values for *entries* range from 2 through 1024. The default value for *entries* is 64.

The /e or /a switch directs RAMDRIVE.SYS to create the RAM drive in extended or expanded memory, respectively. If omitted, the RAM drive is created in conventional memory.

HIMEM.SYS

The HIMEM.SYS driver controls all extended memory in the PC, establishes the XMS (Extended Memory Specification), and creates the HMA (high memory area). It should be the first device driver loaded in your CONFIG.SYS file, after any hard drive configuration device drivers. Here is the format for HIMEM.SYS:

device=*pathname*\himem.sys *options*

pathname indicates the location of the HIMEM.SYS device driver, complete with drive letter and directory.

options can include one or more of the following optional switches:

■ /a20control:On ¦ Off, which determines whether HIMEM.SYS will control the A20 line, which gives access to the HMA. The default setting,

On, gives HIMEM.SYS control even if the A20 line was on when HIMEM.SYS was loaded.

■ /cpuclock:On¦Off, which allows HIMEM.SYS to deal with clock speed changes. The default is *Off*.

■ /hmamin=*m*, which indicates a minimum program size for programs that want to use the HMA. Values for *m* range from 0 through 63, with 0 as the default. (A value of 0 means that the first program to request the HMA gets it.)

■ /int15=*xxx*, which allocates memory for interrupt 15, the "Vdisk" method of extended memory allocation. Values for *xxx* range from 64 through 65535, with 0 as the default.

■ /machine:*xxx*, which selects the proper A20 line handler to be used, depending on your PC. Values for each PC are listed in the Windows manual; however, HIMEM.SYS usually selects the right one by default.

■ /numhandles=*n*, which specifies the number of simultaneous extended memory blocks. Values for *n* range from 1 through 128, with 32 as the default.

■ /shadowram:On¦Off, which controls whether your PC uses shadow RAM. If you have less than 2 MB of RAM, *Off* is the default.

EMM386.EXE

EMM386.EXE is both a device driver and a program. As a device driver, it's used to manage expanded memory and convert extended memory to expanded memory on '386-based PCs, and it creates the UMBs. Under Windows, you will most likely use it only to create UMBs. Here is the format for EMM386.EXE, when it's used as a device driver in CONFIG.SYS:

device=*pathname*emm386.exe *mode* [nohigh] *memory options*
[noems¦ram]

pathname indicates the location of the EMM386.EXE device driver, complete with drive letter and directory.

mode turns the EMM386.EXE driver's expanded memory support on or off, or sets it to auto (automatic). The default is *On*. If you use *Auto*, EMM386 creates expanded memory only if a program requests it. This setting can be changed using EMM386 at the MS-DOS prompt.

The nohigh option directs EMM386 not to load part of itself into a UMB. Normally, EMM386 loads part of its code high. The nohigh option prevents this from happening and gives you approximately 3 KB of extra upper memory.

memory is the amount of extended memory to be converted to expanded memory. Values for *memory* range from 16, for 16 KB, through as much extended memory as is available, or 32768. The default is 256 KB.

options represents the following optional switches:

- a=*altregs*, which specifies the number of alternate register sets to use. Values for *altregs* range from 0 through 254, with 7 as the default.

- b=*address*, which sets the bottommost address to be used for LIM 4.0 EMS banks that are swapped into and out of the page frame. The default is 4000, for bank 4 of memory. You can specify values from 1000 through 4000.

- d=*nnn*, which indicates the amount of RAM needed for DMA (direct memory access) buffering. Values for *nnn* are specified in kilobytes and range from 16 through 256, with 16 as the default.

- frame=*address*, which specifies the EMS page frame address. The frame option is followed by one of the addresses listed in Table A-1.

x	address	x	address
1	C000	8	DC00
2	C400	9	E000
3	C800	10	8000
4	CC00	11	8400
5	D000	12	8800
6	D400	13	8C00
7	D800	14	9000

Table A-1. *EMS page frame addresses.*

Note: You can use only one of the frame, m, or p parameters in the device driver format for EMM386.EXE.

■ h=*handles*, which specifies the number of handles EMM386 can use for accessing expanded memory. Values for *handles* range from 2 to 255, with 64 as the default.

■ i=*mmmm–nnnn*, which specifies an area of upper memory for use as an upper memory block. EMM386 normally scouts out all available areas of upper memory for conversion to upper memory blocks. However, it may occasionally miss a chunk of memory, which you can then specify using the *i* option. The values *mmmm* and *nnnn* are hexadecimal addresses that define the start and end of the memory block.

■ L=*minXMS*, which tells EMM386 how much extended memory to preserve, ensuring that it doesn't convert all the extended memory into expanded memory. The *minXMS* value specifies the number of kilobytes of extended memory to be preserved.

■ m*x*, which gives the expanded memory page frame address. Values for *x* are specified in Table A-1.

■ /p=*address*, which is yet another way to specify the page frame address. The frame and p parameters are identical. Note that this parameter starts with a slash, however.

■ p*n*=*address*, which is used to set the address for a specific page in the page frame. There can be 255 pages, as specified by *n*. Pages 0 through 3 must be contiguous in memory. *address* is a memory address, specifically one of the addresses listed in Table A-1.

■ w=On¦Off, which turns support for the Weitek coprocessor on or off.

■ x=*mmmm–nnnn*, which excludes an area of upper memory from being used as an upper memory block. This exclusion prevents conflicts with adapters in the upper memory area. The *mmmm* and *nnnn* values are hexadecimal addresses defining the start and end of a range of upper memory to be excluded.

noems is used to create UMBs while not converting any extended memory to expanded memory. This is the option you want to specify when running Windows.

ram creates UMBs in addition to converting extended memory to expanded memory. Do not use this switch with Windows.

Note: HIMEM.SYS must be installed before EMM386.EXE. The noems and ram switches cannot be used simultaneously, nor can they be used with MS-DOS versions prior to 5.0.

As a program, EMM386.EXE is used to display the current status of the EMS driver and to turn expanded memory support on or off. Here is the format:

emm386 *state weitek*

Without any options, EMM386 displays information about expanded memory use and the upper memory blocks in your system.

state turns the EMM386 driver on or off or activates auto sense mode. The default is *On*. Note that you cannot turn expanded memory support off when UMBs have been created.

weitek activates support for the Weitek coprocessor. The settings for *weitek* are *w=On* or *w=Off*, with *w=Off* as the default.

Appendix B

Company and Product Reference

Disk Technician Gold
Disk Technician Corporation
1940 Garnet
San Diego, CA 92109
(619) 274–5000

Faxit for Windows
SOFNET, Inc.
380 Interstate North Parkway, Suite 150
Atlanta, GA 30339
(404) 984–8088

Mace Utilities
Fifth Generation Systems
10049 N. Reiger Road
Baton Rouge, LA 70809
(504) 291–7221
(800) 873–4384

Microsoft Windows
Microsoft Windows Resource Kit
Microsoft TrueType Font Pack
Microsoft Corp.
One Microsoft Way
Redmond, WA 98052–6399
(800) 426–9400

Norton Utilities
Norton Desktop for Windows
Symantec
10201 Torre Avenue
Cupertino, CA 95014–2132
(408) 253–9600

PC-SIG Library
PC-SIG
1030 East Duane
Sunnyvale, CA 94086
(800) 245–6717
(800) 222–2996 (in California)

PC Tools
Central Point Software
15220 NW Greenbrier Pkwy., Suite 200
Beaverton, OR 97006
(503) 690–8090

SpinRite II
Gibson Research, Corp.
35 Journey
Aliso Viejo, CA 92656
(714) 362–8800

Super Dual VGA Adapter
Colorgraphic Communications
P.O. Box 80448
Atlanta, GA 30366–0448
(404) 455–3921

Vopt
Golden Bow Systems
PO Box 3039
San Diego, CA 92163–1039
(619) 298–9349
(800) 284–3269

Whoop it Up!
Advance Support Group
11900 Grant Place
St. Louis, MO 63131

WinFax
Delrina
6830 Via Del Oro, Suite 240
San Jose, CA 95119–1353
(800) 268–6082

WinSpeed
Panacea Inc.
24 Orchard View Drive
Londonderry, NH 03053
(800) 729–7420

Index

Page numbers in *italics* indicate figures or tables.

Dan Gookin

Dan Gookin struggles to make computers understandable to all by writing about them in a light, non-threatening manner. His dream is to own his own espresso machine (the copper kind with the big eagle on top), and bounce his new baby on his knee as he sits watching bugs draw lazy circles in the summer afternoon air from his 113-acre ranch in Small Dot, Idaho.

The manuscript for this book was prepared and submitted to Microsoft Press in electronic form. Text files were processed and formatted using Microsoft Word.

Principal editorial compositor: Christina Smith
Principal proofreader: Polly Fox Urban
Principal typographer: Bill Teel
Interior text designer: Kim Eggleston
Principal illustrator: Connie Little
Cover designer: Rebecca Johnson
Cover illustrator: Henk Dawson
Cover color separator: Color Service

Text composition by Microsoft Press in Times Roman with display type in Futura Heavy, using Ventura Publisher and the Linotronic 300 laser imagesetter.

Printed on recycled paper stock.

Great Resources for Windows™

WINDOWS™ 3.1 COMPANION
The Cobb Group

"Covers the basics thoroughly....An excellent reference featuring dozens of live examples....Beautifully produced." **PC Magazine**
This thorough, comprehensive resource covers Windows 3.1 and its built-in applications and desktop accessories for beginning to advanced users. First-time users will appreciate the tutorial-style introduction to Windows 3.1; more experienced users will find this reference invaluable. Packed with a wealth of examples, helpful tips, and techniques.
544 pages $27.95 ($37.95 Canada)   ISBN 1-55615-372-4

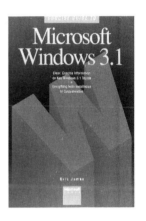

CONCISE GUIDE TO MICROSOFT® WINDOWS™ 3.1
Kris Jamsa
The handiest and most readable reference to Windows 3.1, offering information on everything from installation to customization. It's the ideal computerside reference! For beginning and intermediate users.
208 pages $12.95 ($17.95 Canada)   ISBN 1-55615-470-4

VISUAL BASIC™—GAME PROGRAMMING FOR WINDOWS™
Michael J. Young
Here's a great way to learn Visual Basic programming techniques and have fun as well. VISUAL BASIC—GAME PROGRAMMING FOR WINDOWS, a one-of-a-kind book-and-software package, is a complete hands-on course in game programming. It's packed with solid advice on using animation, generating fractals, controlling sound, and programming in Microsoft Windows. Includes 12 ready-to-run Visual Basic games and fractals complete with online help, playing instructions, and source code.
528 pages   softcover with one 5.25-inch disk
$39.95 ($54.95 Canada)   ISBN 1-55615-503-4

Microsoft Press books are available wherever books and software are sold.
*To order direct, call **1-800-MSPRESS** (8AM to 5PM central time).*
Please refer to BBK when placing your order.* Prices subject to change.

anada, contact Macmillan Canada, Attn: Microsoft Press Dept., 164 Commander Blvd., Agincourt, Ontario, Canada M1S 3C7, or call (416) 293-8141.
In the U.K., contact Microsoft Press, 27 Wrights Lane, London W8 5TZ.

Unbeatable References from Dan Gookin

DAN GOOKIN'S PC HOTLINE
Dan Gookin

Here's candid advice for all PC users on boosting performance, safe-guarding data, and troubleshooting system problems. Discover how to:

- Prevent a potential crash
- Create an Emergency Boot Disk
- Deal with unreadable disks
- Compress files to save disk space
- Defragment your hard disk
- Locate and remove a virus
- Determine when you need—and don't need— utility programs
- And more!

You'll be on your way to trouble-free computing with DAN GOOKIN'S PC HOTLINE!

256 pages $14.95 ($19.95 Canada)   ISBN 1-55615-473-9

THE MICROSOFT® GUIDE TO MANAGING MEMORY WITH DOS 5
Dan Gookin

Now that MS-DOS version 5 has opened the door to megabytes of extra memory, what's the next step? This official guide shows you how to capi-talize on the extra memory now available on your PC. Here's what's covered:

- The basics of memory—what it is and how your computer uses it
- The differences between conventional, extended, and expanded memory—in English
- The whys and hows of buying, installing, and using RAM chips and memory boards
- The secrets of moving device drivers and memory-resident programs into upper memory
- Optimizing memory with MS-DOS 5
- And more!

If memory is the question, this book is the answer.

208 pages $14.95 ($19.95 Canada)   ISBN 1-55615-381-3